T4-AIG-416

Computer Support Web Sites

Computer Support Web Sites	Description	Address
Inquiry.com	The best place to look for product information and to search computer publications.	www.inquiry.com
Microsoft	The best place for upgrades and support for Windows 95 and Internet Explorer.	www.microsoft.com
SupportHelp.com	Looking for the correct URL or newsgroups for a company's site? Look no further. Search here.	www.supporthelp.com/

Search Engines and Directories

Search Engines and Directories	Description	Address
Alta Vista	One of the best search engines on the Internet.	altavista.digital.com/
AOL NetFind	Good search directory, especially for computer-related information.	www.aol.com/netfind/
DejaNews Newsgroup	The only place to go for newsgroup postings.	www.dejanews.com
Excite	A great consumer-oriented search directory, also offering TV listings and news.	www.excite.com/
HotBot	The search engine to use if you are looking for graphics and multimedia files.	www.hotbot.com/
InfoSeek	A great directory for finding mainstream information.	www.infoseek.com
MetaCrawler	The place to go if you want to search all the major search engines in one fell swoop.	www.metacrawler.com
SearchEngineWatch	Want to know how to really search the engines? Excellent site all about search engines.	www.searchenginewatch.com

People Finders

People Finders	Description	Address
Bigfoot	You'll find millions of people here, plus a free e-mail forwarding option.	www.bigfoot.com
PC411.com	The only place to search by phone number. Links to Mapquest to show you where folks live.	www.pc411.com
Switchboard	An excellent, fast engine for finding addresses and phone numbers of people and businesses.	www.switchboard.com
Whowhere	The quickest and easiest people search engine on the Net.	www.whowhere.com

Miscellaneous Sites

Miscellaneous Sites	Description	Address
Amazon.com	The best place on the planet to find and buy any type of book.	www.amazon.com
Expedia	The best travel site on the Internet. Great for booking airline reservations.	www.expedia.com
HotMail	Need an e-mail address? Excellent web-based e-mail.	www.hotmail.com
Microsoft's Investor	The only place to go for online investing and financial information.	www.investor.com
NetGrocer	Too tired to shop for diapers? They deliver via FedEx in two days.	www.netgrocer.com
NetGuide's Online Happenings	An excellent place to find out who's talking about what, where.	www.netguide.com/Happenings
No Thank You	Get your name off those junk e-mail lists.	www.nothankyou.com
The FAX FAQ	Learn to send a fax through the Internet.	www.northcoast.com/savetz/fax-faq.html
Tile.net	A great place to look for e-mail lists and information on signing up.	www.tile.net
TimeCast	Looking for live radio broadcasts over the Net? This is the place.	www.timecast.com

ISP Comparison Sites

ISP Comparison Sites	Description	Address
Online Connection	An excellent site offering comparative reviews of ISPs.	www.barkers.org/online
The Provider List	A complete listing of service providers around the world.	thelist.iworld.com

Shareware Sites

Shareware Sites	Description	Address
ClNet's Shareware.com	One of the best places to go to search for shareware of any kind.	www.shareware.com
FileZ	You name it. You can search for it. Even for software posted in newsgroups.	www.filez.com
TuCows	One of the world's largest repositories of all sorts of software.	www.tucows.com
Windows95.com	An excellent site for Windows 95 and NT shareware and demoware.	www.windows95.com
WinSite	THE world's largest repository of Windows software.	www.winsite.com

Internet & Web

Answers!
Certified Tech Support

ABOUT THE AUTHOR...

Cheryl Kirk has been a computer consultant and trainer since 1983. She co-hosts *Computer.Radio,* a live call-in computer talk show, writes the computer column for the *Anchorage Daily News,* and occassionally contributes to national magazines such as *Internet World.* She also speaks frequently at major computer trade shows across the country and in Canada. She has authored and co-authored about ten different books about the Internet and various Internet and server applications.

Ms. Kirk lives in beautiful downtown Anchorage, Alaska, but constantly wonders what it would be like to live in the real world. She has no children, no dogs, no cats, and no social life. She spends all her time on the Internet or in therapy.

When she's not writing she is usually staring out the window or avoiding phone calls.

Internet & Web

Answers!
Certified Tech Support

Cheryl Kirk

Osborne **McGraw-Hill**

Berkeley • New York • St. Louis • San Francisco
Auckland • Bogotá • Hamburg • London
Madrid • Mexico City • Milan • Montreal
New Delhi • Panama City • Paris • São Paulo
Singapore • Sydney • Tokyo • Toronto

Osborne **McGraw-Hill**
2600 Tenth Street
Berkeley, California 94710
U.S.A.

For information on translations or book distributors outside the U.S.A., or to arrange bulk purchase discounts for sales promotions, premiums, or fund-raisers, please contact Osborne/**McGraw-Hill** at the above address.

Internet & Web Answers
Certified Tech Support

Copyright © 1998 by The McGraw-Hill Companies. All rights reserved. Printed in the United States of America. Except as permitted under the Copyright Act of 1976, no part of this publication may be reproduced or distributed in any form or by any means, or stored in a database or retrieval system, without the prior written permission of the publisher, with the exception that the program listings may be entered, stored, and executed in a computer system, but they may not be reproduced for publication.

34567890 AGM AGM 901987654321098

ISBN 0-07-882380-3

Publisher	**Copy Editors**
Brandon A. Nordin	Timothy Barr
	Judith Brown
Editor-in-Chief	
Scott Rogers	**Proofreader**
	Stefany Otis
Acquisitions Editor	
Joanne Cuthbertson	**Indexer**
	Rebecca Plunkett
Project Editor	
Nancy McLaughlin	**Computer Designers**
	Michelle Galicia
Editorial Assistant	
Gordon Hurd	**Illustrator**
	Lance Ravella
Technical Editor	
Dan Logan	**Cover Design**
	Matt Nielsen

Information has been obtained by Osborne/**McGraw-Hill** from sources believed to be reliable. However, because of the possibility of human or mechanical error by our sources, Osborne/**McGraw-Hill**, or others, Osborne/**McGraw-Hill** does not guarantee the accuracy, adequacy, or completeness of any information and is not responsible for any errors or omissions or the results obtained from use of such information.

To every Internet user who has ever had a question and just couldn't find the answer—this book is for you.

Contents @ a Glance

Contents

Acknowledgments

There are three people I'd especially like to thank for making sure this book was produced: Joanne Cuthbertson, Nancy McLaughlin, and Gordon Hurd.

A special big thanks goes to Joanne for never giving up, sticking with me, lending her ear and giving me a wealth of advice. Joanne makes you realize that computer book publishing is more than just about writing a decent book—it's about people. Not only does she care about the trials and tribulations of the always late computer book author, but she really cares about the reader. That shows in her pushing and prodding to make this book what I think you'll agree is more than just your average Internet FAQ book.

To Nancy, poor overworked Nancy, no words could thank Nancy enough for all her hard work. She and her staff did an excellent job of designing and laying out what is an incredibly easy-to-read book. A truly dedicated editorial and production team makes every Obsorne book a masterpiece.

Osborne has a real gem in Gordon. He always knew where everything was and went the extra mile to keep things going on the right track. I certainly appreciate all his effort.

I'd also like to thank Brandon and Scott for not being too hard on Joanne, and for giving me another opportunity to work with some great people.

Finally I'd like to thank the usual suspects: Many thanks to Mom and Dad for always thinking good thoughts (keep it up). Thanks to Linda for letting me come over and watch *The Real World*; to Clint Swett for getting my name in the Sacramento Bee on a regular basis, to my agent Matt Wagner of Waterside, and of course, to Aunt Jane and Ruthie, for just being who they are.

—CK

Introduction

The Internet is a wealth of information at your fingertips. But as easy as it seems to use, at times it can be nothing but a nightmare. Your email bounces, files don't transfer, you keep getting "File Not Found" errors when you try to click a link on a web page. Just about this time you're ready to tear your hair out. You try to contact your service provider, but they keep telling you the problem isn't on their side. You try to call the manufacturer of the software, only to be put on permanent hold. You ask your best friend if his nerdy son will come over and see if he can fix it, but instead he loads up your computer with all sorts of bells, whistles, and online games that only serve to confuse you. You need straightforward answers you can understand without a whole litany of buzzwords or extraneous fluff. You simply need answers, and you definitely need them now. And you've come to the right place.

The questions and answers found in this book, some 400 different ones, are the same questions Stream International answers ever day in their role of providing technical support to users of popular Internet related software such as Internet Explorer and Netscape Navigator. I've added additional information to many of the answers in an effort to relay what I've learned in my more than ten years of using online commercial services and more than five years of using the Internet. I've checked hundreds of newsgroups, downloaded thousands of programs, read just about every Frequently Asked Question (FAQ), and used just about every version of browser starting with Netscape's original version, 1.0. I've run into just about every problem you can imagine—from my modem dropping my Internet connection, to figuring out how to ignore Instant messages on America Online, to understanding how to uncompress and download files to a variety of file servers, all the while protecting my system from viruses. As a result, I've found some of the best solutions for many of the common Internet problems, and I've referenced many of them here.

Internet and Web Answers is divided into 12 chapters, along with an Appendix outlining common error messages you'll run into using the Web and e-mail. Each chapter tackles the most frequently asked questions about a particular topic, such as sending and receiving e-mail or creating Web pages. And within each chapter, the questions and answers are divided further into subtopics, such as sending and receiving e-mail on commercial services, or downloading files using popular file transfer programs. Each chapter starts with an **@ a Glance** section outlining key terms used within the chapter.

If you're looking for the answer to a particular question, use the table of contents to identify the chapter and the section you need, read the key terms in the **@ a Glance** sections, then use the keywords to narrow down exactly what question you seek an answer to. But don't stop there. Take a look at some of the similar questions, and I'm sure you'll find plenty of additional information and support. Even if you don't know exactly what question to ask, browse through each chapter for plenty of Tips, Notes, Sidebars and Cautions, all intended to enhance your use of the Internet and its associated programs.

? Conventions Used in This Book

Internet and Web Answers uses several conventions designed to make it easier to find the information you need and follow the instructions outlined in the book. These include:

⇨ **Bold type**, which is used for text that you are to type from the keyboard. For example when you need to type a web page address, such as **http://www.osborne.com**, the address will appear in bold.

⇨ *Italic type* is used to call your attention to certain important terms or words and phrases that deserve special emphasis, such as "You should *never* open an e-mail attachment from someone you don't know."

⇨ SMALL CAPITAL LETTERS are used for keys on the keyboard, such as the ENTER key or the SHIFT key.

 Remember   *When you should enter a keyboard command, you will be told to press the key(s). If you are required to enter text or numbers, you'll be told to type them.*

? One Word of Advice

Before you venture out on your quest of Internet knowledge I strongly recommend that if you haven't upgraded your version of Windows 95 with the Service Pack 1 upgrade, you do so *immediately*. Available on

Microsoft's web site at **http://www.microsoft.com/support/**, the Service Pack 1 patch is simple to install, and it fixes many of the problems that plagued the original versions of Windows 95. And while you're at it, if you want to learn more about Windows 95, why not pick up a copy of Marty Matthews' *Windows 95 Answers!*, also published by Osborne/McGraw-Hill. Not all your problems may be related to the Internet or specific Internet applications. Sometimes it's just a matter of tweaking your system, and Marty's book offers a great guide for doing just that.

❓ Are You Ready to Get Going?

Now that you know what this book offers, you're probably chomping at the bit to get going. But before you do, I suggest you first spend some time investigating your system. Find out what version of the Web browser you are using, what email application you use and what online service you use. I also suggest you sit yourself down in front of your computer with this book in hand, so you can follow the instructions step by step. And if you have any problems with any of the answers not working exactly the way you think they should, feel free to e-mail me at **mailto:ckirk@alaska.net**. Let me know what page and exactly what question you are having problems with; oftentimes things change quickly on the Internet, and what used to work last week may be slightly different this week. I'll be happy to answer any questions I can, or at least try to point you in the right direction.

So now, not only do you have the entire Stream International organization's top Internet and Web questions and answers in your hand, you also have a friend in the business. Good luck—and let's get to your questions!

Top Ten FAQs

Answer Topics!

The Top Ten Frequently Asked Questions @ a Glance

The Internet is a vast repository of all sorts of information presented in a multitude of ways. From discussion groups to animated Web pages to streaming audio and video, the Internet delivers tons of information. Finding your way around and getting answers to your questions can be tough. But don't fear. Help is here. This chapter gives you the answers to ten of the most frequently asked questions about the Internet.

? What's the best search engine to use?

It depends on what you're looking for. There are *search engines* and then there are *directories.* Search engines, also called "spiders" or "crawlers," are automated programs that seek out Web sites on the Internet in order to create catalogs of Web pages. These catalogs are then searched using keywords and phrases, returning results that best match the search query.

Unlike search engines, directories are created by humans. Web sites must be submitted to the directory, then the directory company assigns the site to the appropriate category. Directories provide less volume, in terms of Web pages that match a certain keyword, but oftentimes provide better results when you're searching for general information such as health issues, sports, children, or computing.

Here is a list of popular search engines and directories:

Search Engine	URL
Alta Vista	http://altavista.digital.com/
AOL NetFind	http://www.aol.com/netfind/
Excite Search	http://www.excite.com/
HotBot	http://www.hotbot.com/
InfoSeek	http://www.infoseek.com/
Lycos	http://www.lycos.com/
OpenText	http://www.opentext.com/
WebCrawler	http://www.webcrawler.com/
Yahoo	http://www.yahoo.com/

❓ What do I need to <u>create a Web page</u>?

All you really need is a text editor and a little knowledge of the HTML programming language. Web pages are simply text files with special HTML code that have embedded into them pointers to graphics, links, and other information stored on servers across the Internet.

If you plan to do some serious Web page creation, you should probably purchase a graphics editing program such as Photoshop in order to speed up the process. Programs like Photoshop not only provide the tools to create Web page graphics but also let you manipulate and fine-tune images so they load quickly and display clearly.

You might also consider Web page creation programs such as Adobe's PageMill, **http://www.adobe.com**; HotDog Pro, **http://www. sausage.com**; or Microsoft's FrontPage, **http://www.microsoft. com/frontpage**.

❓ I don't want the Netscape home page as my <u>default Start page</u>. How do I change it?

First, go to Netscape's Options menu. Choose General Preferences, then click on the Appearance tab. In the field labeled "Browser starts with …" fill in the URL for the home page you want to automatically display every time Netscape opens up or every time you click the Home button. Finally, make sure that the Home Page Location button is selected.

❓ How can I <u>find an individual 's e-mail address</u>?

If you have the latest version of Netscape Messenger or Navigator you can use the Find People option to locate someone's e-mail address. Or if you have Internet Explorer you can choose Start | Find | Find People. You can also use a variety of Web-based search engines, some of which are listed here:

➪ Four11, at **http://www.four11.com**

➪ WhoWhere, at http://www.whowhere.com

➪ Internet Address Finder, at **http://www.iaf.net**

➪ SwitchBoard, at **http://www.switchboard.com** (SwitchBoard allows you to search not only for e-mail addresses but also for phone numbers)

➪ Yahoo's People Finder, at **http://www.people.yahoo.com**

➪ BigFoot, located at **http://www.bigfoot.com**

⇨ The World E-mail directory, at **http://www.worldemail.com** (contains links to all sorts of e-mail directories)

If you know the company or domain where the person you are trying to find works or receives his or her e-mail, you can also send a message to **postmaster@***domainname*, where *domainname* is the domain name of the company or service provider. For example, if you know that the person has signed up for service at Netcom, you can send a message to **postmaster@netcom.com** asking if he is registered.

If you and the person you are trying to find use the same service provider you can do the following: Check to see if your ISP has enabled fingering on its site. If so, you can use telnet to log on to the ISP's computer. After logging on, issue the command **finger** *name*, where *name* is the name of the person whose address you're searching for. Say you're looking for someone with the last name "Simler." If you type **finger Simler**, your service provider's finger server will respond with a list of all users whose login names contain the word "Simler."

With both America Online and CompuServe you can also search the member directories for members who have similar interests or are located in a particular geographic area. Use the keyword MEMBERS in AOL or GO DIRECTORY in CompuServe.

Why don't I get full 28.8Kbps or 33.6Kbps access with my connection?

There could be several problems. First, you should make sure you have the right modem driver selected in Control Panel | Modem | Properties for the particular modem you are using. Next, make sure you have the hardware handshaking flow control turned on and that you're using the right modem INIT string for your modem. Check your modem's documentation for the correct INIT string to use, or contact your ISP. Finally, double-check your phone line. You may have noise on your line which is causing the modem to drop in speed.

How do I convert existing Netscape Navigator bookmarks to Internet Explorer's Favorites sites?

From the File menu in Internet Explorer, click Open, and then click Open File. Locate the bookmark.htm file in your Netscape folder and click Open. Use the right mouse button to click a bookmark in the Internet Explorer window, and then click Add To Favorites on the menu that appears. Repeat for all bookmarks you want to convert.

You can also use the Bookmarks Converter tool to automatically convert Netscape Navigator bookmarks to shortcuts on the Favorites menu in Internet Explorer for Windows 95. The Bookmarks Converter tool is a file named WINBM2FV.EXE. You'll find WINBM2FV.EXE by searching Shareware.com's index, located at **http://www.shareware.com**.

Are the e-mail or newsgroup postings I send really private? Can someone trace newsgroup postings back to me?

Never consider e-mail messages or newsgroup postings to be private forms of communication. E-mail messages usually travel through many different computers before reaching their intended destination, and newsgroup postings are *meant* to be public.

So never, ever assume any e-mail messages you send are private, even if they are within your own company's network. Not only could someone forward your e-mail without your knowledge, but also, because e-mail messages are stored and then forwarded from one computer system to the next, anyone along the way could read your e-mail.

In addition, remember that computer system tape backups can store e-mail messages. Similarly, any messages you post to a newsgroup or mailing list are open to the public and oftentimes are kept on publicly accessible archives such as DejaNews, located at **http://www.dejanews.com**.

Why can't I save my password in Windows 95 Dial-Up Networking?

Password caching only happens if you install a Windows 95 network client or enable User Profiles on a stand-alone computer. By default, the Internet Setup Wizard only installs the TCP/IP protocol and the dial-up networking components, which are all you really need. To save your password, first make sure you have Client for Microsoft Networks listed when you double-click the Network icon in the Control Panel. If it's not listed, select Add | Client, then select Client for Microsoft Networks. Or, in Control Panels | Passwords, simply set a password for the Windows logon. If you type in a password when Windows starts up, the password will be saved on the Dial-Up Networking screen as well.

How do I <u>unsubscribe to a mailing list?</u>

Normally, you simply issue the command **unsub listname**, where *listname* is the name of the list you have subscribed to, in the body of a message. Some lists require you to spell out the entire word, **unsubscribe**, while others may simply want you to type **signoff**.

For ListServ mailing lists, send a message with the following in the body:

unsub *conference name*

For Majordomo, send a message with the following in the body:

unsubscribe *conference name*

Note   *Sometimes mailing list commands are case-sensitive. When subscribing to a list make sure you follow the commands listed exactly, including typing the words such as "subscribe" or "unsubscribe" exactly as the instructions show.*

How do I send an e-mail message to a group of people without having their names listed on the message?

Most e-mail software programs offer a cc: option, which stands for "carbon copy." This feature lets you send a single message to multiple people. However, the Blind cc: option, which stands for "blind carbon copy," is not always displayed in the standard "compose e-mail" window.

In Netscape, click the To:Mail button, then select Mail Bcc from the View menu to display the bcc: option. With Microsoft's Internet Explorer, click in the Bcc: field and include the e-mail address of the recipient you want to send the message to. America Online requires that you place parentheses around any addresses that you want to hide.

Connection Basics

Answer Topics!

Connection Basics @ a Glance

⇨ There are plenty of ways to get connected to the Internet. From standard telephone lines to elaborate networks, the method you choose often dictates how fast and how easy your connections will be. You can use analog modems, ISDN terminal adapters, Ethernet connections that tie into an existing network, or more advanced technology such as wireless modems or even cable modems, which deliver both Internet connections and cable TV. All these options provide the essential framework for connecting electronically with your coworkers, your neighbors across town, or people worlds apart from you. The first step in exploring the Internet is **getting connected.** And the first step in getting connected is knowing which options will work the best in various situations and configurations.

⇨ Of course, most home and small business Internet users will opt for an analog modem, the cheapest and easiest way to connect to the Internet. But with all the new modem choices available, what should you look for when **buying a modem**?

⇨   Local Internet service providers (ISPs) have popped up all over the place offering low monthly fees. Picking the right one for personal use is relatively easy, but choosing one for business use can be more difficult. There are plenty of features to look for when **choosing an ISP** to host your business or personal account.

⇨   Once you've decided on the connection, configuring your software and **troubleshooting** any problems are not that difficult. Most problems arise with the Windows 95 Dial-Up Networking software. Understanding where to look to change various properties, modem setup strings, or passwords is the key to having a smooth-running, Internet-connected computer.

GETTING CONNECTED

? Can I use my trusty old <u>286 PC</u> to send e-mail files? This computer runs at 12 MHz and uses DOS 5.0.

You certainly can, but you most likely will be shut out of using any graphic-oriented e-mail software. Make sure you buy an internal modem in order to get the highest speed possible. Otherwise, you'll have to upgrade the UART chip in your system. You should be able to use text-only communications software to connect and get your e-mail through a shell account.

? I have an older <u>386 computer</u>. Someone told me I can't use a high-speed modem with it. Is this true, and if so, why not?

You may have an older-style communications port that does not have the 16550 Universal Asynchronous Receiver-Transmitter (UART) chip. This chip provides storage buffers that allow data to be transferred at high speed. If you are using Windows 3.1 or DOS, you can find out exactly what type of chip you have by running MSD.exe. If you have Windows 95, check the Control Panel | Modems | Diagnostics | Com port setting. Make sure you click the "More info" button to see exactly what chip you are using. If it says you have a 16450 UART chip, you'll need to upgrade.

You can add a 16550 UART chip by purchasing an interface card that has one, or by considering purchasing an internal modem that comes with the faster chip technology right on the internal modem card itself.

An Internet Buzzword Primer

Bandwidth

The amount of data a communications circuit can accommodate. A slow modem delivers low bandwidth; an ISDN line offers high bandwidth.

Cache

A directory on the computer used to store Web page graphics and pages for faster access when displaying the page again.

Cyberspace

Coined by author William Gibson, this term denotes a world of networked computers and the people who control them.

Domain

The service provider or company network that gives you access to the Internet. The domain name refers to the unique name, such as *aol.com* or *alaska.net*, that your provider has chosen to identify itself.

Download

The process of transmitting files from a remote computer to your computer. Upload is the process of sending files from your computer to another computer.

Electronic mail (e-mail)

A way to send text messages and/or binary files as attachments from your computer to another user's electronic inbox.

FAQ

An abbreviation for *frequently asked questions.* FAQs exist on either Web pages or e-mail messages. They explain particular topics or answer questions for a particular newsgroup or mailing list.

File transfer protocol (FTP)

The protocol used to transfer files from a file transfer server to your computer.

Anonymous FTP

The ability to log into a file server and download files without having to have a valid account on the server. Anonymous FTP logins use the word "anonymous" as the username and (usually) your e-mail address as the password.

HTML

An abbreviation for *hypertext markup language.* It's the page description language used to create Web pages. HTML files are actually text files that, when viewed by a Web browser display formatted text and graphics in a browser window.

HTTP

An abbreviation for *hypertext transfer protocol.* HTTP is the protocol used to send Web pages to your computer.

IRC

Internet relay chat is the Internet's version of online chat rooms. People converse with each other by typing messages to each other in real time.

ListServ

An automated system that allows a group of users to discuss topics via e-mail.

PPP

An abbreviation for *point-to-point protocol*, a method for connecting a PC computer to an Internet host computer. PPP and SLIP (serial line Internet protocol) both allow computers to use multimedia programs such as Netscape Navigator and RealAudio.

Search engine

A service that lets you search for Web pages, e-mail messages, or newsgroup postings.

Usenet

The worldwide electronic bulletin board system.
A good Internet glossary index can be found on the Web at **http://www.msn.com/tutorial/glossary.html**.

? What computer enhancements do I need to connect to the Internet?

You will need four basic things. The first is a modem, which is a device that connects you to the Internet using standard phone lines. The modem you choose should support at least 28.8Kbps transfer rates.

Next, you will need an analog telephone line. Your telephone line at home is an analog line, and you should have no problem using it to connect. Digital telephone technology, which means the phone line in your office that is connected to the PBX system most likely will not work unless you use a digital-to-analog converter. You need to check with your phone company to ensure the phone line you want to use will work with your analog modem.

Besides a phone line, you will need special software that enables you to dial the phone with your computer and connect to the Internet. Your system may already have this software installed.

Finally, you will need an Internet service provider (ISP).

? **I've been having problems downloading stuff from the Net on my machine at work. Our systems manager says it's probably due to the company <u>firewall</u>...what is she talking about?**

A firewall is either a computer or a series of computers or routers that limits entry into a company's network. There are two different types of firewalls used on the Internet today. The first is called a *packet filtering router*. This router elects whether to forward or block data based on a set of rules programmed into the router itself. The second type, known as a *proxy server*, relies on daemons to provide authentication and to forward packets, possibly on a multi-homed machine which has kernel packet forwarding disabled.

If your company uses a firewall, you may not be able to access certain Web sites or newsgroups, be able to transfer files from file transfer servers, or work with streaming audio or video files. Your company and network administrator decide which options are restricted.

Note   *People often think that having a firewall between their company's internal network and the Internet will solve all their security problems. A firewall can add another layer of security to a network but cannot always stop a determined hacker (or someone within the network) from browsing files or causing havoc.*

? **Can I configure my system to work behind a <u>firewall</u>?**

Yes, *if* you can get access to the necessary information. You will need to know what the settings are for your company's proxy server and what restrictions the firewall has in place. Some firewalls are set to restrict access to certain sites and certain types of data or to limit the traffic coming into the network. You will need to consult with your network administrator for the correct gateway and network numbers and include those numbers in your Control Panel | Network settings and in your Web browser, file transfer software, and other specialized software such as Internet telephones, streaming audio, or video.

? A phone company sales rep has been trying to sell me an ISDN connection for my home office. Would it really save me time?

ISDN stands for *Integrated Services Digital Network,* and it gives you a digital connection from your PC to your service provider. Without such a connection, digital information coming from your PC must be converted to analog information so it can travel over telephone lines via your analog modem. ISDN can transfer the digital information without conversion, so you can get anywhere from 64Kbps to 128Kbps transfer rates to and from your computer. If you're on the Net a good part of the day, ISDN might be a cost-effective option for you.

? What's an ISP?

ISP stands for *Internet service provider,* the company that provides you a connection to the Internet. An Internet service provider can be either local or national. An ISP gives you the software you need as well as an e-mail account and access to other options on the Internet for a monthly fee.

? Our office doesn't need an elaborate network; we just need to log on and off to get our e-mail and do some occasional browsing. Is it possible to connect multiple PCs to a single modem?

There are several hardware solutions that allow you to create a miniature network without all the hassles of elaborate wiring, cabling, and network software. A Canadian company called Protec lets three PCs access the Internet simultaneously using just one telephone line, one modem, and one internet address. You can find Protec Microsystems at **http://www.protec.ca**. The price is around $350.

? What's the difference between an online service and an ISP?

Online services, often referred to as commercial service providers or commercial information service providers, organize the information and display it usually in a menu-driven fashion using specialized software. ISPs usually provide only access to the Internet, without offering any specialized content such as chat rooms, worldwide news, or online games. Also, online services usually have specialized information you can only get on their service. For example, America Online is the only place where you can find Oprah Winfrey online. The Microsoft Network also offers specialized travel services for its members, not found elsewhere on the Internet.

Note   *There's a web page at* **http://www.mindspring.com/ ~lmcgatney/isprate.html** *which offers a relatively complete listing of Internet service providers, along with comments from consumers who use the various services. Another site, called the Online Connection* (**http://www.barkers.org/online**) *compares both regional and national service providers and includes a long list of links for a wide variety of service providers. Both of these sites are worth checking out if you are trying to decide which service to go with.*

What are the most popular commercial providers?

That changes daily. At present, America Online is the largest in terms of sheer numbers of users. Here is a list of the major providers:

Name of Service	Location	Year Started	Number of Subscribers	Customers per Modem	Price
America Online	Dulles, Va.	1989	8 million	30	$19.95 per month for unlimited Internet access.
AT&T WorldNet Service	Bridgewater, New Jersey	1996	More than 600,000	Information not released	$19.95 per month for unlimited Internet access.
CompuServe Interactive	Columbus, Ohio	1979	2.2 million	Information not released	$9.95 for five hours per month, then $2.95 for each additional hour, or $24.95 per month for unlimited access.

Name of Service	Location	Year Started	Number of Subscribers	Customers per Modem	Price
The Microsoft Network	Redmond, Washington	1995	More than 2 million	Information not released	$6.95 for five hours per month, then $2.50 for each additional hour used. (Note that pricing is subject to change.)
SPRYNET	Bellevue, Washington	1996	More than 277,600	Information not released	$19.95 per month for unlimited Internet access.

? What's the difference between a PPP account and a SLIP account?

PPP accounts are faster, offer better error correction, don't require you to use a terminal window to log in, and do not require you to manually enter your Internet address. SLIP is an older technology; most service providers do not use it any more because it's slower than PPP and does not offer as many features as PPP.

? How much RAM do I need to cruise the Internet using Internet Explorer or Netscape Navigator?

You should have at least 16 megabytes. More memory will help in caching the Web pages you visit, or will allow you to run more than just a few programs at a time. Consider upgrading to 32MB if the cost is reasonable.

? What is involved in setting up my brand new Windows 95 computer so it can easily connect to the Internet?

Windows 95 comes with the necessary software to handle connecting to the Internet. So, unlike Windows 3.1, you don't have to do much in the way of adding software, but you do have to accomplish these three main tasks:

⇨ Install Dial-Up Networking if if wasn't included when you installed Windows 95. If you purchased Microsoft Plus! the Internet Wizard will guide you through the necessary steps.

⇨ Set up your Network Configuration using TCP/IP, and supply the DNS server IP address and name.

⇨ Set up your Dial-Up Connection using the Dial-Up Networking software supplied with Windows 95 in order to connect to your provider.

❓ Do I need any kind of special phone line to connect to the Internet?

No. There are several ways to connect to the Internet using your standard telephone line. You can use an analog modem with speeds that range from 28.8Kbps to 56Kbps. This type of modem requires no additional hardware or changes to your existing phone line and will work without additional per-minute costs outside the cost to connect to your provider. If your phone company offers it, you can also connect using what is called ISDN, or Integrated Services Digital Network, which uses a special plug with standard phone lines to connect you directly to a digital phone switch. ISDN offers the ability to transfer data without having to convert analog signals into digital signals. The result is a faster transfer rate—up to 128K, twice as fast as current analog modem speeds..

❓ I've tried cruising the Net on my lunch hour, but it's so slow! Some of my friends and co-workers say the same thing. Is there a better time of day to use the Internet?

Yes, definitely. The very, very early morning hours and very late at night are probably the best times to go cruising. Between the hours of 4 P.M. and 11 P.M. on weekdays, regardless of where you live, the Internet is bogged down with people who get off work and jump on commercial and local ISPs to get their personal e-mail and browse. You do see a decrease in traffic in the summer, early on Sundays, Wednesday afternoons, and during the day on holidays because government and universities are usually not as active online at those times.

? Why can't I <u>use my telephone</u> while I'm on the Internet? I do have call-waiting.

Even though you have call-waiting, you only have one phone line. When you are using the Internet you are essentially occupying the telephone line, which makes it unavailable for voice calls. Call-waiting can interrupt your Internet transmissions and it's recommended that you turn it off before connecting.

? I keep hearing about <u>WebTV</u>. What exactly is it?

WebTV is actually hardware, manufactured and sold by both Sony and Philips-Magnavox, that works with the WebTV Networks ISP. The WebTV box has a built-in modem (33.6Kbps at the time this book was produced) and the necessary hardware to connect you to the Internet using your TV as the means to display the information. You can send and receive mail, view Web pages, chat with others online, and view newsgroups through Web page-based newsgroup reader services.

? I'm all set up with a <u>Windows 95 computer</u>. Now how do I use it to get onto the Internet?

First, you need to install the Dial-Up adapter and the TCP/IP networking protocol if it hasn't already been installed. The Microsoft Plus! CD, which comes with many new systems or can be purchased in any software store, offers what is called the Internet Wizard, an application that will step you through the process of getting your Windows 95 computer connected to the Internet. The Wizard will guide you through installing the proper Internet software, configuring your modem, and entering the proper information about your Internet service provider. If you don't have the Microsoft Plus! CD, you can still manually configure a new dialup session with the Dial-Up Networking option installed on your Windows 95 system.

? What is <u>Winsock</u> and why do I need it?

If your computer has not been preconfigured to connect to and interact with the Internet, you need special software that tells your computer how to do just that. That's where Winsock comes into play.

Windows Sockets, or Winsock, is a standard application programming interface, basically configuration files for Microsoft Windows allowing you to use TCP/IP, the language of the Internet. Without Winsock you would not be able to cruise the Net, since your computer would not be able to communicate with other computers connected to the Internet.

BUYING A MODEM

? I have a 28.8Kbps modem, but now I'm seeing faster ones in the store. What's the advantage of a 33.6Kbps modem? Should I upgrade?

A 33,600 bits-per-second (bps) modem is 4,800 bits per second faster than a 28,800 bps modem. If your service provider utilizes 33.6Kbps modems, you should see a noticeable difference, granted your telephone lines are relatively noise-free.

If you already have a V.34 28.8Kbps modem, ask the manufacturer if the modem is software upgradable to 33.6Kbps technology. Many of the better modems can be reprogrammed via flash read-only memory using software to upgrade them.

? Why would anyone want to buy a 33.3Kbps modem? Wouldn't it be best just to get a 56Kbps modem?

First, not all ISPs have 56Kbps modems installed at their sites because such modems require proprietary digital terminal equipment. So before you run out and buy a new modem, check with your provider to see if it even offers such a service. Second, unlike that of 28.8Kbps or 33.3Kbps modems, the technology used in 56Kbps modems does not rely on a standard protocol, so many of the brands are simply not compatible with each other. Therefore, if you are considering buying a 56Kbps modem, you'll first need to check to find out what brand your ISP has so you can buy the same and be compatible. Eventually there will be a standard.

 Note   The three current chip sets for 56Kbps modems are the US Robotics' X2 chip, Rockwell's K56flex, and AT&T/Lucent's K56flex.

? Is a 56Kbps modem really twice as fast as a 28.8Kbps modem?

No. Because 56Kbps modems use digital-to-analog technology, the 56Kbps speed only works in one direction—from your ISP to you. Going the other way, from you to your provider, the speed is about 33.6Kbps. Overall, you should get a combined speed of between 40 and 50Kbps.

? If I buy a 56Kbps modem, will I need a special phone line?

No. Unlike an ISDN terminal adapter, which uses a standard phone line for transmission but which does require a special phone jack, a 56Kbps modem won't require any special wiring or equipment. However, because of its increased speed capabilities, your new 56Kbps modem will require a clean, relatively noise-free telephone line. If you haven't been able to get optimum speed with your existing modem because of your phone line, you may need to have the telephone company take a good look at your wiring or remove repeaters or multiplexers in the telephone path between your system and your ISP. If your ISP offers 56K service, ask if it offers loaner modems so that you can verify the speed of your connection before you spend the money on a 56K modem.

? Which is better—a 56Kbps modem or ISDN?

It depends on what you want—faster speed at a high price or slower speed at a lower price. 56Kbps modems only offer that speed going one way, whereas ISDN moves along at 64Kbps both ways. ISDN does cost more, not only because the terminal adapter (modem) is more expensive but also because it requires special installation by the phone company. Also, consider that most ISDN service is charged on a per-minute basis during prime-time hours, whereas 56Kbps modems use standard phone lines that don't have per-minute charges attached. If it's true speed you need, with clean digital access, then definitely ISDN is the way to go. If you need relatively fast speed, slightly faster than a 33.6Kbps modem can provide, and you don't have money to burn, then choose a 56Kbps modem.

? **Why should I spend money on a 56Kbps modem? Aren't standard analog phone lines only capable of handling about 35Kbps?**

That's true if both ends are connecting in the traditional analog method. The actual bandwidth of a pure digital channel like ISDN is 64K. If your ISP has powerful enough equipment, then a 56Kbps modem will take advantage of digital connections on the ISP's end, allowing you to connect over your regular phone lines at 33.6Kbps.

? **What do all those blinking lights on my external modem mean?**

Those lights are giving you indications of what is happening behind the scenes between the phone and the telephone line. Here is a quick rundown of what they mean:

Signal	Condition of Modem
RI	Receiving ring signal
HS	Connected at highest speed
M	Set to auto-answer
CD	Picking up carrier detect signal
OH	Off hook
RD	Receiving data
TD	Sending (transmitting) data
TR	Terminal is ready (sometimes MR for "modem ready")

? **What should I look for when I buy a modem?**

You should look for a brand name, such as U.S. Robotics, Zoom, or Supra, to name a few. The modem manufacturer should have a Web site where you can download updated modem drivers. The modem should also be flash-ROM upgradable, meaning you can boost the speed and capabilities of the modem with software instead of a hardware fix. You should also buy at least a 33.6Kbps modem.

? The documentation says that my modem is flash-ROM upgradable. What does that mean?

If you have a V.34 28.8Kbps modem, it might be upgradable to a faster speed through what is called flash-ROM. Flash-ROM offers the ability to speed up your modem by using software to send instructions to the read-only memory of the modem. Many of the better modems can be reprogrammed via flash read-only memory.

? How do I find out how fast the connection is between my modem and my ISP?

Simply move your mouse pointer over the connection icon in your System Tray (located in the lower right-hand corner of your task bar), then double-click. The number of bytes sent and received along with the current connection speed will be listed, as shown here:

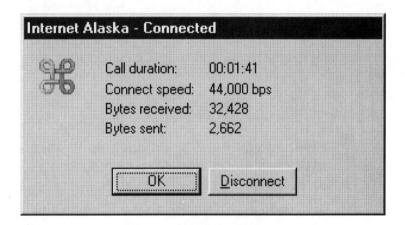

? How do I set the modem INIT string in Windows 95?

Select Control Panel | Modem. Select the modem you want to configure, then click the Properties button. Next, click the Connection tab, then click the Advanced button, and enter the modem INIT string in the "Extra settings" field. You'll see a box that looks something like this:

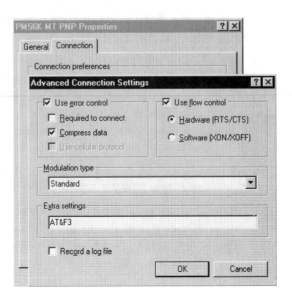

Make sure you do not include an AT command. Windows 95's dial-up settings take care of sending the AT command to the modem. All you have to do is include the actual string, which looks something like this:

s27=48s32=6s54=0#cid=0.

? I'm trying to install my modem in Windows, but I don't see my brand on the list. What should I do?

Check your box or owners manual to see if your modem is using the Rockwell chip set. If so, choose "Rockwell" first. If that doesn't work, or if your modem doesn't have the Rockwell chip set, try choosing the "standard" or generic modems next. Also, make sure you either check your modem manufacturer's home page or Microsoft's site (**http://www.microsoft.com**) for updates to modem driver files for Windows 95 users.

? Is there a place on the Web that gives me all the skinny on modems?

One of the best places that has links to virtually every modem manufacturer, along with technical notes, reviews, and tips is Modems, Modems, Modems, located at **http://www.rosenet.net/~costmo/**.

? I've tried to install my modem, but am having all sorts of problems getting it to work, including getting Windows to recognize it. Have any suggestions?

If you have problems with your modem installation, the best thing to do is to simply start the installation process from scratch. But before you do that, check the Control Panel I Modems I General option and make sure you remove all previous modem installations. Next, in the Control Panel I System I Device Manager window, shown here,

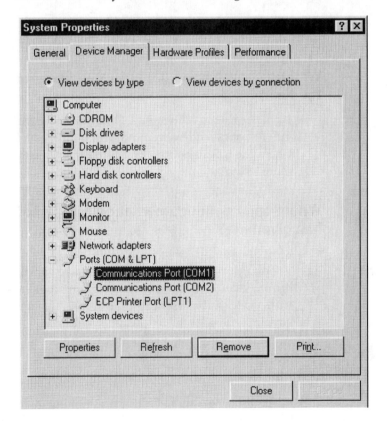

make sure you remove the COM port installations. Then, in the Control Panel I Add New Hardware option, have Windows 95 detect new hardware. If Windows still can't find your modem or picks the wrong modem, select the modem manually from the list of modems presented. Once installed, restart your machine and try again.

? **Is there some way I can <u>test my phone line</u> to make sure it will handle a 56Kbps modem?**

U.S. Robotics has a test line you can use to dial in with your existing V.34 modem to find out if your phone line supports the new 56Kbps X2 technology. If your phone line passes that test, it's likely you will be able to use a 56Kbps modem. You can find the instructions and phone number on the U.S. Robotics Web page at **http://x2.usr.com/ linetest1.html**.

CHOOSING AN INTERNET SERVICE PROVIDER

? **Why do I sometimes get abruptly <u>disconnected from the Net?</u>**

It may be due to call-waiting. Or, if you are using a Rockwell-based U.S. Robotics modem, your modem may need a firmware upgrade. Check the U.S. Robotics site at **http://www.usrobotics.com** for more information.

? **Where can I get <u>documentation for the software</u> my ISP has given me?**

Most likely online or in a bookstore. Most ISPs will also create technical support Web pages with links to various online documentation for the software they provide. Rarely do you get a full manual for the browser or e-mail software ISPs include. You can find support online for the following products:

Product	URL
Netscape	http://www.netscape.com
Microsoft Internet Explorer	http://www.microsoft.com/explorer
Eudora e-mail software	http://www.qualcomm.com
Pegasus Mail software	http://www.pegasus.com

? **I'm considering signing on with an Internet service provider. Can I expect a <u>good connection?</u>**

You should expect that there will be between 12 and 20 users for every modem, which means you will probably get a few busy signals during peak hours (4 P.M. to 11 P.M.). You should expect a relatively reliable connection; however, frequent service interruptions, which can last anywhere from one hour to five days, are common with providers that experience rapid growth. You should also expect that an ISP specializes in one platform of computer, either Mac or PC. You may experience long delays for phone support, and a fee may be charged if a technician must visit your site to fix your problem.

What should I look for in a good ISP when I first sign up?

Nowadays, there are plenty of Internet service providers to choose from, so that means finding the right one to meet your unique needs. Here are some questions to ask before signing up:

⇨ What kind of equipment do I need at my site?

⇨ What computer platforms do you support? Mac or PC?

⇨ What connection options do you offer and how are they priced?

⇨ Do you offer a flat rate for unlimited Internet access? And is there a limit on the amount of hours I can be on at any one time or during any 24-hour period?

⇨ Do you charge a start-up fee?

⇨ Do you offer a free trial period?

⇨ Do you include the software?

⇨ If I decide I want to use my own software, can I?

⇨ Is there a local access number for where I live?

⇨ What speeds do your modems support?

⇨ How often will I get a busy signal?

⇨ Do you provide user support by answering questions via telephone, electronic mail, or both? What are your hours of operation?

⇨ Do you provide any Internet documentation locally, such as useful files on the host computer?

⇨ Do you offer any free or fee-based training? On-site or at your location?

⇨ Do you have a toll-free access number in case I'm away from home?

⇨ Do you support ISDN connections?

⇨   Do I get space for my own Web page? How much?

⇨   Do you provide toll-free tech support?

? I'm about to make that first call to my service provider. What <u>information</u> should I ask for?

You need the following information in order to set up your computer to connect to the Internet:

⇨   Username

⇨   Password

⇨   Local access phone number

⇨   Your host and domain name

⇨   DNS server IP address

⇨   Whether your connection uses a static IP address or not

⇨   The IP subnet mask

? Where can I find a <u>list of service providers</u> in my area?

The yellow pages is usually the first place to go. Look under either Internet Service Providers, or check the Computer section. Another option is to use a friend's Internet connected computer and go to **http://thelist.iworld.com** to search for service providers in your area. You can also find a list of Internet service providers that supply Netscape software with each account by visiting Netscape's home page at **http://www.netscape.com**.

? Can I <u>sign up for an ISP online</u>?

Several Internet and commercial service providers allow for you to sign up online. America Online, CompuServe, and Netcom offer this option. You can also use Netscape's ISP select program to find an ISP in your area, then sign up directly online. Check **www.netscape.com/ focus2/ assist/isp-select/index.html** on the World Wide Web.

? **What should I ask my ISP to do to <u>speed up my Internet</u> connection?**

There are a couple of things you can do. First, find out what brand of modem the ISP uses and buy the same brand. Oftentimes using the same brand with the same type of compression will increase your connection speed. Next, find out whether your ISP uses either a T1, T2, or T3 line to connect to the Internet. If it isn't using any of these high-speed lines, find one that does. Also, ask the prospective ISP if it uses UNIX servers or standard PC servers, and inquire as to the amount of hard disk space and RAM it has installed as well as the number of simultaneous users it has at peak times.

TROUBLESHOOTING

? **I can log on to the Internet but I can't <u>access a Web site I want</u>. What could be the problem?**

There are several possibilities:

⇨ Check that your TCP/IP protocol is configured properly to use your service provider's DNS server.

⇨ If you're using Internet Explorer prior to version 3.0, make sure you don't have both the Use Auto Dial and Use Proxy Server options in the Internet Properties dialog box enabled.

⇨ Try emptying the cache to your Internet Explorer browser. Then try the site again.

⇨ Verify that you haven't accidentally replaced the Wsock32.dll file included with Windows 95 with another third-party DLL file.

? **I'm getting the message <u>"comm errors [FRAME] = x"</u> after loading Trumpet or trying to use Netscape. What does this mean?**

This usually means you have your MTU size set too high. Try lowering your MTU settings down from, say, 1500 to 576 or even lower (if 576 doesn't fix the problem).

? When I double-click to launch an Internet-related application, why doesn't my Windows 95 <u>computer invoke the dialer automatically</u>?

If you have Autodial installed, and it just doesn't seem to be working, you're experiencing a common problem with Microsoft's Dial-Up Networking. The workaround is not to use Autodial. Instead, double-click on My Computer, then Dial-Up Networking, then your connection, and then click Connect to dial manually.

? How do I stop the Dial-Up Networking window from appearing and making me click the <u>Connect button</u> every time I want to log on?

Open the Dial-Up Networking folder, then click to select the connection you want to configure. Select Connections | Settings, and check Redial. This will automatically prompt the software to redial if the connection is lost. Next select "Don't prompt to use Dial-Up Networking," as shown here, and click OK to save the changes.

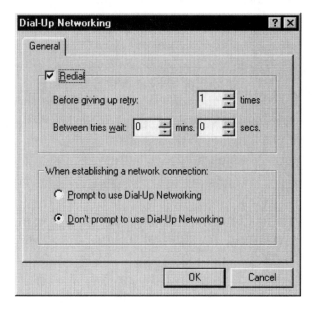

Now each time you go to use your Dial-Up Network connection it will automatically dial without asking you to connect.

? **Why does it take so long for my Windows 95 system to connect to my service provider?**

Most likely your system is set up to allow too many network protocols, thus slowing down the login process. If you are only using the dial-up networking and your computer is not connected to another network, select Dial-Up Networking, then click the icon for your ISP's connection. Select File | Properties, then click the Server Types tab, and uncheck the boxes next to NetBEUI and IPX/SPX compatible. Since you are only using one protocol, TPC/IP, you don't need to have the others checked.

? **What do CRC errors mean?**

CRC errors, especially if you get them while downloading, are usually a sign of overrunning data, or incoming data being lost because the computer is unable to process the information in a proper amount of time. There are a variety of reasons for CRC errors including not having a 16550A UART chip installed, having the wrong hardware flow control settings, problems with your Windows VGA monitor driver, or conflicts with memory managers or drive caching. Check your modem manual for more information on resolving CRC errors.

? **Windows 95 doesn't automatically load the Dial-Up Networking software when I launch Netscape Navigator. Can I configure it to launch automatically?**

You could install Microsoft's Internet Explorer, since Explorer will launch a Dial-Up connection when you type an Internet address. But you still have to click the Dial-Up Connect button to initiate the connection. If you'd rather not do that, you can download Vector Development's free Dial-Up Networking Connection Enhancer, which will launch the Dial-Up Networking and click the Connect button automatically. You can find Enhancer at **http://www.vecdev.com**.

? **Can I disable call-waiting from within Windows 95?**

Yes, if you choose Control Panel | Modems | Dialing Properties. The following dialog box will appear:

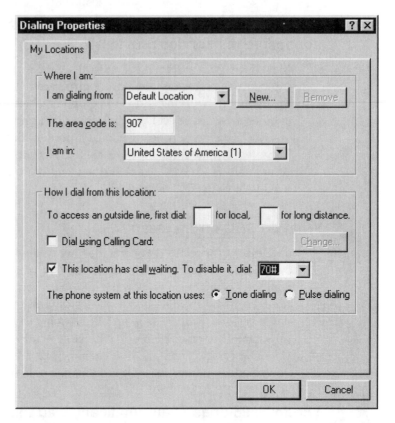

Make sure you check the box labeled "This location has call-waiting."

❓ Every time I try to get online, my computer <u>disconnects</u> <u>me</u>, then asks me if I want to reconnect. What's wrong?

You might be experiencing problems with your modem or the INIT string used to initialize it. Or you might have a problem with your service provider. The first thing you should do is check to make sure you are using the right modem by checking the Control Panel | Modems | Properties option. If the modem is set correctly, and you have the proper settings to connect to your ISP, try selecting Control Panel | Internet | Connection, then unchecking "Connect to Internet as needed." Click OK, then restart your system and try connecting again.

? When I try to connect to a site I get the following error message: "DNS error Site not found." Do I have something configured wrong?

If you do not have the correct DNS server in your networking setup, your computer may not know which server within your Internet service provider's network is responsible for changing addresses such as this, **http://www.alaska.net**, into Internet addresses computers actually understand that look like this, 206.149.99.3. If your computer is not properly configured to connect to a DNS server, it will not be able to locate Web pages, file transfer servers or e-mail addresses. Check with your ISP for the right DNS server number.

? For some reason I can't seem to connect to my ISP at the full 33.6Kbps speed. What's up?

There could be several problems.

⇨ Check to see that the correct modem driver is selected in Control Panel | Modems | Properties for the particular modem you are using.

⇨ Verify that you have the hardware handshaking flow control turned on.

⇨ Make sure you're using the right modem INIT string for your modem.

⇨ Check your modem's documentation for the correct INIT string to use, or contact your ISP.

⇨ Double-check your phone line. You may have noise on your line which is causing the modem to drop in speed.

? How can I find out how long I've been on the Internet?

Double-click the connection icon in the System Tray. A dialog box will appear displaying the amount of time you've been connected and at what speed. I get only the bytes received and transmitted.

? How can I find out what my IP address is?

Windows 95 comes with a utility called WinIPCFG, which will tell you not only your IP address but also the address of the DNS server you are using. To run WinIPCFG, simply click the Start button, choose

Run, and then type **winipcfg** and hit ENTER. You'll see a box that looks something like this:

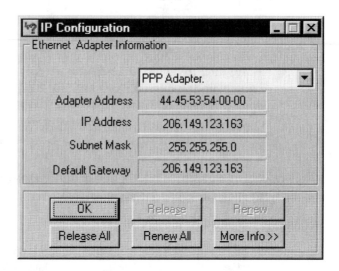

? **I have disabled the "disconnect after *x* minutes" option in the software setup, but I lose the connection to my ISP anywhere from 2 to 30 minutes after I log on even when I'm actively cruising the Internet! What can I do to make it stop dropping me?**

Pinning down the source of your problem means double-checking your system setup. You may have the wrong modem selected in the Control Panel | Modems option, or you could be using the wrong modem INIT string.

But you could also have a noisy phone line which is causing disruption in your Internet connection. Also, if you have call-waiting you will need to disable it in the Control Panel | Modems | Dialing Properties | General tab.

? **What are some common mistakes I can avoid making with my Internet setup?**

Here are the top five:

⇨ Using a Windows 3.1 TCP/IP protocol, such as Trumpet Winsock, with a Windows 95 computer. You're likely to encounter all sorts of problems and delays in your connection.

⇨ Installing Netscape Navigator Personal Edition and using its dialer instead of the Windows 95 dialer. You should make sure you always use the Windows 95 dialer when connecting.

⇨ Installing a provider's setup disk for Windows 3.1. It may end up overwriting your Windows 95 DLL files. Beware of older software from providers such as America Online or CompuServe—it might contain outdated or incompatible DLL files.

⇨ Leaving the "File & Print Sharing for MS networks" option turned on over TCP/IP. This will slow down your connection to the Internet and open up your system, making it possible for someone on the Internet to see, delete, move, or rename your files.

⇨ Not getting the right connection and server information from your provider, or placing the right information in the wrong fields.

❓ Why does it say "No Dialtone" when I try to connect to the Internet?

It could be that you don't have the telephone line connected to the proper plug in the back of the modem. Many modems have two plugs, one that goes directly to the telephone wall jack and another that you can connect a handset to so you can take voice calls when you're not on the Internet. Another problem might be that an extension in your house is off the hook.

❓ Is there anything I can ask the phone company to do to make my network connection faster?

There are several things. First, you could have the phone company check the lines in and outside your house for noise or bad telephone connections. The phone technicians can oftentimes pinpoint problems with telephone lines that may be causing delays or interference. Also, ask the phone company to have repeaters removed from your phone line if such repeaters are installed. Repeaters boost the telephone signal so it can travel longer distances but can interrupt data transmissions, thus slowing down your connection to the Internet. Finally, ask whether your connection can bypass any multiplexers installed within your connection to the phone company's switch. They can also slow down a connection.

I just set up my computer and I'm having problems connecting to my ISP. The modem chirps and buzzes, but I can't get much further than that. What's wrong?

First, make sure your server type is set up correctly on the Dial-Up Networking | Properties | Server type tab for the icon of your Internet provider. If you are set up to use a PPP account, make sure the server type is set to PPP, not SLIP or CSLIP.

I can connect to my ISP, but I'm having problems getting my e-mail and browsing Web pages. Is something wrong with my modem?

It's probably not your modem; it's more likely a problem with the server settings you're specifying in the Mail and Web preferences settings. Double-check the servers specified in the applications and make sure they are the ones your ISP has specified.

How do I get Windows 95 Dial-Up Networking to redial the phone when the line to my ISP is busy?

Open the Programs | Accessories | Dial-Up Networking folder, and locate the icon for your ISP. Click once, then select Connections | Settings and check the Redial checkbox, specifying the number of times to redial and the interval to wait between each attempt.

Can I find out the route a message takes when I send it from my computer to another computer?

Sure! Windows 95 has a utility called tracert, which actually traces the route information takes as it travels from your computer to your service provider to the intended destination. You can supply any device you are trying to contact, whether it be a Web server, e-mail server, individual machine, or FTP server. To run tracert, click the Start menu and choose Run, then type **tracert** *name* where *name* is the name of the device you want to trace the route to. You can also supply an IP address. Tracert will display all the devices that are used in order to get from one location to the next.

? Can I create <u>scripts</u> to automate my Dial-Up Network connection?

Yes, you can, if you install the Dial-Up Scripting software. Check **http://www.microsoft.com** if you need a copy of the Scripting software. First you install the Dial-Up Networking Scripting tool, then assign a script file to the network connection you are using.

? Where do I get <u>SLIP</u> software for my Windows 95 computer?

You can install the Windows 95 SLIP support files. Check the Windows 95 CD-ROM for the directory \Admin\Apptools\Slip\. Inside this directory are the necessary files to add to your system. You can also get the SLIP files online at Microsoft's Web site. Search for the Windows 95 SLIP Scripting package, which is free.

? What other things can I do to <u>speed up my network connection</u>?

There are plenty of factors that can affect network and modem speed throughput. Here are some things to check.

⇨ If you are using an internal modem, make sure you have a real 16550A or 16550F UART chip. Run the MSD utility to find out which chip is installed. If you are using an external modem, check your COM port for the version of UART chip that's installed in your computer.

⇨ If you're using a 28.8Kbps modem, you should set the speed of your modem to at least 115.2Kbps.

⇨ If your phone line is noisy or you get frequent radio-type interference, remember that different brands of modems can handle noisy phone lines with varying results. You do get what you pay for.

⇨ If you plan on purchasing a new modem, check with your ISP first to see which kind it uses. If you and your ISP have the same kind of modem, connections may be faster, especially with all the new compression technology being used.

❓ I'm having a problem connecting to a site on the Internet. When I do, invariably my <u>system locks up</u>. What's going on?

It could be a problem with the site. But if other people can access it, it may be a problem with your Web page cache. Clear your Web browser's memory cache first, then try reloading the site.

❓ What is the most recent version of <u>Trumpet Winsock</u>?

The latest version of Trumpet Winsock is 3.0d. It includes both 16-bit stack and Windows 95 support. You can find copies at Shareware.com, located at **http://www.shareware.com**.

❓ Trumpet Winsock gives me the error message <u>"Unable to load TCP"</u> when I first start it up. What could be wrong?

Most likely you have supplied in the BOOTP field an IP address in Trumpet's configuration. BOOTP should always be set to 0.0.0.0. If it isn't change it, then, exit, and relaunch Trumpet Winsock. If you still get the error message you may have a corrupted or misconfigured trumpwsk.ini file. Try replacing that file with one you know works. If you don't have a good trumpwsk.ini file available, download a fresh copy of Trumpet Winsock and reinstall the application.

❓ I get an <u>"Undefined Dynalink"</u> error message when I try to use Netscape or other applications. What's the problem?

First, if you are using Trumpet Winsock, you should first check for duplicate Winsock.dll files. If you have more than one Winsock.dll file, you should remove all but the one being used by Trumpet Winsock. Delete any files outside the Trumpet Winsock or Windows directories.

? **I've <u>upgraded from a 14.4Kbps modem to a 28.8Kbps</u> modem, but I don't see any substantial increase in speed. Why not?**

There could be several problems. First, you may not have changed the settings in your modem software. Check the Control Panel I Modems I Properties I Maximum Speed setting to ensure you've updated the modem speed.

If the speed matches, you might have problems with a noisy phone line. If you are using an extension or a long phone cord strung across the floor or across flourescent lights, try a shorter cord or try running the cord away from lights, radios, or other things that may be emitting interference.

If your computer has an old UART chip, upgrading to a 28.8Kbps modem will not improve actual performance. You must first upgrade your UART chip to a 16550 version in order to see increased speed.

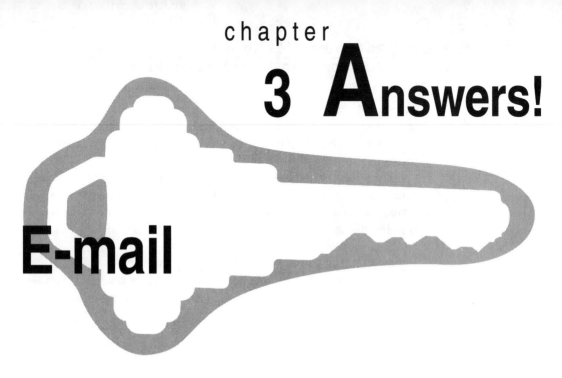

chapter

3 Answers!

E-mail

Answer Topics!

E-mail @ a Glance

⇨   Sending and receiving e-mail. You do it every day. Sure, you know the basics, enough to get by on the job, but there are plenty of **advanced e-mail functions** that you may never have explored. Features such as sorting and filtering help keep your inbox clean and organized. Searching for addresses, adding nifty signature files to your messages, and organizing your address book can expand your e-mail capabilities.

⇨   **Mailing lists** offer a way to chat about all sorts of things with people around the world. You name it—whatever you are looking to discuss, there most likely is an e-mail list on that topic. Finding out which lists are available, how to subscribe, and what commands can be sent to a list server can help you maximize your subscription.

⇨   Many people get their e-mail through **commercial services** such as CompuServe or America Online. Each commercial service comes with a variety of unique features and options specific to the provider's e-mail system. Learning the intricacies of the system will help speed up your day-to-day e-mail chores.

⇨   Regardless of how hard you try not to, you may run into problems sending and receiving e-mail. It may be a simple bounced e-mail message or problems sending attachments. You may just need a little push in the right direction to know where to start **troubleshooting problems**, since many e-mail glitches can be solved by checking e-mail addresses, understanding how to decode file formats, knowing where the options are in your favorite e-mail program, or preventing spammers from sending unsolicited e-mail your way.

ADVANCED E-MAIL FUNCTIONS

 Is an e-mail <u>address</u> meant for one person only?

No. Groups of people, the postmaster, or the person who takes care of a company's e-mail can also have addresses. In addition, there are special mailboxes that send specific information back to you if you send them a certain command, and they use addresses as well.

? Isn't there just one directory somewhere that contains e-mail <u>addresses for everyone connected</u> to the Internet?

Not exactly. First of all, people change their e-mail addresses frequently because they leave their jobs or change providers. Keeping track of the minute-by-minute changes worldwide would be extremely time-consuming. However, directory services such as WhoWhere and Four11 do try to provide some form of worldwide directory.

Also, consider the privacy aspect. Many companies do not want to advertise their employees' e-mail addresses simply to keep e-mail traffic flow to a minimum. If the address of every employee in every company were advertised in a global database, just think how many unsolicited e-mails would be sent!

? What is an e-mail <u>alias</u>?

An e-mail alias is basically a fake e-mail address that diverts mail sent to the alias address directly to your real e-mail address. E-mail aliasing is also called "e-mail forwarding." E-mail aliasing/forwarding lets you change service providers without having to change e-mail addresses. Services such as BigFoot (**http://www.bigfoot.com**), Iname (**http://www.iname.com**), RocketMail (**http://www.rocketmail.com**), PoBox.com (**http://www.pobox.com**), and MailCity (**http://www.mailcity. com**) offer free and fee-based e-mail forwarding services.

In some mail programs, "aliases" also refers to nicknames you give people in your Address Book.

? Sometimes e-mail I send is received instantly. Other times it seems to take hours or even days. Why is there such a difference in the <u>amount of time</u> it takes to send and receive messages?

Some mail sites only connect to the Internet periodically, while others connect every few seconds. The traffic one site may be experiencing can slow down the transfer of e-mail, especially if the site has only limited bandwidth capacity. Also, the site you are trying to send to may be down for maintenance or it may be improperly configured.

❓ How exactly does <u>anonymous remailing</u> work?

An anonymous remailer strips the personal details from your e-mail message, then forwards your message to the intended recipient. Anonymous remailers are often used when posting to newsgroups so that any personal information cannot be traced back to the poster. Although the recipient doesn't know who the sender is, he or she can respond via the anonymous remailer.

For a list of active anonymous remailers, check the Remailer List on the Web at **http://www.cs.berkeley.edu/~raph/remailer-list.html**.

❓ What is <u>bulk e-mail</u>?

Bulk e-mail refers to sending the same message to a large number of recipients. It is different from spamming or unsolicited e-mail in that bulk mail is usually sent to recipients that have previously requested to be sent the e-mail or are part of a network mail system. Many ISPs have restrictions, however, on the number of messages that can be sent within a 24-hour period as well as on the number of recipients a single e-mail message can have. Check with your ISP to find out what its restrictions are.

❓ Are e-mail addresses <u>case-sensitive</u>?

As a rule, most e-mail addresses should be typed in lowercase. Some university systems, BITNET systems, and military systems, however, are case sensitive, whereas commercial systems such as America Online or Netcom are not case sensitive.

❓ What is the <u>cc: field</u> for? Why not just use the To: field instead?

When you are sending a message that you want the recipient to act on, you type his or her name in the To: field. When you want to send a carbon or courtesy copy to other people, you include their e-mail addresses in the cc: field.

❓ Can I set my mail program to <u>check for messages automatically</u>?

Most e-mail programs allow you to check for messages every so many minutes and alert you of new messages by either playing a sound file or displaying an icon depicting new messages. You can find the settings for checking e-mail every X minutes either under your Mail and News Preferences or Configuration in the Edit or Options menu. For example, in Netscape Mail you would choose Options | Mail and News Preferences, then choose Servers, as shown in Figure 3-1.

Finally, check the "Check for mail every X minutes" box, supplying the number of minutes.

? Is there a way to convert my address book file from Pegasus Mail to Netscape?

There is a utility called Interguru which will, through the use of scripts, convert address books, a.k.a. nicknames or aliases, from Eudora, Pegasus, Netscape, Pine, and Elm format to the Netscape address format. You can find it on the Web at **http://www.interguru.com/ mailconv.htm**.

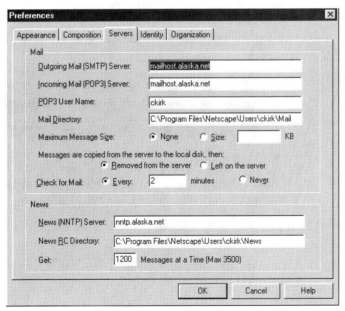

Figure 3-1.   With Netscape's Server options, you can choose how often your system checks for new mail.

? **Is it safe to use my <u>corporate e-mail account</u> for personal matters? I've heard that many companies are restricting Web browsing to only company-related sites. Could the same apply to e-mail?**

Consider e-mail, like any other business communication tool your company supplies, to be available for the sole purpose of conducting business, not for chatting with your long-lost relatives and friends across the country. Also, remember that the contents of your e-mail messages are considered company property—and may be stored in company archives.

? **How much will it <u>cost to send an e-mail message overseas?</u>**

Nothing! There is no cost for sending e-mail messages to any country. Any e-mail-enabled computer connected to the Internet can receive and send messages to any other computer free of charge—excluding the monthly or hourly connect charges—regardless of its geographic location.

? **Can I check to see if a message has been <u>delivered</u>?**

Yes. With CompuServe you can request a return receipt, and with America Online you can select Show Status when clicking on an e-mail message in your Sent Mail box. You'll see a message much like this one:

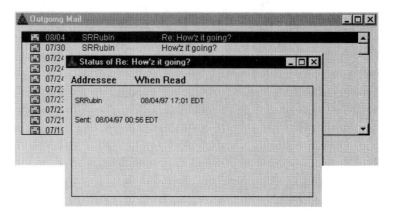

With cc:Mail you can check the Receipt option. Netscape Communicator's Messenger also has a receipt feature. Check the Configuration or Preferences options of your e-mail program for this feature.

? Can I get my e-mail through the Web?

Yes, there are several services that will let you do this, granted you are using a POPMAIL server. The most popular is a service called "Hotmail." You can also use Hotmail as a permanent e-mail address to which all your mail will be forwarded. You can find Hotmail at **http://www.hotmail.com**. RocketMail is another service that lets you get your e-mail through a Web browser.

Hotmail isn't the only service available however. Also check out RocketMail (**http://www.rocketmail.com**), MailCity (**http://www. mailcity.com**), BigFoot (**http://www.bigfoot.com**), and Netaddress (**http://www.netaddress.com**). These are just a few of the free Web-based e-mail forwarding services popping up all over the Web.

? Is there a list of e-zines I can get via e-mail?

There are tons of e-zines popping up every day; one of the best ways to get a list of them is by sending an e-mail message to **Agora.dna. affrc.go.jp**. Leave the subject blank, but in the body of the message type the following:

SEND http://propagandist.com/tkemzl/full.htm

You can get the same list on the Web by simply supplying the URL:

http://propagandist.com/tkemzl/full.htm

? How do I send an e-mail message to a fax machine?

If your company or service provider does not offer e-mail to fax gateways, such as is the case with CompuServe and America Online, you should check out the many free and commercial services for sending e-mails to fax machines listed in the *E-mail to FAX FAQ*, found on the Web at **http://www.northcoast.com/savetz/fax-faq.html**.

A commercial service called Jfax, located at **http://www.jfax.com**, can also send your faxes, voice mail, and e-mail to a single mailbox.

? How do I forward my e-mail to somebody else?

If you're on a Unix system, you can have all of your mail forwarded to any valid Internet e-mail account by creating a text file called .forward. This file, which should reside in your home directory should contain a single line of text. This single line of text should be the complete Internet e-mail address to which you want your messages forwarded. You can also visit the Mail Tools page on the Web, at **http://charlotte.acns.nwu.edu/mailtools**.

? Isn't there any company that provides free e-mail accounts?

Juno.com is one company that provides a free e-mail account to anyone using a Windows-based computer system. You dial into Juno's system using its specialized software, and you can then send and receive Internet mail. Contact Juno at 1-800-654-JUNO or on the Web at **http://www.juno.com**.

A service called FreeMail offers Windows users in the United Kingdom a free e-mail address. Like Juno.com, you simply dial in to the service using the company's software to retrieve and send e-mail. You can contact them at 0990 99 33 22 or on the Web at **http://www.emarkt.com**.

? I'm using Microsoft's Internet Mail, and I need to send one message to a group of people. How do I do it?

Probably the easiest way to send one message to multiple recipients is to use the Groups feature found in the Address Book option of Internet Mail. To create a new group containing the list of people you want to send a single message to, select Address Book from the Use File menu, then click New Group. Follow the instructions for adding people to the group.

? I want to be able to check and work with my messages at home as well as at work. How do I do that?

When you want to read messages both at home and at work you'll need to leave your e-mail messages on the server. That way you can

E-mail Acronyms

Every day your boss sends you e-mail asking where this or that report is. You respond by typing, "I'll have it to you as soon as possible." Why not save some time and just use an acronym or two, like "I'll get it 2 u ASAP." Or "Your request had me ROTFL," as in "rolling on the floor laughing." There are a ton of e-mail acronyms, but here are some of the most common ones you'll un into:

Acronym	What It Means
AAMOF	as a matter of fact
AFAIK	as far as I know
AFK	away from keyboard
ASAP	as soon as possible
BBL	be back later
BTW	by the way
CUL(8R)	see you later
DAMIFINO	damned if I know
FAQ	frequently asked questions
FWIW	for what it's worth
FYI	for your information
GAL	get a life
IAC	in any case
IDGI	I don't get it
IMHO	in my humble opinion
IMNSHO	in my not so humble opinion
IMPE	in my previous/personal experience
IOW	in other words
IRL	in real life
LOL	laughing out loud
NC	no comment
ONNA	oh no, not again!
OTOH	on the other hand
REHI	hello again (re-Hi!)
RO(T)FL	rolling on the floor laughing
SO	significant other (e.g. boyfriend, wife, pet dog)
THX	Thanks

Acronym	What It Means
TIA	thanks in advance
TTFN	ta-ta for now
TTYL(8R)	talk to you later
YGWYPF	you get what you pay for
YMMV	your mileage may vary

read messages from any location. If you want to leave messages on the server in Microsoft's Internet Mail, choose Mail | Options | Server | Advanced and click the checkbox labeled "Leave a copy of messages on server." This feature also allows you to read messages at one location but retain and store them at another location.

In Netscape, choose Options | Mail and News Preferences and select "Left on server" to keep the messages on your e-mail server.

? How big a message or file can I send to others?

You shouldn't try to send files larger than one megabyte in size; many service providers restrict inboxes to accommodate no more than that amount of data. If you plan to send larger files, first contact the person you want to send the file to and confirm that he or she can receive large files. If you need to transfer multimegabyte-sized files, consider using an FTP server instead.

? Can I import addresses from Netscape Mail to Microsoft's Internet Mail?

Yes, as long as you have at least Build 1162 of Internet Mail, which contains tools that enable you to import addresses from Netscape Mail and Eudora (both the Pro and the Light versions) and to migrate your messages over to Internet Mail. If you already have Netscape or Eudora installed on the computer you are using Internet Mail on, those applications will be recognized when the update is installed, and you will be asked if you want to import your mail messages and address book for use with Internet Mail and News.

? Is there a way to import my address book from CompuServe to Microsoft Exchange?

Microsoft Exchange can use any existing CompuServe or MSN address book you might have. All you have to do is download a utility called CS2Exchange 1.01. CS2Exchange can also import WinCIM file cabinets and messages directly into Exchange from your CompuServe account. You can find CS2Exchange by searching Shareware.com's indexes on the Web at **http://www.shareware.com**.

? Can I include links or graphics in a signature file?

You can include a text file or include mailto: or HTTP links within a standard signature file. You can also include ASCII art in an effort to spruce up your signature file. However, most e-mail programs allow for text-only signature files, so that means you cannot include a GIF or JPEG graphic as part of your signature file. If you do, some e-mail systems may not be able to handle the graphic as a proper MIME type, resulting in gibberish text or an attachment being sent instead of the graphic itself.

? What is Mailer-Daemon?

Mailer-Daemon is the program most e-mail systems use to interpret error messages. It also supplies a more English-like "translation" of the error message to the sender. The Mailer-Daemon program can help you isolate specific problems you may encounter when sending e-mail, including "Host Unknown" and "User Unknown" alerts.

? What does MAPI stand for?

MAPI stands for Microsoft's *messaging application programming interface*. This programming interface lets Windows applications interact with other mail systems. Applications such as Word, Excel, or Office 97, which allow you to send e-mail messages, interface with MAPI-compliant servers, allowing you to send files as attachments to other users across networks.

❓ Can I use my CompuServe account to send and receive e-mail via Microsoft Exchange?

Yes, if you download a special add-on program for Exchange. Type **GO CIS:CSMAIL** for more information on using Exchange to both send and receive e-mail from your CompuServe account.

❓ When I'm using Pine, how do I include a Microsoft Word file with a message?

First, you need to save the Word file with line breaks, using the File | Save As option and specifying Text Only with Line Breaks. Once it is saved as a text file, you should then FTP it to your user account. When it is uploaded, compose a new e-mail message in Pine, then press CTRL-R. This will invoke the Rich Header option, which displays a field for specifying Attachments. Address your e-mail, press CTRL-J on the Attachment field, and specify the filename you've uploaded. Type the rest of the message, then press CTRL-X to send the message.

❓ What does MIME stand for?

MIME stands for *multipurpose Internet mail extensions*. E-mail was originally intended only for sending text messages; MIME extends the capabilities of text-based e-mail by allowing you to attach pictures, sounds, and binary or compressed files to your mail messages. MIME encodes, then decodes all the nontext-related information and identifies the content type to the computer.

❓ What services offer news, weather, and stock quotes delivered directly to my e-mail box?

There are a plethora of sites popping up every day that offer news, weather, sports scores, TV listings, and more delivered to your e-mail inbox every day. If you're using an HTML-compatible e-mail program such as Internet Mail or Netscape mail, you can receive full HTML-formatted messages that are much like Web pages, complete with clickable links.

The best place to go to sign up for all sorts of information is Netscape's InBox Direct, located on the Web at **http://form.netscape.com/ibd/html/ibd_frameset.html**.

Other sites that offer e-mail news include the following:

⇨ C | NET Central's Digital Dispatch, at **http://www.cnet.com**

⇨ Microsoft's MSNBC, at **http://www.msnbc.com**

⇨ Excite's News Service, at **http://www.excite.com**

⇨ Mercury Mail, at **http://www.merc.com**

⇨ InfoSeek's Personal News Service, at **http://www.infoseek.com**

⇨ NewsLinx Daily Web News, at **http://www.newslinx.com**

? Are there any <u>newsgroups</u> specifically for the different e-mail programs?

You can find a list of newsgroups that specialize in e-mail programs on the Web at **http://www.lib.ox.ac.uk/internet/news/ comp.mail.html**, or check out the comp.mail.* hierarchy for a list of e-mail newsgroups.

? Is there a list of <u>newspapers and news services</u> I can get via text-based e-mail?

Yes. You can get a list of services that offer daily news, weather, sports, and stock quotes by sending an e-mail message to **Agora@dna.affrc.go.jp**. Leave the subject blank, but in the body of the message type the following:

SEND http://www.cix.co.uk/~rnet/text/newsmail.txt

This service will send back to you a list of services you can, in essence, subscribe to and receive news and information from each day. You can sign up for some services via the Web, while others allow you to sign up directly through an e-mail message.

? I really need to <u>organize all my mail.</u> Any suggestions?

The easiest way is to create folders for the type of mail you receive, then either use the Filter feature of your e-mail program to have

Smileys

It's hard to emote through e-mail. How can you let the people you are writing to know how you feel? They can't see you smile or frown, but you can use a combination of keystrokes to let your e-mail recipients know exactly how you feel. These special keystroke combinations are called *emoticons* or *smileys*. Look at them sideways and you'll see a whole range of emotion! This list shows you the more popular emoticons. You can get a longer list of smileys by sending a blank e-mail to **SMILEYS@Newbie.net**.

:-)	The basic smiley
:-(	The basic unhappy smiley
;-)	Winking (indicating light sarcasm)
:->	Devilish grin (indicating heavy sarcasm)
:--I	Indifference
:--D	Shock
:-/	Perplexed
:-*	Blowing a kiss
:-p~~~	Blowing raspberries
8-)	User wears glasses
%-)	User has been spending too much time in front of her screen
:*)	User is drunk
:-{)	User has a mustache
:-{}	User wears lipstick
{:-)	User wears a wig
(:-)	User is bald
:-~)	User has a cold
:-@	User is screaming
[:-)	User is listening to music
_O-)	User is scuba diving
O :-)	User has a halo
C=:-)	User is a chef
*<:-)	User is a wearing a Santa hat
*:o)	User is a clown
+-:-)	User is wearing a pope's hat
X-(	User is dead
>>>>>:============	User is an asparagus

messages automatically sorted into designated folders or manually transfer the messages to those folders yourself, as shown in Figure 3-2.

You can also use your e-mail program's Sort command to sort messages according to date, sender, or subject. Most e-mail programs let you click once on the column header to sort the e-mail listing by that column. Click again on the same column heading and the column is sorted in descending order.

You might also consider using the Priority feature many e-mail programs offer. By prioritizing your e-mail, either manually or through automatic filters, you'll know exactly what messages you must act on and what messages can wait for replies. Moving e-mail messages with low priorities to another folder is a good idea.

If you need to delete or move a group of e-mail messages, simply click on the first message to highlight it, then hold down either the SHIFT key (to select a contiguous group) or the CTRL key (to select noncontiguous messages).

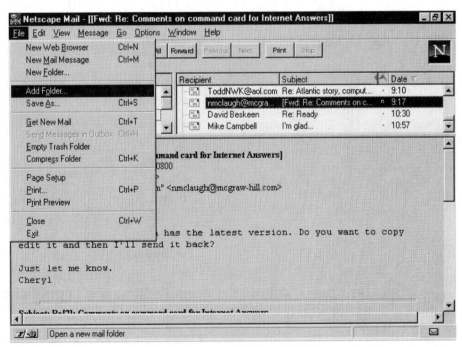

Figure 3-2. Organizing your messages in folders will help you find them when you need them.

The best advice for easy mail management is to delete messages regularly and to go through your folders monthly, cleaning out those messages you have no more use for. And make sure you only use your inbox for new incoming messages, not as a storage bin for all your messages.

 Note   *You should always compact your e-mail boxes and delete the items in your e-mail trash can (check the File or Special menu for the Delete option). Otherwise, you may find your e-mail box bloats to an unmanageable size.*

? I get e-mail from all over the world. Is there a quick way I can glance and see if a message has come from <u>outside the United States?</u>

Sure is. Simply look at the end of the e-mail address. Addresses that contain country codes are stored on servers located outside the United States. For example, in the address *jdoe@apple.oz.au*, the *.au* indicates that the message originated in Australia.

Here are a few of the more popular top-level domain country codes:

Country Code	Country
AQ	Antarctica
AU	Australia
BR	Brazil
GR	Greece
JP	Japan
KR	Republic of Korea
MX	Mexico
NO	Norway
RO	Romania
ZA	South Africa
UK	United Kingdom

? How can I find out the e-mail addresses of <u>politicians and government workers?</u>

One of the best e-mail directories, not only for government addresses but also for university and online locations, is the World E-mail Directory, located on the Web at **http://worldemail.com**.

? What does <u>POP</u> stand for?

POP stands for *post office protocol*. POP servers are the incoming mail servers. POP is a protocol designed for handling requests to get mail from client mail programs. Therefore, you really receive your messages from a POP server and send your messages using an SMTP server.

? Can I send e-mail <u>postcards</u> over the Internet?

There are tons of sites that let you send free e-mail postcards over the Internet. @loha is a separate application you would need to download in order to create an animated e-mail message. You can find @loha at **http://www.elitemall.com/aloha**.

You can also send e-mail postcards from a variety of Web sites. Some of the more interesting e-mail postcard sites include MaxRacks (**http://www.maxracks.com**), BuildACard (**http://www. buildacard. com**), Digital Postcards (**http://www.all-yours. net/postcard**), and Send a Postcard (**http://www.media- magic.com/digital**). Or, if you happen to be visiting Seattle and want to send an electronic postcard complete with snapshots of tourist hotspots, try Seattle Square (**http://www. seattlesquare. com/postcard**).

? Are the messages I send <u>private</u>?

No. Never ever assume that any e-mail message you send is private, even if it's within your own company's network. Not only could someone forward your e-mail without your knowledge, but since your messages are stored and then forwarded from one computer system to the next, it would be possible for anyone along the way to read them.

Also, remember that computer system tape backups can also store e-mail messages. In addition, any messages you post to a newsgroup or mailing list are open to the public, and oftentimes are stored on publicly accessible archives such as DejaNews.

? How do I set up my e-mail so I automatically <u>quote a message</u> in the reply?

Check your Mail Preferences, usually available under the Edit or Options menu. For example, in Netscape Mail you choose Mail and News Preferences, then click the Composition tab, shown in Figure 3-3. Finally, check "Automatically quote original message when replying."

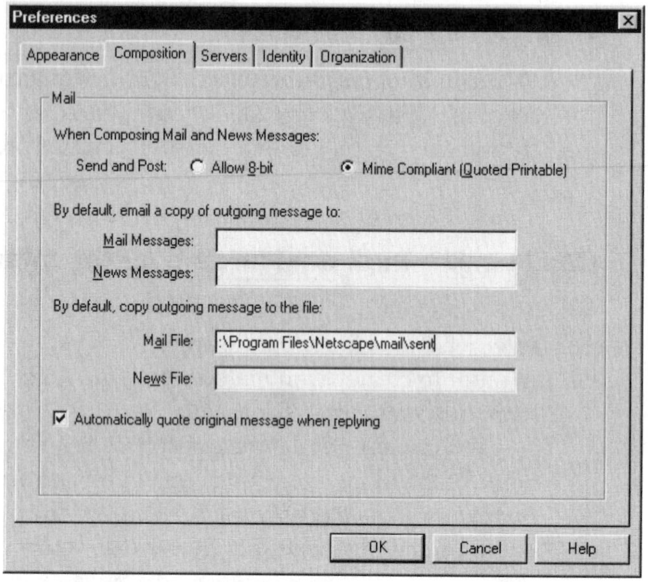

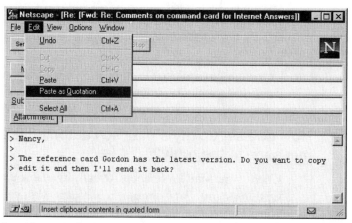

Figure 3-3.   Most e-mail programs have composition preferences that let you customize your messages.

How can I quote a portion of a message in my reply?

It depends upon the e-mail software you are using. With certain programs, you highlight the portion you want to quote, then click an icon or button to compose a reply. With Netscape, you can highlight, choose Copy from the Edit menu, as you see in Figure 3-4, and paste the text into your message reply.

Figure 3-4.   You can clarify your reply to an e-mail message by pasting in a section of the original.

? How do I know what my <u>real e-mail address</u> is?

The best way to find out what your e-mail address is is to send yourself a message.

• • • • • • • • • •

Who Am I?? Where Am I??

If you happen to be on one of the following services and would like to know what your Internet e-mail address is, follow the examples, replacing *user* with your username.

AOL   Make sure you change the AOL address to lowercase, then add @aol.com to the end of the username:

> *user*@aol.com

AT&T mail   To e-mail a user at AT&T mail, add @att.com to the username:

> *user*@att.com

BIX   To e-mail a user at BIX, add **@bix.com** to the username:

> *user*@bix.com

CompuServe   CompuServe addresses are in either the numeric format *xxxxx,xxx* or *Username*. Replace the comma with a period and add compuserve.com:

> *xxxxx.xxx*@compuserve.com

FidoNet   To e-mail John Smith at 1:2/3.4, follow this example:

> john.smith@p4.f3.n2.z1.fidonet.org

GEnie   To e-mail a user at GEnie, add @genie.geis.com to the username:

> *user*@genie.geis.com

? **It would really help me out to have <u>reminders</u> of important dates and meetings sent to my e-mail address. Is there such a service?**

> There are several companies that will perform this service for you. An excellent one is the Free E-mail Reminder Service, located on the World Wide Web at **http://calendar.stwing.upenn.edu**. You can also sign up for reminder services with BigFoot, which is an e-mail forwarding service (among other things). BigFoot is located at **http://www.bigfoot.com**. Or you can use a service called PlanetAll, located at **http://www.planetall.com**.

? **I only have access to an e-mail account, but I want to be able to <u>retrieve files</u> as if I were using an FTP server. Can I do that?**

> Yes, you can retrieve files via e-mail, granted you use what is called an FTPMAIL server. This server takes your e-mail message, uses the information you supply to log on to the FTP server, and retrieves the files you've specified in your e-mail message. You can get a list of FTPMAIL servers by sending a message to **mail-server@ftfm.mit.edu**. In the body of the note include the following:
>
> Send usenet/news.answers/ftp-list/sitelist/part1
> Send usenet/news.answers/ftp-list/sitelist/part2
> Send usenet/news.answers/ftp-list/sitelist/part3... etc.
>
> There are 21 parts, so include a line for each part up to 21 if you want to retrieve all 21 parts, but be careful. Each part is approximately 60K in size, so if your e-mail account can't accommodate more than one megabyte, you might request only a few parts at a time.

? **Is it possible to <u>save a message</u> so I can work on it later before sending it?**

> If you are using Netscape Messenger, you can use the File menu's Save Draft option. If you are using another version of Navigator or Internet Explorer, you can create your message in a text editor such as Notepad, then save it. When you're ready to send it simply bring up the file, copy its contents, and paste it into your e-mail message.

❓ How do I save the messages I send to people?

You can do a couple of things. First, you can carbon copy or blind carbon copy yourself on every message, or you can change the settings in your e-mail program. In Netscape, you would choose Options | Mail and News Preferences | Composition. In the Mail Messages field (refer to Figure 3-3), under the "By default, e-mail a copy of outgoing messages to:" line, type the name of a file in which you want to save all your outgoing messages.

❓ How do I send secure, private e-mail that no one but the intended recipient can read?

The best way to ensure your e-mail is read only by the intended recipient is to use some form of encryption. The best encryption program is one called Pretty Good Privacy. You can find PGP at **http://www.pgp.com**. PGP is a computer program that scrambles, then unscrambles the information you send using what are called *encryption keys*.

 Note *Netscape's Communicator Messenger application includes an e-mail encryption option. Check the Mail Preferences to turn this option on.*

❓ Can I get Internet Mail to send my messages right away instead of keeping them in the outbox?

Yes you can. First select Mail | Options | Send, then check the box labeled "Send messages immediately." As a default, messages are placed in the outbox, awaiting the command for you to send them.

❓ I've seen some pretty nifty signature files using ASCII characters. Is there an easy way to create this type of signature file?

The best place to go is a service called Figlet, located at **http://www. inf.utfsm.cl/cgi-bin/figlet**. You type in the text you want turned into an ASCII masterpiece, and Figlet does just that.

❓ What does SMTP stand for?

SMTP stands for *Simple Mail Transfer Protocol*. SMTP is a set of rules for transferring e-mail messages from the source to the destination. Each host that wants to receive e-mail sets up an SMTP server. When a host receives an e-mail message from a user and wants to send it to another server, it contacts the SMTP server. The SMTP server then responds with either a confirmation, an error message, or specific requested information. You send your e-mail messages using SMTP and receive your messages using the POP3 protocol.

? Can I make my browser start up automatically into the e-mail portion of the program?

Yes. Check the General Preferences in your Web browser for the feature that automatically launches the e-mail portion of the program when the browser is started. In Netscape, you'll see a screen that looks something like the one in Figure 3-5.

? I'm back from vacation...so how do I stop forwarding my e-mail?

Simple. Just delete the .forward file from your home directory, or visit Mail Tools on the Web at **http://charlotte.acns.nwu.edu/mailtools**, a site that allows you to forward, stop forwarding, or send vacation mail.

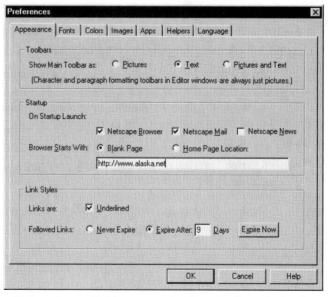

Figure 3-5.   To launch your Netscape e-mail automatically, go to the Appearance tab.

? How long is my e-mail <u>stored on the system</u>?

If you're using a local Internet service provider, you should check with them. Most providers will store your e-mail on their servers indefinitely, or until one of two things occurs: you stop paying for your account, or your mailbox becomes overloaded with e-mail messages.

If you're on a commercial service, such as America Online, your unread e-mail stays on the system for 27 days and your read e-mail stays on for only 3 to 5 days. If you want to save your e-mail longer, you should download your messages to your computer's hard drive.

If you're on CompuServe, ASCII messages stay on the system for 90 days and binary messages for 30 days.

? What <u>types of files</u> can I send?

You can send just about any type of file. However, not all mail servers are capable of handling large files, and some e-mail/server programs require that you first encode files so they can be sent in text instead of binary format. Also, before sending any file outside of a simple text message, you should ensure the other person can read the type of file you are sending. If you are using a PC and the recipient a Mac, you need to make sure the file formats are compatible.

? What do <u>Uuencode and Uudecode</u> mean?

Uuencode is an encoding format used throughout the Internet, specifically within e-mail messages and newsgroup postings, for sending programs and data. Uuencode is primarily used to send and post binary files such as pictures, sounds, programs, and documents. Uuencode takes an 8-bit file and essentially encodes it into text. The file in its uuencoded format can be sent through the Internet without becoming corrupted or damaged while passing through various e-mail systems.

Uudecode is the method or program that takes uuencoded files (basically binary files that have been encoded into 7-bit text) and turns them back into their original binary file formats. In order to read a uuencoded file you need a uudecoder program. You'll find such programs (for any platform of computer) at Shareware.com, located on the Web at **http://www.shareware.com**.

? **What's the easiest way to send a message to tell people that I'm on <u>vacation</u> and not getting my e-mail?**

The easiest way is to fill out the form at the Mail Tools page located at **http://charlotte.acns.nwu.edu/mailtools**. If your e-mail system is run on the UNIX platform, you can also type **vacation** at the UNIX prompt and follow the prompts to set up your vacation mail file.

Or you can set up an account using MailCity's free Web-based email program, located at **http://www.mailcity.com**, and turn on MailCity's vacation notification option.

? **How can I get a personalized <u>"vanity"</u> e-mail address?**

There are several services that allow for "vanity" e-mail addresses. One such service, Iname, lets you choose your preferred name and domain. You can find Iname at **http://www.iname.com**. Iname will also forward e-mail to another account you specify.

? **Can I get a <u>virus</u> through an e-mail message?**

Because viruses require you to "run" or "execute" them, yes, you certainly can receive viruses through e-mail attachments! However, unless you *execute* the attachment the actual process of retrieving the e-mail message will not cause your system to become infected.

To ensure that you do not infect your system, follow these guidelines:

⇨ Never open attachments from people you do not know.

⇨ Always run virus-checking programs against all attachments you receive.

⇨ Never place attachments in system-related or program-related directories. Instead, store them separately in a folder all their own. This will prevent you from accidentally overwriting important files.

? **Can I send a mail message from a <u>Web page</u> without logging on to an e-mail service?**

If you want to send a quick message from a Web page without having to log on to an e-mail program or Web-based e-mail service, try going to the Web2Mail form page at **http://www.middlebury.edu/cgi-bin/Web2Mail.pl**.

Tips for Effective Business E-mail Communications

⇨ Make sure your subject grabs 'em.

In the subject line, make sure you clearly state the need or urgency of your message. For example, sending out an e-mail with the subject line listed as "Monthly Billing" is not as effective as "Account To Be Terminated Tomorrow," if your intent is to collect for money owed.

With the volume of e-mail increasing daily, you have to write subject lines that immediately stand out. Many people take one glance at the subject line, and if it doesn't pique their interest, they immediately delete the message without reading it.

⇨ Don't be too casual or too sloppy.

E-mail is just another form of communication. Make sure you say exactly what you mean, and that you don't ramble on and on. Oftentimes long messages never get read, so you're better off being short and to the point. Use your e-mail program's spell checker, and don't be sloppy with grammar or capitalization. Don't type messages in all CAPS.

The best way to construct an e-mail is to do it the same way you would a good one-page letter. Make sure you summarize the reason for the e-mail in a single sentence as an opener. Then, outline what action needs to be taken, including any necessary details. Close by briefly summarizing the contents of any electronic files you've attached.

⇨ Ask for a response, if one is required, in the first or second sentence.

If you need something from someone, ask for it up front, in the first or second sentence of your e-mail. Many times people skim through e-mail messages looking for names, addresses, phone numbers, and action items. Make it easier for them to find those things by including the most important information near the beginning in a concise fashion.

Check out *A Beginner's Guide to Effective E-mail* on the Internet if you need more help on e-mail etiquette. The Guide is located on the Web at **http://www.webfoot.com/advice/email.top.html**.

? Are there any Web-based e-mail forwarding services?

You can always use a Web-based e-mail forwarding service such as BigFoot (**http://www.bigfoot.com**), RocketMail (**http://www. rocketmail.com**), or Hotmail (**http://www.hotmail.com**). However, these services will only forward from the address you set on their service. Only Hotmail will allow you to grab your POP3 mail and display it while logged on to Hotmail.

? How can I find out where a message really came from?

If you choose Show All Headers from the View menu of your e-mail program, you can see the route the message took before it got to you. Remember, however, that someone can send an e-mail message from a variety of locations or use an e-mail forwarding address, so there are times you may never know exactly who/where the message came from.

MAILING LISTS

? How exactly do electronic mailing lists work?

A mailing list is basically an ongoing discussion about a particular topic. But instead of standing around the water cooler, the participants conduct their discussion via e-mail. Messages are sent to a central computer where the list is stored, and the computer forwards the messages to the others on the list. You join in on the discussion by subscribing or putting your name on the mailing list so you can receive the e-mail messages others send to the list.

There are an estimated 35,000 mailing lists, and more are created every day. They cover everything from airplanes to pigmy goats to new Web sites. There are mainly two types of mailing lists: moderated and unmoderated. On a moderated list, a list administrator ferrets out the noise, sending along only the worthwhile messages. An unmoderated list usually involves little or no human intervention and is mainly run by the computer serving up the list, most commonly called a list server. There are three main types of list server software—ListServ, ListProc, or Majordomo—but there are hundreds of other e-mail list server products out there.

There are two addresses used with almost every mailing list—the address used to issue commands to the list server and the address used to send messages to the rest of the group. When you subscribe to the list, you send the Subscribe command to the list server computer. After subscribing, you start sending your e-mail discussion messages to the mailing list address.

? How do I subscribe to an e-mail list?

With most lists you simply send a subscribe command to the list server, but you should check the instructions for subscribing to a particular list before sending the command. With automated mailing lists you send a subscribe command to the subscription address. The command is usually placed in the body of the message. The subscription address may be for a computer or a person. Some lists require you to confirm that you want to subscribe. Usually this means the list server will send you an e-mail message asking for confirmation. Normally, all you have to do is send the message back or include just your e-mail address in your response. Read the instructions carefully if the list server computer asks you to confirm your subscription.

For lists running on LISTSERV server software you would send this in the body of the message to the ListServ address:

> sub *listname your full name*

For lists running on Majordomo servers you would send this in the body of the message:

> subscribe *listname*

 Remember   *There are usually two addresses used with most mailing lists—the address for the list server computer and the address for the list. You send commands, such as* **subscribe***, to the list server computer, and messages to the list address.*

? I'm going on vacation but don't want to unsubscribe to the mailing list I'm on. Is there a command I can use to limit the amount of mail I get while I'm away?

Depending upon the list server software running, you could issue the command **set nomail** in the body of a message to the list server address. This will set your account to not receive e-mail. When you get back from vacation, you should send a message with the command **set mail** in the body of the message to the list server address.

❓ Can I get a list of available mailing lists?

You bet. The best place on the Internet is a Web site called Liszt.com, located at **http://www.liszt.com**. Liszt.com offers an enormous list of mailing lists you can join (there are over 35,000 entries), or you can search for mailing lists that meet your particular interests. Complete instructions on how to subscribe, along with a description of what the mailing list offers, are included with each mailing list entry.

Internet Mailing Lists Guides and Resources, located at **http://www.nlc-bnc.ca/ifla/I/training/listserv/lists.html** is another great Web site with information on all sorts of mailing lists and how to subscribe. And E-Mail Discussion Groups, located at **http://alabanza.com/ kabacoff/Inter-Links/listserv.html** is another fine source for e-mail discussion lists as is the Publicly Accessible Mailing Lists page, located at **http://www.neosoft.com/internet/ paml/index.html**.

You can find a ton of mailing lists on the Publicly Accessible Mailing Lists Index Web site located at **http://www.neosoft.com/internet/paml**. You can search PAML either by using the keyword index or by using the handy search engine.

Another good source is Tile.net. You can search not only for mailing lists but also for newsgroups, FTP archives, and hardware and software vendors. If you'd rather read through the entire list by keyword or by description you can also click the links for either format. The direct link that will take you to mailing list discussion groups is **http://www.tile.net/tile/listserv**.

❓ How do I get a listing of commands that can be used on the mailing list I'm subscribed to?

You can usually send the command **help** in the body of your message for ListServ, Majordomo, and ListProc list servers.

Note   *Almost all automated mailing lists require you place the commands in the body of the message, not in the subject. However, there are exceptions. If placing the command in the body doesn't work, try placing it in the Subject line.*

? I've heard that companies can get <u>my address</u> from list servers. Is there some way I can prevent them from doing this?

Depending upon the list server software running, you may be able to conceal your address by issuing the **set conceal** command in the body of a message to the list server address.

? How can I tell whether I'm sending an e-mail message to a person or a list server?

Just look at the return address. If you see something like **listproc@ mysite.com**, **LISTSERV@mysite.com**, or **Majordomo@mysite.com**, you are sending your message to a list server.

If, instead, you see a return address such as **info-requests@ mysite.com**, you could either be sending your message to a person, a group, or an automated mailer account set up to return a specific message.

? I'm getting too much e-mail! What if I don't want to get every single posting to a mailing list? Is there some way I can <u>pick and choose among incoming messages</u>?

Many mailing lists do have condensed versions of all the messages sent to the list; these are called *digests*. Normally, you will see information about subscribing to the digest in the Help file you receive after subscribing to the list. Most lists run on ListServ and ListProc have digests. Majordomo lists may or may not have digests. List digest addresses are identified much like *barbiedolls-digest*.

? Do I have to include anything in the <u>Subject field</u> of messages I send to the list server software?

No. With ListServ, ListProc, and Majordomo, you don't have to include anything in the Subject field. The commands used to get information from the list server software are all placed in the body of the message. However, lists running on different server software may require commands to be placed in the subject field. Check the instructions provided to you when you first signed up to join the mailing list before you send the message.

? I've **unsubscribed** from a mailing list, but I'm still getting posts. What's their problem?

Some mailing lists may be administered manually, and the process may take a day or several days, sometimes several weeks, depending upon when the administrator can remove your e-mail address from the list.

If the list is not administered manually, the list server may be busy processing other requests. Also, because of the nature of the Internet, you may still receive posts for a few days after signing off. You should contact the list owner if you continue to receive mail several weeks after signing off.

? Can I find out who else is on a mailing list?

Depending upon what list server software is used, you can normally issue the command **review [listname] by [field]**, for ListServ and ListProc, or **who [listname]** for Majordomo list servers, in the body of your message to the list server address. *Listname* is the name of the list you are subscribed to, and *field* is the field you want to sort by, just like country, name of subscriber, or User ID.

COMMERCIAL SERVICES

? I'm trying to send a file using America Online, but I keep getting a message saying it can't attach large files. What's the problem?

America Online has a one-megabyte file size limitation. If your message and attached files goes over the one megabyte limit, America Online will alert you with this error message.

? **Does CompuServe allow me to send binary files to and from the Internet?**

> Presently, you can only send ASCII files, not binary files. If you want to attach a binary file to an e-mail message, you first must encode the file, which basically turns it into ASCII text. The recipient must be able to decode the ASCII file you are sending and turn it back into a binary file.

? **How do I send a blind carbon copy to someone using America Online? There doesn't seem to be a "bcc" field, only a "cc" field.**

> To denote that an address should not be listed, but rather blind carbon copied, put parentheses around the name.

? **Can I have both CompuServe addresses and Internet addresses in the same group?**

> Yes. Just make sure you include the INTERNET: designator before any Internet addresses in your group address entries. You only have to include the member's name or number, not the @compuserve.com designator if you also want to send to CompuServe members in the same group as Internet members.

? **How long does it usually take for an e-mail message to be delivered via CompuServe?**

> It can take anywhere from a few minutes to 48 hours. The average delivery time runs around 30 minutes but can be longer depending upon traffic on the Internet.

? **Does America Online allow me to use another e-mail package for sending and receiving e-mail? I would really rather use Netscape or Eudora than AOL's e-mail program.**

> Although America Online has plans to offer POP3 services, at present you can only send, not receive e-mail through a third-party e-mail program. To set up your system to send e-mail through the AOL SMTP gateway, change the SMTP server to a.mx.aol.com.

? **Can't I use my own e-mail program instead of using Compuserve's Information Manager software?**

Yes, you can use CompuServe as a bona fide Internet service provider, which means you can pick and choose which applications you want to use to access such things as the Web and e-mail. However, you must set up your Dial-Up network connection to use CompuServe's IP address as its host, first. Type **GO:WINSOCK** or **GO:PPP** for more information on the IP address used.

SMTP and POP3 mail server settings for CompuServe both are "mail.compuserve.com."

Unfortunately, while you can send e-mail via CompuServe using any mail program, to receive mail you must still use WinCIM or the Microsoft Exchange add-on. However, Compuserve has gone semipublic with its POP mail beta test, and it should be in production by the time you read this. For more information about CIS's e-mail option, check **http://www.csi.com/mail**.

? **Can I include formatted text from my word processor in an e-mail message?**

You can send text you've prepared in a word processor by simply highlighting, copying, and then pasting the text into the e-mail message. However, you will lose the formatting you've created, and you can only send text, not special characters. Another option is to include the entire file as an attachment to your e-mail message by clicking the Attachment button while in your e-mail program. However, the recipient must have a word processor capable of reading the file you create. Check first to see what word processor and version of the software that person is using before sending the file as an attachment.

? **I use America Online for my e-mail, but am going to switch over to another provider soon. Is there a way to forward my AOL e-mail?**

At present there is no option to forward your America Online e-mail. However, this feature may be available in the future. Keep checking the E-mail Message center or the What's New feature on America Online.

? **I'm using CompuServe to send e-mail over the Net. How long can my messages be?**

> The largest a message coming or going to the Internet through CompuServe can be is two million characters in length.

? **How long will my messages be stored in my CompuServe mailbox?**

> ASCII messages are automatically deleted 90 days after being sent, whereas binary messages are deleted after 30 days.

? **On CompuServe, how many addresses can I send one message to at a time?**

> You can send a single message to up to 50 people at one time, including those on the Internet.

? **How many messages can I keep in my CompuServe e-mail box?**

> Your CIS mailbox can hold up to 100 messages at a time. When your limit is reached, anyone sending messages to your mailbox will receive a return message stating that your mailbox is full.

? **Can I include a hypertext link to one of my favorite Web sites in the AOL message I'm sending?**

> Yes. First, create a new message using the Mail menu's Compose Mail option. Then, open the Favorite Places window by clicking the Favorite Places icon on the toolbar. Next, simply drag the heart next to the name of the favorite place you want to include as a hypertext reference in your e-mail message. The full hypertext reference will be sent. The recipient can then click the link to your included favorite site, and if it is compatible, the recipient's e-mail program will open the browser and take him or her directly to the Web site.

? **How do I send Internet e-mail through my CompuServe account?**

> If you have CompuServe version 2.*x* or above, or WinCIM version 2.44 or above, or MacCIM, you should have an option that allows you

to specify Internet addressing as one of the options. You must select this option in order for e-mail to be sent through CompuServe's Internet e-mail gateway. If you are using earlier versions of any WinCIM, MacCIM, or CompuServe software, you must first include in your recipient's e-mail address the following: **INTERNET.**

You must type the word "INTERNET" in all caps, by the way.

For example, if you wanted to send an e-mail message to ckirk@alaska.net, you would type the following:

INTERNET:ckirk@alaska.net

? I'm on America Online and I keep getting junk mail. How can I end this avalanche?

The best thing to do is block all messages from the junk mailer's domain, or simply restrict all but a select few people from sending you e-mail. To do this use the keyword PreferredMail. This will take you to the e-mail filter tool that will block most spammers from sending unsolicited e-mail to your AOL address.

? Someone sent me a document in MIME format. The instructions call for me to decode it using a MIME decoder. What does this mean?

It means your mail system couldn't interpret MIME format, so you will have to decode the document. Wincode, a MIME decoder which can be found by searching the Shareware.com archives (**http://www.shareware.com**), will decode the saved MIME file.

? How do I get a name instead of a mysterious number for my CompuServe e-mail address?

You must register with CompuServe by typing **GO REGISTER.** Follow the instructions for registering your own unique name on CompuServe. Once registered, you can use that alias instead of the member ID number. For example, if you registered the name JohnDoe for your member account number 777,7777, then instead of your address being **777.7777@compuserve.com**, it would be **JohnDoe@compuserve.com**.

? Sometimes I log on to America Online and it says I have mail waiting, but I don't have any mail. Other times I know I have mail, but there is no <u>notification of e-mail</u> in my inbox. What's the problem?

Oftentimes America Online has experienced e-mail problems, specifically with what is called the "e-mail flag." Instead of clicking the icon for your e-mail box, try using the Read New Mail option from the Mail menu. Also, try resetting your e-mail flag by sending a message to yourself with the following in the subject line:

SET MAIL FLAG

? Doesn't CompuServe's <u>Receipt feature</u> work when I send Internet e-mail messages?

No. The receipt feature only works when you send e-mail to other CompuServe members. On the Internet, service providers use a variety of e-mail servers. Some can use receipt features and some cannot.

? Why is it that I can check the <u>status of a message</u> sent to another America Online member, but not one sent to an Internet address?

America Online utilizes special software that allows you to check the status of a message you've sent. However, since a variety of e-mail servers are used throughout the Internet, there is no conventional way to check the status of all the e-mail sent.

? I know I can send text and pictures, but can I also send <u>voicemail</u>?

If the recipient is using a compatible system that can understand .wav files, you essentially can use your Sound Recorder program to record messages, then send them as attachments. A company called Bonzi, however, makes it even easier. They've created voicemail add-ons for a variety of e-mail programs such as Eudora and Netscape Mail. The company has also created software for America Online and CompuServe users. The cost of the program runs under $50 and includes a free player for the recipient of your voicemail message. You can find Bonzi at **http://www.bonzi.com**.

TROUBLESHOOTING E-MAIL PROBLEMS

How can I get rid of that annoying = sign that appears at the end of each line when I'm using Microsoft Exchange?

First, open the Internet Mail Properties window, then click the General tab. Next, select Message format, then click Character set. Change the character set from ISO-8859-2 to US ASCII.

I haven't had any success sending an attachment in Microsoft's Internet Mail. What am I doing wrong?

You should first check to see if the attachment you're trying to send is larger than what your service provider allows for in a single message. If it is, you can use Internet Mail's "break apart" messages option, found in the Mail | Options window. You should set the Kilobyte (KB) limit to what your service provider allows.

When I try to send an attachment I get the following error message: "File in Use and Cannot Be Sent." What am I doing wrong?

Most likely you are trying to send a file that is currently open. You should close the document before trying to send it. For example, if you have Word open with the memo you are trying to send, you need to first save, then close the memo before you can e-mail it. To be totally safe, you might consider closing the application as well as the document to ensure there are no problems with temporary files.

What does "Host Not Found" mean? I sent a message that bounced back to me with that line added to it.

Host Not Found means the domain name you've specified in the e-mail address is wrong or has been removed. For example, if you sent a message to **johndoe@ibm.nte**, the message would bounce back because you misspelled the word *net*. Double-check your spelling, or use the Ping command to see if the host is alive and active. And make sure the address listed in the message header is correct.

? **Someone's just sent me a message that's <u>indecipherable</u>. What could be the problem?**

Several things could have occurred:

⇨ If both you and the sender are using a mail program such as Microsoft's Internet Mail, which allows font formatting, you may not have the font the sender used loaded in your system. Ask the sender to resend the message using a standard font.

⇨ The sender may be using a language character set that is different from yours. You will need to install that language on your e-mail system if you want to read the message.

⇨ The sender may have used an encoding format your e-mail program cannot understand or may have used encryption technology. Ask the sender if the message is encrypted or if any special encoding format was used, or have her resend the message using a plain text format.

? **I've been getting a lot of <u>junk mail</u> lately. Where are these companies and people getting my e-mail address?**

Most likely from a variety of locations, including the following:

⇨ Usenet newsgroup postings

⇨ Sites that might have requested you fill out some form and supply your e-mail address

⇨ Service providers' member profiles

⇨ Web pages that list mailto: links

⇨ Companies that sell e-mail directories

⇨ Chat rooms you've visited

? **How can I keep my e-mail address off <u>junk mail lists</u>?**

It's somewhat difficult if you spend a lot of time interacting on the Internet. The best thing to do is simply restrict your newsgroup postings or have two e-mail addresses, one you use only when posting Usenet replies, and another for normal day-to-day business and personal e-mail. You can also register your name on several "Spam Control" lists. There is no guarantee, however, that after you register your name, new spammers won't grab your e-mail address from older newsgroup postings. These services let bulk e-mailers and junk mailers know you do not want your address listed in their databases.

⇨ Internet Spam Control Center, at **http://drsvcs.com/nospam/ns2.shtml**

⇨ Netiquette.net, at **http://www.netiquette.net**

⇨ No Junk Email, at **http://www.glr.com/nojunk.html**

⇨ No Spam, at **http://kenjen.com/nospam/** (also lets you report spammers/junk mailers)

⇨ No ThankYou.com, at **http://www.nothankyou.com**

❓ What is a mail-bomb? Is it the same thing as a spam?

A mailbomb is when one person or a group of people send multiple messages to a single mailbox with the intention of overflowing the recipient's e-mail box. Mail-bombs often are intended to shut down a mailbox, making it impossible for the owner of the mailbox to even open his or her e-mail. Mail-bombers can also disrupt people's service another way: They can subscribe someone to numerous e-mail lists without their knowledge, causing the unsuspecting person's mailbox to flood with messages.

❓ What should I do if I'm the object of a mail-bomber's attack?

You should contact your service provider immediately. Report the problem and let the ISP know where you think the bomb may have originated, be it from a newsgroup posting or a disgruntled customer, coworker, or acquaintance. The ISP can most likely help track down who is doing the damage and help you set up a new account, filtering any "real" messages your way. You should then consider using one account for posting to newsgroups or participating in discussions and another for conducting your day-to-day business. Whatever you do, do not reply to the mail-bomber directly. This may only serve to incite him or her further. You can also complain to the postmaster of the service the mail-bombing might be coming from by sending an e-mail message to **postmaster@domainname**. You should first read the full e-mail headers to decipher exactly where the mail originated from, since many mail-bombers probably won't be using their real e-mail address.

• • • • • • • • • •

Anyone Can Get Spammed

If it can happen to Rush Limbaugh, it can happen to you. Limbaugh, the right-wing radio talk show host, was spammed last year, rendering his electronic inbox almost useless. He'd clear out his mailbox, and within seconds it was full again. Seems someone decided to subscribe him to hundreds of e-mail lists. "I was put on every stupid ListServ out there," Limbaugh told his national radio audience, "including one for discussing the use of Sanskrit as a third language."

But Limbaugh isn't the only one. People as diverse as Sandy Gookin, author of *Parenting for Dummies,* President Clinton, and the speaker of the House, Newt Gingrich, have been spammed. Because many mailing lists do not first check that the request to join is coming from the same address as the one listed in the subscription request, spamming people's mailboxes by signing them up on hundreds or even thousands of mailing lists is relatively easy to do. And if it can happen to Rush, Bill, Newt, and Sandy, it can easily happen to you.

? I get the error message "Mailbox full." How do I send a message to someone whose mailbox is full?

You don't, or at least the e-mail server at that person's provider probably will not let you. Most service providers have a set limit on the number of messages any one mailbox can hold. For example, America Online restricts its members from having more than 550 messages across five mailboxes at any one time, and CompuServe only allows for 100 messages to be stored in a user's mailbox at any one time.

The best way to get in touch with people whose mailboxes are full is to pick up the phone and call them, send them a fax, or drop them a snail-mail postcard.

? Can I stop Microsoft Exchange from coming up every time I click a mailto: link in a Web page?

Simply go to Mail | Options | Send in Microsoft Exchange. Next, select "Make Microsoft Internet Mail your default e-mail program."

? **My mouse stops working after I open and read multiple e-mail messages in Microsoft's Internet Mail. What's the problem?**

You may need to update the mouse driver on your computer. You should visit Microsoft's Windows Support Web page at **http://www.microsoft.com/windowssupport** and search for file pnt32upd.exe. Download and install the latest version of this file and restart your machine. A search on pnt32upd.exe here didn't produce the file; I had to go to /windowsSupport/default-sl.htm, click on Miscellaneous Files and Utilities, and then search for pnt32upd.exe

? **I keep getting a message saying my outbox is corrupted in Internet Mail. Should I replace it?**

You don't have to replace the program per se. Instead, what you'll need to do is delete the outbox.mbx and outbox.idx files, normally located in the Program Files\Internet Mail and News\ [Username] \Mail directory. Make sure Internet Mail and News is not running, then delete outbox.mbx and outbox.idx. The next time you launch Internet Mail and News, these two files will be re-created and you shouldn't get the "corrupted outbox" message again.

? **I've tried to use the Reply button to respond to e-mail, but the mail bounces back with an error message. Why?**

The user who sent you the e-mail message probably filled out his address incorrectly in the Preferences section. Oftentimes people add additional words or characters without realizing it. For example, I know a person whose address is *johnsmith@alaska.net*, but he typed *alaska.net* twice in Preferences. Every time I receive a message from him and click the Reply button my e-mail program places *johnsmith@alaska.net.alaska.net* in the return address box, which causes the message to bounce back.

? **I keep getting the same messages again and again. Am I doing something wrong?**

Your e-mail preferences have probably been set to keep your messages on the server. That means every time you log in and click the Get Mail or Retrieve Mail option you get not only all the new messages but also all the old messages still stored on the server. Check your Mail and News preferences, as shown in Figure 3-6 to make sure your messages are removed from the server once they're delivered.

? When I try to start Microsoft's Internet Mail, I get the following error message: "Unable to Start Application. Some components may be busy or missing." What am I doing wrong?

You will most likely get this error if the Windows Address Book file is damaged. You might try downloading a newer version of Internet Mail and News from Microsoft's Web site at **http://www.microsoft.com**, or you can try to rename the Address Book file, named [username].wab in your Windows folder. Make sure you are not in Internet News or Mail when you rename the file and that you restart your system after you rename the file.

? OK, what does this mean: "Undelivered Message - Message not delivered in four hours. Will continue to try"?

This error message simply means the system has tried to deliver the e-mail but hasn't successfully delivered it within the time limit set up

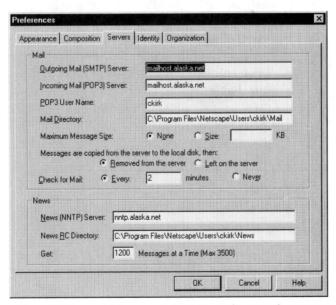

Figure 3-6.   To avoid those déjà vu experiences, make sure that your messages are removed from the server upon delivery.

in the e-mail program. The system isn't giving up, just letting you know there may be a delay. The delay may be caused by a power outage, a downed e-mail system, or problems with the network link. As with any e-mail message, you should look past the subject header for more detailed information in the body of the message. The mailer-daemon or the automated e-mail administration program usually will specify exactly how many hours or days the system will continue trying to deliver the message. You should not resend the message.

? My e-mail bounced back with the message "Unknown User." What did I do wrong?

Unknown User means the host's e-mail database does not contain the username or ID you specified in the address. In other words, you probably either typed in the user's name wrong or the person has left the company or changed her e-mail address.

? How do I stop Microsoft Exchange from sending out that WINMAL.DAT attachment with each e-mail message I send?

First, choose Control Panel | Mail and Fax, then click the Services tab and select Internet Mail from the list. If Internet Mail is not listed, click Add to add Internet Mail as one of your services. Next, click Properties and choose Message Format. Make sure you turn off the option entitled "Use MIME when sending messages." Click OK to save your changes.

chapter

4 Answers!

Cruising the Web with Netscape Navigator

Answer Topics!

NETSCAPE NAVIGATOR 3.0   84

Choosing between the **16-bit and the 32-bit** version

Accessing your bookmarks for easy editing

Adding addresses to your e-mail address book

Adding up numbers with your Web browser

Using Navigator in conjunction with **America Online**

Creating and using Web **bookmarks**

Netscape's **"Can't Read Newsgroup"** error message

Toning down gaudy Web page **colors**

Determining whether you're **connected to a Netscape server**

The **"Connection Reset by Peer"** message

How to tell when a site is asking for a **cookie**

How to **copy a URL to an e-mail message**

Preventing your system from **crashing** when running Netscape Navigator

How to **cycle through** your open windows

How to **delete the history file**

How to quickly **delete a message** from your inbox

Deleting a group of e-mail messages at once

What happens if you leave the **domain name** off of an e-mail address?

Getting rid of the URL Location **drop-down list**

Changing the way your **e-mail is displayed**

Moving **Eudora e-mail messages** to Netscape

Why does it take forever to **exit Netscape**?

Finding the page you want from your bookmark list

Getting your e-mail without the Netscape Mail option

Going directly to a newsgroup

A shortcut for **Gopher servers**

A keystroke for **jumping between Web pages**

Keeping copies of the e-mail you send

How to **know when you have e-mail**

Troubleshooting Conference on a **Packard Bell computer**

Figuring out which **plug-ins Communicator has installed**

Fixing **problems with your e-mail messages**

Publishing a Web page using Page Composer

A **quick way to send a message** to someone in your address book

Resuming a download after getting the boot from Internet

Searching for unknown addresses

Composer **shortcuts**

How to **start Communicator** without being on the Net

Conference **support for video**

About Communicator and those **tags for Internet Explorer**

Using Conference to call a **traditional phone**

How to **undelete e-mail messages**

Turning off the **underlining of hyperlinks**

Viewing the text in compressed columns

Winsock error 10061

Netscape Navigator @ a Glance

⇨   **Netscape Navigator 3.0** is the most widely used browser on the market today, offering e-mail and newsgroup and Web page browsing in a single program. You can read HTML formatted messages and read and post to newsgroups, and it offers some file transfer capabilities.

⇨   **Netscape Communicator** is the latest entry into the browser market. Netscape's upgrade to Navigator 4.0, Communicator offers a ton of new features, including full integration of e-mail, browsing, file transferring, Web page composing, calendar features, and Internet telephony in a single package. It's much more memory intensive than Navigator 3.0—and has much larger hard drive requirements as well.

NETSCAPE NAVIGATOR 3.0

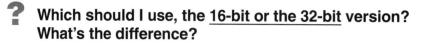 **Which should I use, the 16-bit or the 32-bit version? What's the difference?**

The differences between the versions aren't apparent to the user. The main difference is in the way they handle memory. The 32-bit version may offer slightly faster speed, however. If you are using Windows 95 or Windows NT and the TCP/IP protocol supplied with either operating system, you should be using the 32-bit version. If you're using 16-bit TCP/IP software, such as Trumpet Winsock, you cannot use the 32-bit version. If you do, your system is guaranteed to crash, and certain Internet applications may not run.

? Is there a quick way to <u>access my bookmarks</u> so I can edit them?

Try pressing CTRL-B in Netscape Navigator. The BookMarks should open, allowing you to edit any bookmark entry.

? Is there a quick way to <u>add someone's e-mail address</u> to my address book if they've sent me an e-mail?

The easiest way to add someone to your address book is to select the message and then select Message | Add to Address Book. Then add a nickname, as shown here, or just click on OK to add the entry to your address book.

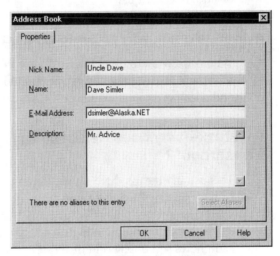

? I know I can <u>add up numbers</u> in my word processor. Can I do the same thing in my Web browser?

You can if you have the JavaScript option enabled. First, make sure it is enabled by choosing Options | Network Preferences. Click the Languages tab and check Enable Javascript, if it is not already checked. Click OK to save your changes. Next, click in the Location field and type **javascript:eval(2+2)** and press ENTER. (You can substitute any operand or number within the parentheses.) Your result will display in a separate Web page.

Tip   *Try typing **about:mozilla** in the Location box of your Netscape browser. You should see an excerpt from the classic Book of Mozilla. Mozilla, by the way, is Netscape Communications' green lizard mascot.*

? Can I use the mail and newsgroup portion of Navigator with <u>America Online</u>?

At present, America Online uses its own proprietary software for both mail and newsgroups, so the answer is no. You can, however, use the Netscape browser if you prefer.

? How do I create a <u>bookmark</u> for a page I want to return to?

If you want to quickly add a bookmark for the page you are visiting, right-click anywhere on a blank area of the page; then, from the pop-up menu, choose Add Bookmark. A bookmark for that page will be added to your list.

? Is there a quick way to <u>bring up my bookmarks</u>?

When you want to quickly access your bookmarks, press CTRL-B from anywhere in Netscape Navigator. The Bookmarks window will open and allow you to edit or select various bookmarks.

? I'm stuck—why does Netscape say "<u>Can't Read Newsgroup</u>"?

This usually means there's a problem with your Internet service provider's news server, or you have configured your news server settings improperly. Check Options | Mail | News Preferences. Click the Servers tab, shown in Figure 4-1, and make sure you have the right news server listed in the bottom frame. If the server name specified is correct, contact your Internet service provider to see if they are having problems.

? My eyes are killing me. Some of these Web page colors are so loud! Is there some way I can tone down the <u>colors</u>?

You can have Navigator override the color schemes of any Web page by selecting Options | General | Preferences | Colors and picking a color scheme that suits you (see Figure 4-2). After you select the color scheme, make sure you check Always Use My Colors, Overriding Document, and click OK to save your changes.

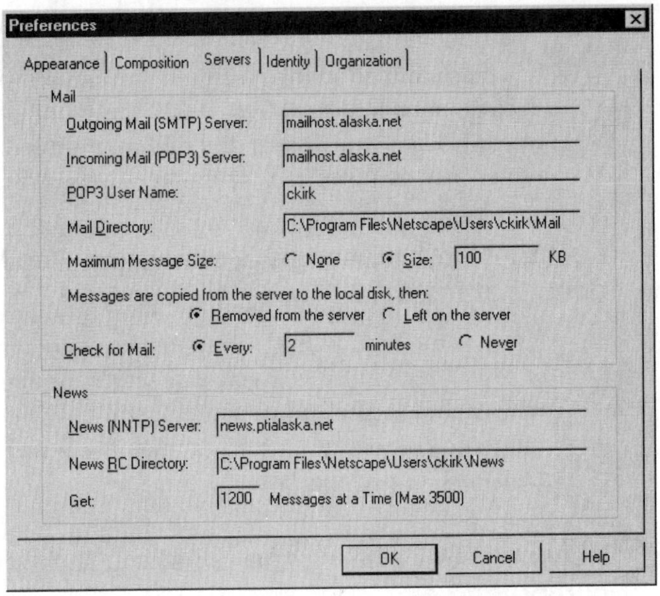

Figure 4-1.   Have you properly specified your news server?

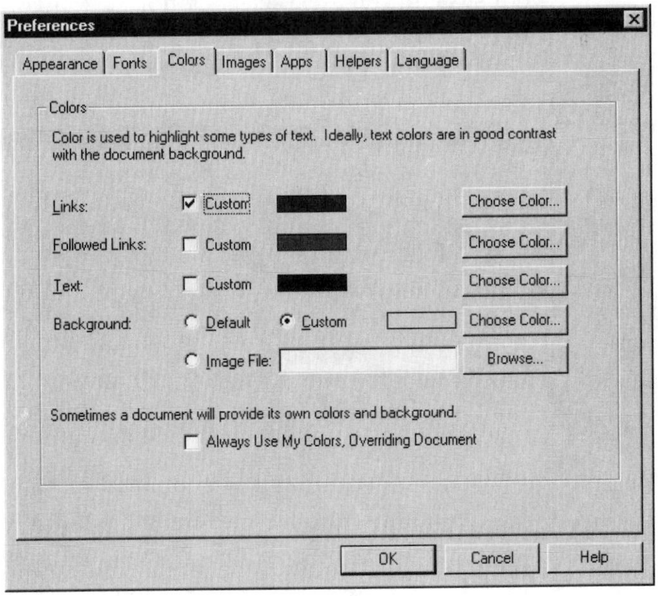

Figure 4-2.   Setting the color options

? How can I tell if I'm really <u>connected to a Netscape server</u>?

If you are connected to a Netscape server, you will see the word "Netsite" next to the Address field instead of the word Location. The word "Netsite" will appear any time you are connected to a Netscape server such as a FastTrack or Enterprise server.

? I get the error message <u>"Connection Reset by Peer."</u> What does that mean?

It means the host, or the Web server, has reset your connection. It may be reset after a failed CGI script or search, or due to network traffic. Simply click the Reload button. If it still says "Reset by Peer," try connecting to the site at another time. The server could be having problems connecting clients.

? How can I tell when a site is asking for a <u>cookie</u> from my computer?

If you want to be notified every time a site requests a cookie from your system, you must select Options | Network Preferences | Protocols and check the option Accepting a Cookie under the Show an Alert Before section, as shown here:

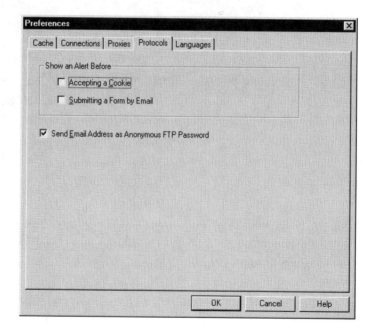

Once you check this option, every time a site requests a cookie from Navigator, you will be alerted through a dialog box.

? I'm tired of all this typing! Isn't there a quick way to copy a URL to an e-mail message?

Yes. Just click on the QuickLink button, which is the little chain icon next to the URL Location field:

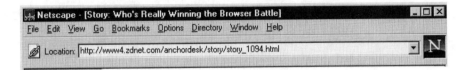

This will copy the URL to the clipboard. Then click the To:Mail button in the e-mail option, position your cursor in the body of the text, and choose paste. The URL will be pasted into the body of your message.

Note   *You can also click and drag the QuickLink chain icon onto your open BookMarks file to create a new bookmark or drag the icon to the desktop to create a shortcut.*

? My computer keeps crashing when I'm using Netscape Navigator. Any suggestions on how to prevent this?

If you have Java support turned on, you may be encountering Java-enabled sites that could cause your system to crash. First, try turning off Java by selecting Options | Network Preferences | Languages and unchecking Enable Java and Enable JavaScript in the Java/JavaScript section.

If that doesn't solve your problem, try emptying the disk and memory caches by choosing Options | Network Preferences | Cache, then clicking the Clear Memory Cache Now and Clear Disk Cache Now buttons. Also make sure your disk cache is set at a reasonable size, such as no more than 10MB.

? Is there a keystroke I can use to cycle through all my open windows?

Yes. ALT-TAB will cycle through all open windows, including Web pages, newsgroups, and e-mail messages. ALT-TAB also cycles through all open Windows 95 applications.

? How can I <u>delete the history file</u>?

Search for a file called Netscape.hst, which should be in your
Netscape directory. Before you delete it, make sure you exit Navigator.

? How do I quickly <u>delete a message</u> from my inbox?

Simply highlight the e-mail message and press DEL.

**? Can't I save some time by <u>deleting a group of e-mail
messages at once</u>?**

Yes, first you'll have to flag those messages you want to delete by
clicking in the Flag field or choosing Message | Flag Message. Then
choose Edit | Select Flagged Messages and press DEL or choose Edit |
Delete Messages.

**? What happens if I leave off the <u>domain name</u> of someone's
e-mail address?**

If the user is part of the domain you are part of, the message will go
through. For example, if you are part of alaska.net and you type **rbd2**
as the username, if rbd2 is a valid user on alaska.net, the message will
be sent to that user. If not, you will receive an error message.

**? Is there a way to get rid of the <u>drop-down list</u> under the
URL Location field?**

It's a little complex and requires editing the Registry file, which is
shown in Figure 4-3. Make sure you back up your Registry file first,
and read and follow the instructions to the letter. Also make sure you
don't have any other applications running, including Netscape, when
you start on your Registry editing journey.

Once you've taken precautions, follow these steps:

1. Click Start, then select Run.

2. Type **REGEDIT** and press ENTER.

3. Expand the HKEY_CURRENT_USER field.

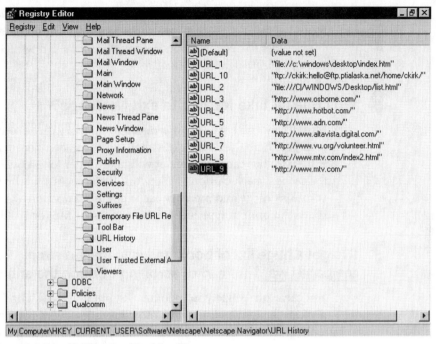

Figure 4-3.   Editing the Registry file

4. Click to expand the Software folder, then expand Netscape, and then expand the entry for Netscape Navigator.

5. Double-click to open the URL History folder.

6. Delete everything except Default.

7. Close the Window, then restart the computer. Reconnect to the Internet, and then launch Navigator.

❓ Can I change the way my e-mail is displayed?

You can change the way your e-mail is displayed by changing the Options | Mail and News Preferences | Appearance option. Here, you can split the screen vertically or horizontally, change the font type to either fixed or variable width fonts, or change the text style or size.

❓ Can I move all my Eudora e-mail messages over to Netscape?

Yes, but first you'll have to copy and rename the files. Navigator mail files are located in the Mail subdirectory by default. Simply copy your Eudora files that end in .mbx to your Netscape Mail directory, then change the extension from .mbx to .snm.

Note   *You do not have to rename the .toc files. These are table of contents or index files that Netscape does not recognize but will create the first time you view the messages in the mail folder.*

Why does it take forever to exit Netscape?

Most likely you have set your disk and memory cache settings relatively high. Netscape does all its cache maintenance when you exit, so if your cache is huge, it will take longer for Netscape to clear the cache. Check Options | Network Preferences | Cache to be sure your disk cache and memory cache are using no more than 10MB of space. An optimum setting for most users is 5MB (or 5000K).

I've got a huge list of bookmarks. Is there a simple way to find the page I want instead of scrolling through the entire list?

You can alphabetize your bookmarks, but if you can't find a bookmark alphabetically and know just a few words of what you're looking for, try the Find option. Simply hold down CTRL-F and type the keywords you're looking for. Netscape will take you directly to the bookmark containing that keyword.

Is there a quick way to get my e-mail without having to choose the Netscape Mail menu option?

Sure. Just click the little mail envelope icon in the lower-right corner of any Netscape window. This will automatically connect to Mail, display the Mail window, and then download your mail messages.

Can I go directly to a newsgroup?

If you know the newsgroup's name, you can type **news:** and the name in the URL Location field. For example, if you wanted to go to the newsgroup called News.Answers, you would type **news:news.answers**.

I know I don't have to enter http:// in the Location field, but what if I'm accessing a Gopher site? Is there a shortcut for Gopher servers?

You bet. If the site you want to access uses a Gopher server, you can leave off the **gopher://**. For example, if you want to access The Well, and the full location is **gopher://gopher.well.com**, you can just type **gopher.well.com**. As long as a site includes the word "gopher," Netscape will assume it's a Gopher server. If you simply type **well.com**, however, Netscape assumes you want to access an HTTP (Web) server.

? ## Is there a keystroke shortcut for jumping between Web pages?

Try using CTRL-TAB. This will cycle you through all the open Navigator windows, including Web pages, newsgroups, and the e-mail application.

? ## Can I keep a copy of e-mail I send to other people?

You can keep track of the messages you send by copying your outgoing messages to a file stored on your computer. Simply select Options | Mail and News Preferences. Click the Composition tab and type the full pathname for the file you want to create to store all your outgoing messages. For example, if your Netscape application is stored in Program Files\Netscape\, you can create a file called Sent by specifying Program Files\Netscape\Sent.

• • • • • • • • • • • •

Keyboard Shortcuts and Navigation

Don't want to lift your hand off that keyboard? Getting mouse-induced carpal-tunnel syndrome? There are plenty of keyboard shortcuts for navigating through Web pages, Web sites, dialog boxes, and windows. Here's a list of some of the best ones that will make your navigating easier:

ALT-LEFT ARROW moves backward.

ALT-RIGHT ARROW moves forward.

CTRL-TAB cycles through all the open Communicator windows.

CTRL-A selects everything on a page.

CTRL-B opens the Bookmark window.

CTRL-C copies the items or text selected.

CTRL-D adds a bookmark.

CTRL-F opens the Find window.

CTRL-H displays the History window, where you can point and click on URLs you've recently visited.

CTRL-M opens the New Message Composition window.

CTRL-N opens a new window displaying the page set as your home page in Communicator's Preferences.

CTRL-O displays the Open Page window.

CTRL-P displays the Print window.

CTRL-R reloads the current page.

CTRL-U displays the page source.

CTRL-W closes the currently opened window.

CTRL-X exits Communicator.

CTRL-1 displays/opens the Navigator window.

CTRL-2 displays/opens the Messenger window.

CTRL-3 displays/opens the Collabra Discussion window.

CTRL-4 displays/opens the Page Composer window.

CTRL-5 displays/opens the Conference window.

CTRL-ALT-S removes or displays the status bar at the bottom of the Netscape screen; this is useful if you need more screen landscape.

CTRL-ALT-T displays status information about the files and URLs being transferred to your computer.

ESC cancels the currently loading page.

F1 brings up the Communicator Help window.

F6 cycles through all the open windows in Communicator.

F10 activates the menu bar.

PAGE UP and PAGE DOWN scroll up and down through the currently opened window.

SPACEBAR moves you down a page.

TAB cycles through the links on a Web page.

❓ How do I <u>know when I have e-mail</u>?

Simply look for the exclamation point in the lower-right corner of your Netscape screen, as shown in Figure 4-4. If you see a question mark instead of an exclamation mark, you may not have connected to your server, or you may have set your mail preferences so they do not check for new messages.

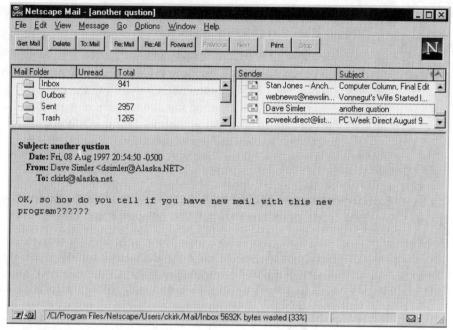

Figure 4-4.   The exclamation point in the lower-right corner notifies you of new mail.

 ## How do I print a <u>list of my bookmarks</u>?

First open the bookmark file in a Web page window. To do that, select Bookmarks | Go to Bookmarks, then select File | Save As. Type a name other than bookmark.htm in the Save As dialog box and click Save.

Next, close the Bookmark window, then choose File | Open File from the browser window. Select the bookmark file you just saved. A formatted HTML version of your bookmark should open. From there, choose File | Print to print your list of bookmarks.

Tip   *If you have a lot of bookmarks and want to keep them handy, why not make them the page your browser starts with each time you open Navigator? To do this, select Options | General Preferences; then in the Browser Starts With field, type* **c:\Netscape\Bookmark.html** *(if that's where your Netscape bookmark.html file is stored) and select the Home Page Location radio button.*

? **Can I mail an entire Web page to someone else? Will they get all the text and graphics?**

Netscape lets you mail any document to anyone using an e-mail application capable of reading HTML. To send a page to someone, choose File | Mail Document while viewing the page you want to e-mail. If you want to send just the text of the page, click the Quote button instead. The recipient should receive all the text and graphics within the body of the e-mail message.

? **How do I set up Navigator so I can use more than one provider or have more than one person use the system?**

First, you will need to create a new directory for each person who will be using Navigator. Create these directories in the c:\program files\netscape\navigator\ directory. Within each new directory, copy your original address book and bookmark file. Next, create two subdirectories named Mail and News. Then select Start | Run and type **REGEDIT** in the dialog box.

On the left side of the Registry Editor window, open HKEY_CURRENT_USER\Software\Netscape. Next, highlight the Netscape entry, and select Registry | Export Registry File. Save this file as netscape.reg in the Netscape directory. This creates a backup file just in case problems arise.

Now, for each person who will be using Navigator, or for each ISP you plan to use, make a copy of this original netscape.reg file, replacing "netscape" in each copy with the name of the person or ISP and keeping the .reg extension.

Open one of the files with a text editor and edit the file, supplying the correct settings for the user or ISP, including the username, e-mail address, and the paths to the mail and news directories and to the cookies and history files. Make sure you point to these new directories you've created for each user or ISP. Save and close the file, and repeat the steps for each .reg file you've created.

Now, users can simply double-click their .reg file to launch Navigator with their settings. When finished, they should exit Navigator so the next person's (or ISP's) options can be loaded.

? **I can't seem to get <u>Navigator installed</u>. I keep getting install errors; what's wrong?**

Previous installations may still be lurking in your hard drive. Try searching your drive for files that start with "uninst." Within Windows 95 select Start | Find | Files or Folders. Next, type **uninst*.exe**. Once you locate these files delete them.

You can also open your C:\temp or C:\windows\temp folder and delete all files in the folder.

? **How do I make <u>Navigator start with mail</u> (or newsgroups) instead of a Web page?**

To make Navigator start with mail or newsgroups instead of a Web page, select Options | General Preferences and click either Netscape Mail or Netscape News in the Startup section. You can choose either to have Navigator start with mail, news, or the browser, with all three, or with any combination of the three. In Figure 4-5, you can see that the system is set to start with just Netscape Mail and Netscape News.

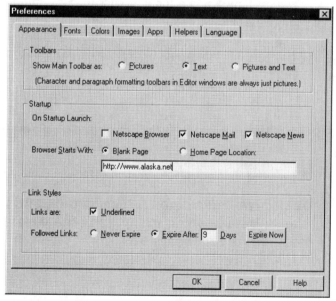

Figure 4-5.   Setting up Navigator to start with your favorite application

Can I use Navigator to browse the pages I like later, <u>offline</u>?

> You can, but you'll need to increase the size of your hard disk cache substantially through the Options | Network Preferences | Cache option. Then choose the Never radio button in the Verify Documents section of the Cache tab.
>
> Next, connect to the Internet, and visit every page you want to browse later so those pages and accompanying graphics will be copied to your cache. Then disconnect and browse the pages at your leisure.

> *Note*   *Imagemap navigational buttons won't work offline, since imagemaps need the Web server to find the accompanying links associated with imagemap.*

 Can I compose e-mail messages <u>offline</u> using Netscape?

> You sure can. Simply start Netscape Navigator and compose your e-mail message. Before you click the Send button in the e-mail composition window, choose Options | Deferred Delivery. This will place your message in the Outbox folder. Once you've composed all the e-mail you want offline, connect to the Internet, then choose File | Send Messages in Outbox or press CTRL-H. This will send all the messages stored in the outbox to the intended recipients.

> *Note*   *If you choose this option, subsequent e-mail messages will be placed in the outbox until you compose a new message and choose Options | Immediate Delivery.*

A lot of my messages are important, and I want to keep them...but I have so many! Isn't there some way to <u>organize my messages</u>?

> Yes; in electronic folders. You can create as many folders as you need by choosing File | New Folder, then typing a name for the folder and clicking OK. Then you can drag and drop messages from your inbox into the new folders.

❓ I know I can type http:// to see pages stored on Web servers, but are there other <u>protocol commands</u> I can use?

Yes. The hypertext transfer protocol isn't the only protocol you can use with any Web browser. Other types of protocols you can use include the following:

Protocol	Usage
FTP	ftp://*domain name* Example: ftp://netscape.com
HTTPS (for secured servers)	https://*domain name* Example: https://www.netscapesecure.com
FILE	file://*localfile* Example: file://c:/windows/deskop/index.html
NEWS (also SNEWS for secure news)	news:*newsgroup.newsserver* Example: snews:secnews.netscape.com
TELNET	telnet:*host:port* Example: telnet:alaska.net
MAILTO	mailto:*user@domain* Example: mailto:ckirk@alaska.net

❓ Why do I sometimes see a messages saying <u>"Reentrant call to interrupt"</u>?

You may see this when you click the Stop button while loading a Web page. If you see this message when you try to access the page again, simply open a new browser window and access another site. Wait a few minutes, and then try the previous site that gave you the error. If the error appears again, exit Netscape, then relaunch Netscape and try again.

❓ Sometimes I reload a page and the response is really slow. Is there a way to make a page <u>reload faster</u>?

You can reload a page faster by holding down the SHIFT key while clicking the Reload button. This will accelerate the reload process.

? **Help! I've <u>reloaded a page</u>, but nothing seems to be happening.**

If pressing the Reload button doesn't work, try holding down the SHIFT key while you choose Reload from the toolbar. This will force Netscape to reload the page from the server rather than from the disk or memory cache of your machine.

? **Can I <u>save copies of all the messages I've sent</u>?**

To keep track of all the mail you send, you should create a mailbox for your sent mail. First, select Options | Mail and News Preferences | Composition. In the Mail File: field, look for the "By default copy outgoing messages to the file" section and type the full pathname of the directory where you want to store your sent mail. For example, if you wanted to save your messages in the Sent Mail folder, you would type **C:\Program Files\Netscape\Navigator\Mail\Sent**.

From that point on, all sent messages will be saved in the Sent directory and displayed in the Sent Mail folder.

? **How can I <u>save a Web page</u>, along with the images I see there?**

If you'd like to save a Web page with both the text and images in Netscape Navigator, you have three options:

⇨   If you have Netscape Navigator Gold, click on the Edit button to save HTML as well as graphics.

⇨   Save the HTML file, and then save all the images separately. To save GIF and JPEG images to disk, right-click on the image. From the pop-up box, select "Save this image as." You can then enter the path where you want to save the image.

⇨   Use a third-party utility to save an entire Web page or even a Web site (try **http://www.ffg.com**, **http://www.evolve.co.uk/unmozify**, or **http://www.talentcom.com**).

? **Can I put my <u>schedule on the Web</u>? I'm not using Communicator.**

If you are using Office 97, you can use Internet Assistant for Microsoft Schedule+. This application lets you save your schedule as an HTML document, which you can publish on a Web page. You select the information you want to be shown or hidden, and the software creates an HTML-formatted page. You can download the Internet Assistant software extension directly from Microsoft's Web site at **http://www.microsoft.com/schedule** or from WinMag's Web site at **http://www.winmag.com/win95/software.htm.**

I've turned off all the toolbars and location bars, but I'd still like more <u>screen space</u> to see Web pages. Any suggestions?

About the only thing left to hide at this point is the status bar. You can turn it off by pressing CTRL-ALT-S.

Note   *To bring back the status bar, just repeat the keystroke combination.*

Someone told me I can easily jump to databases where I can <u>search for friends and relatives</u>. I can't seem to find such an option.

You may not have the Directory buttons showing. First, choose Options | Show Directory Buttons. Next, click the People button. This will take you to a Web page with a list of different "People" search engines.

Can I <u>search for newsgroups</u> within Navigator?

There is no search option, but you can use a third-party Web-based search engine to find newsgroups you're interested in viewing. The following table outlines some of the more popular newsgroup search engines:

Search Engine	Location
DejaNews	http://www.dejanews.com
Infinite Link	http://www.ii.com/internet/messaging/newsgroups/
Usenet Info Center Launch Pad	http://SUNSITE.UNC.EDU/usenet-i/home.html
Tile.net	http://WWW.TILE.NET

? How do I know a site is <u>secure</u>?

There are several ways. If the site's URL starts with **https://**, the Web server hosting the pages is a secured server. Or if the little key in the lower-left corner of your browser window is not broken, but a solid key with a blue background, that's also an indication of a secured site. You can also double-click the key an the security information about this site will be displayed. You can also check the View | Document Source option. This window will display the security options for this page.

 Tip   *If the key only has one tooth, the site has medium security. Two teeth mean high-grade encryption.*

? If I browse a Web page, does Navigator automatically <u>send my e-mail address</u> to that site?

No, although version .09 of Navigator did. But you shouldn't be using that version by now. If you are, make sure you upgrade to the latest version, either 3.*x* or 4.*x*. The only thing Web servers are able to see about you is what version of Navigator you are using and what platform you are on, such as Windows 95 or Windows NT.

The e-mail address you supply in the Mail and News preferences is only used when you send e-mail or post newsgroup messages.

? Why can't I <u>send a message to everyone on my mailing list</u>?

When you first created your mailing list, you should have created a nickname or alias. Then, when sending a message, you would enter that nickname or alias for the mailing list you want to use. If you don't have a nickname, and simply click on the mailing list name in the address book, only the address of the first person on the list will be placed in the To:Mail field, and the message will only be sent to that person. If you haven't included nicknames in your addresses, go back through your address book and add them, then try recreating the message again.

? **How do I <u>send a message to a group of people</u> without each person's name appearing at the top of the message?**

If you want to send a message to a group of people and don't want to have the entire list of recipients show in the header of the mail message, use the Bcc: option. To display the Bcc field, compose a new e-mail message, and then choose View | Mail Bcc. Include the addresses you don't want to show in the Bcc field, and make sure you have at least one valid e-mail address in the To: field.

? **Can I create a <u>shortcut</u> for my favorite Web page and place it on my desktop?**

You sure can, simply by right-clicking when you're on the Web page you want to create the shortcut for. Once you've right-clicked your mouse, choose Internet Shortcut from the pop-up menu. Enter a description for the page if you don't want to use the name of the page, then click OK. An icon representing that Web page will appear on your desktop.

Another way to create a shortcut is by clicking and dragging the QuickLink icon next to the Location field directly onto your desktop. This will create a shortcut with the name of the page for the title. Or you can drag any entry in your bookmark list to the desktop, and an Internet shortcut will be created.

? **Someone told me I can use <u>shortcuts in the URL field</u>. What are some of those shortcuts?**

You can use all sorts of shortcuts in the URL Location field. Here are a few examples:

What You Can Omit	The Long Way	The Short Way
http://	http://www.netscape.com	www.netscape.com
ftp://	ftp://netscape.com	netscape.com
.com and http://	http://www.netscape.com	netscape
http:// and the home page	http://www.netscape.com	www

? **Is there a quick way to skip back to a site I visited several pages ago?**

You could use the Go menu, but if the page you are looking for is not listed, try Window | History. This will display a list of all the pages you've visited while in the current window. You can then double-click any entry, or click to select a URL, and bookmark it.

? **Can I sort my e-mail messages by subject instead of by the date I received them?**

You can sort by any of the column designators simply by clicking the heading of the field you want to sort by. Click once on Subject, and your messages will be sorted by Subject in ascending order. Click again on the Subject header and your messages will be resorted. You can click on any header to sort by that header. The field your messages are sorted by is indicated by an inverted arrow in the column heading.

? **How can I speed up the downloading of Web pages?**

An effective and easy way to speed up download times is to turn off the graphics. To do this, click Options, then deselect Auto Load Images. No graphics will be loaded, which can greatly improve download times. If you find a graphic you want to view, you can right-click on the Graphic button and choose View Image from the shortcut menu.

? **I've heard you can load Navigator using different switches. What are some of these switches?**

Navigator has special switches that you can use to launch the application in a variety of ways. You can either include these switches using the Start | Run option, as in c:\program files\netscape -k, or you can add the switches to the properties of the Netscape icon. Following is a list of switches that you can use to launch Navigator in any way that you like.

Switch	Purpose
-k	Opens navigator in kiosk mode, meaning no menu bar, toolbar, or other controls are made available. You might want to do this when Netscape is used in a public location or when you want to prevent kids from accessing newsgroups.
-news	Opens directly into the newsgroup option.
-mail	Opens directly into the e-mail option.
-h URL (or file)	Specifies the file or home page to open to as Navigator launches.
-l filename.ini	Specifies an alternative .ini file. You would use this option if you have multiple users and configurations of Netscape on one machine. It's definitely handy if you have more than one mailbox and you don't want to change the settings each time.

❓ Can I snag some text from a Web page and include it in an e-mail message?

Simply highlight the text you want to copy, then choose Edit | Copy. Next, click the To:Mail button, address your e-mail message, click in the body of the message, and select Edit | Paste. The text will be placed at the cursor location.

 Tip *You can also paste text from a Web page into any application you choose by copying the text, then jumping to the application you want to paste the text into and choosing Edit | Paste.*

❓ When I compose an e-mail message, Netscape automatically wraps the text. Can I control exactly where the text wraps in an e-mail message?

Yes you can. Netscape Mail automatically wraps text on the right-hand side of the mail composition window based on the size of the window. When the mail message is received, however, the message will wrap at the 72nd character. If you want the message to wrap exactly as you have written it, when sending a message, choose the View menu and uncheck Wrap Long Lines. Now the text will wrap within the constraints of the window.

? I keep getting an "Unable to launch external viewer! error code=16" message when I try to download a file through Navigator. What's wrong?

This error message usually means your helper applications haven't been configured properly, so Netscape doesn't know what to do with this type of file. You can try bypassing Navigator's file checking by holding down the SHIFT key while clicking the link to download the file. This will cause Navigator to download the file directly to your hard drive.

If you'd rather configure Netscape to accept the file format the next time you download the same type of file, select Options | General Preferences | Helpers. Scroll down to the line for Mime Type "application/octet-stream," then click to select that line, or click the New button to create a new entry. In the Extensions field add the extension of the file you're trying to download; then set the action to Unknown:Prompt User, and click OK to save the changes. The next time you try to download this type of file, a dialog box will pop up asking you to save the file.

? When I'm using CoolTalk I get an "Undefined Dynalink Error." What could be the problem?

You may not have the proper video driver installed, or you may have two different video driver versions installed in different locations. This can cause a DLL conflict. Check your system for the file msvideo.dll, which should be located in the \Windows\System\ directory. If you don't have version 1.1e or above, download the latest version at **ftp://ftp.netscape.com/pub/navigator/3.01/windows/wv1160.exe**.

? I store a lot of messages in my inbox. Is there a quick way to show only the unread ones?

Yes, Netscape has included such an option under the Options menu within the e-mail application. To activate it, choose Options | Show Only Unread Messages. This will show only those messages that have not been read. To show all messages again, select Options | Show All Messages.

What's the quickest way to upload files to my file server?

All you have to do is connect to your file server using Navigator, then simply drag the file you want to upload to the open browser window.

How do I find the URL of a frame?

To find out what the actual URL is of a frame, right-click the frame and select Frame Info. This will display the URL for that frame. If you copy it and paste it back into the Location field, the same site will appear without frames.

How can I find out what version of Navigator I'm using?

The easiest way is to type **about:** in the URL Location field and press ENTER. That will tell you what version you are currently using. An example is shown in Figure 4-6.

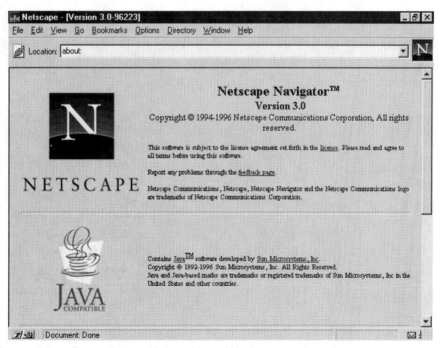

Figure 4-6.   Determining which version of Navigator you're using

• • • • • • • • • •

Interested in Seeing the Netscape Development Team?

If you have version 2.0 or below of Navigator, you can type **about:photo** in the Location box and see a photo of the Navigator developers. You can try typing **about:authors** and see a text listing of authors. Unfortunately, these options have been removed in version 3.0 and above.

However, if you want to know more about those wacky workers at Netscape, check out each person's home page by typing **about:** and the person's name in the Location field of Netscape's browser. Here are some of the people you'll find:

about:ari	Ari Luotonen
about:atotic	Aleks Totic
about:blythe	Garrett Blythe
about:chouck	Chris Houk
about:dmose	Dan Mosedale
about:dp	dp Suresh
about:ebina	Eric Bina
about:hagan	Hagan Heller
about:jeff	Jeffrey M.Treuhaft
about:jg	John Giannandrea
about:jsw	Jeff Weinstein
about:jwz	Jamie Zawinski
about:karlton	Philip Karlton
about:kipp	Kipp E.B. Hickman
about:marca	Marc Andreessen
about:mlm	Mike McCool
about:montulli	Lou Montulli
about:mtoy	Michael Toy
about:paquin	Tom Paquin
about:robm	Rob McCool
about:sharoni	Sharon Iimura
about:terry	Terry Weissman
about:timm	Tim McClarren

? I have Auto Image Loading turned off. Occasionally, though, I would like to <u>view an image</u>—can I do this?

Anytime you want to view a specific image but have the Auto Load Image option turned off, simply right-click on the icon of the image, then select View Image from the pop-up menu. This will load just that image. Repeat the same steps for as many graphics as you want to view. These images will then be added to your memory cache and will be displayed the next time you view that page, even if you have Auto Image Loading turned off.

About the about: options

There's more to about: than finding out the status of your memory cache. How about finding out what version of Netscape you're working in—or simply displaying the Netscape logo? You can use the about: option to view all sorts of information in Netscape Navigator. The following table outlines what you can see:

Command	What It Does
about:	Shows the version number. Typing **about:** is the same thing as choosing About Netscape in the Help menu.
about:logo	Displays the Netscape logo. Useful if you need to include the logo on your Web page. You can right-click to save the file or make the logo your desktop wallpaper.
about:javalogo	Displays the Java logo. Same use as displaying the Netscape logo.
about:*URL* Example: about:http://www.netscape.com	Displays information about a particular URL cached in your browser.
about:cache	Displays status information about the size of your disk cache and the files stored there.

Command	What It Does
about:memory-cache	Displays information about each file stored in your memory cache. A quick way to jump back to previously visited links.
about:image-cache	Displays information about only the image files stored in your memory cache. Details each image in terms of URL location, byte size, and actual dimension of image.
about:plugins	Displays what plug-ins are installed in your browser, including the full pathname of where the plug-in is stored, the company that created the plug-in, and whether the plug-in is active. Useful for troubleshooting problems with plug-ins.
about:document	Displays information about the last URL you visited. Same as choosing View	Document Info.
about:global	Reads in, then displays the history.db file. This file contains every visited link.

? Can I view my "cookies" file?

You bet. Your cookies file is not for other people to view. If you've ever wondered what your cookies file holds, just search for a file called cookies.txt, which should be stored in your Netscape directory. You can either open the file through Netscape's File | Open option or use your favorite word processor. What you'll find in this file is such information as your name, password saved for a particular site, the last time you visited sites, and more.

? Can I check which Web sites my kids have visited?

You can easily find out which Web sites your kids, you, or anyone else has visited by typing the following command in the Location field of your Netscape browser:

about:global

Caution   *This may take quite some time to load the results. Make sure you don't have any other applications running and that you've saved whatever work you currently have open.*

 ### Is there a way to find out <u>what's stored in my cache</u> before I delete the files from my drive?

Yes. Type **about:cache** in the URL location field of any browser window and press ENTER. A list of all the files and graphics currently stored in your cache will be displayed in a Web page. You can then click any link to display the graphic or URL.

 Caution   *If your cache file is large, trying the about:global option could crash your computer. Make sure you have saved any files you're working on before running this option. It's also probably best if you don't have other applications running.*

NETSCAPE COMMUNICATOR AND COMMUNICATOR PRO

Can I <u>add a bookmarked site to my Personal toolbar</u>?

Yes. If you already have a site bookmarked and just want to add it to your Personal toolbar, click the Bookmarks icon on the Location toolbar, then select Edit Bookmarks from the drop-down list. Locate the bookmark you want to add to your Personal toolbar and drag it to the toolbar. An icon for that page link should immediately appear in your Personal toolbar.

If I'm using <u>AOL or CompuServe</u>, can I use Conference?

As long as you are using a true Internet TCP/IP connection, you should be able to use Conference. However, some commercial providers may use error checking, which can result in decreased performance.

? How can I <u>arrange my address book fields</u> to appear in a different order?

To display the address book fields in a different order, simply click on the title of a field and, while holding down the mouse button, move it to the left or right. To sort the fields in ascending or descending order, click once on the title of a field. A pyramid icon will display next to the field name depicting the sort order. An upside-down pyramid means the field is being sorted in ascending order.

? How do I add an <u>attachment to an e-mail message</u>?

You can quickly add any file to an e-mail message simply by dragging and dropping the file from your desktop or Windows Explorer screen onto the Attach Files & Documents tab in the Composition window. The filename and location will appear in the attachment listing and will be sent when you click the Send button. Or you can press INS while clicking in the Attach tab and the File Attach dialog window will display, then select the file to attach to the e-mail message

? How can I add a different <u>background color</u> to my e-mail messages?

First click the New Msg button, then select Format | Page Colors and Properties. This will bring up the Colors and Background dialog box, shown in Figure 4-7. From there, select the colors you want, or include a background image if you choose to. Make sure you click the "Save these settings for new pages" checkbox so the background or image will be used on each new message you send.

? Can I use Communicator to <u>bookmark my e-mail messages</u> as well as my favorite Web pages?

Yes, you can bookmark your e-mail messages and even newsgroup postings—allowing you to jump directly to whatever you want with a click of a button.

To bookmark an e-mail message, open the message you want to bookmark. Next, select Bookmarks | Add Bookmark from the Communicator menu. You can bookmark newsgroup postings the same way—select the posting you want to bookmark and choose Bookmarks | Add Bookmark.

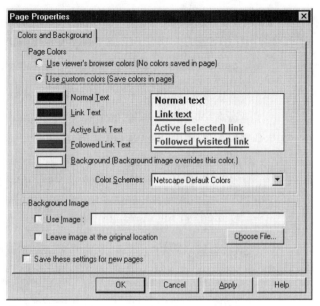

Figure 4-7.   Setting the background color of your e-mail messages

Note   *When you bookmark an e-mail message, this bookmark will only work on your computer—meaning that you can't send your bookmarks to others on your network and assume they will work. However, bookmarked newsgroup postings can be distributed to anyone on a network with the same access to the newsgroup you used to bookmark the posting. Remember, if you bookmark global newsgroup postings, these messages can expire.*

Do I need to be connected to a special server to use the Calendar option of Communicator Pro?

You can use Calendar even if you are not online or connected to a workgroup server. Just click Calendar under the Communicator menu and choose Off-line. Then add your calendar entries.

Note   *If you want to use the advanced features, such as group scheduling, you will need to be connected to the Internet and have access to a Netscape Calendar Server.*

? Can I have Netscape Messenger <u>check for e-mail at a specific time</u> and remember my password?

Yes, if you select the right preferences. To do that, follow these steps:

1. From the Communicator main menu, select Edit | Preferences.
2. Click the plus sign for Mail & Groups to expand this option.
3. Click the Mail Server entry, then select the More Options button.
4. Click the "Check for mail" option, then specify how long you want Communicator to wait between checking for e-mail.
5. To save your password, within the same window, check "Remember my mail password," as shown here, and click OK.

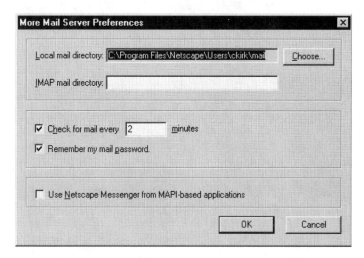

6. Click OK again to save the changes. The changes will take effect immediately.

? Can I change how often Communicator <u>checks my cache</u> or the server for new information on a Web page?

Yes—here's how: select Edit | Preferences from the main menu, expand the Advanced category, and click the Cache category option. Next, select "Document in cache is compared to document on network," and select Once Per Session, Every Time, or Never.

? I'm getting a <u>choppy sound</u> with Conference. Are there any settings I can change to quiet things down?

For really choppy connections, or slow response, select a slower speed compression method from the Compression drop-down list. You can also tweak the number of audio packets (referred to as buffers) using the Advanced button in the Audio tab window. Click the Latency tab, then adjust the slider for more or less buffers. The more the buffers, the better the sound quality, but the slower the playback will be.

? <u>Conference doesn't work with my sound card.</u> Any suggestions?

Conference uses the multimedia Application Programming Interface, mmsystem.dll, for information about your sound card and how it handles sound. If your sound card doesn't write to this API—and many older sound cards don't—Conference may not work with your system and its sound card drivers.

To find out if your system can work with Conference, first check to see if Sound Recorder can play and record audio from your microphone. Since Conference uses the same drivers as Sound Recorder, Conference should work.

If you still have problems, try selecting Windows Control Panel | Multimedia. Check the Preferred Devices under the Playback and Record drop-down list. If the listing is selected on "None," choose the proper sound card for your system. Click OK, then reboot your machine. Try connecting to the Internet, then using Conference.

If you have the proper sound card chosen for recording and playback, but Conference still doesn't work, try right-clicking on the My Computer icon. Select the Device Manager tab, then click the plus sign next to Sound/Video/Game Controllers to expand the listing. If there is a yellow circle with an exclamation mark next to your sound card or recording device, you need to delete, then reinstall, the driver for your sound card.

? Can I add my own links to the Personal <u>custom toolbar</u> in Communicator?

First display the page you want to bookmark. Next, show the Personal toolbar by selecting View | Show Personal Toolbar. Move your cursor over the Page Proxy icon next to the Netsite/Location field, then click and drag the cursor from the Location toolbar to the

Personal toolbar. Release the mouse button, and an icon for the page is displayed on the toolbar.

? Is there a quick way to <u>delete messages</u>? I'm tired of always dragging them to the Trash folder?

Of course. All you have to do is select the items you want to delete in any message or newsgroup view, then press SHIFT-DEL. This will bypass Messenger, placing the message in the Trash folder.

? How do I get Navigator to start with a <u>different home page</u>?

To change the page displayed every time you start Navigator, choose Edit | Preferences. Click the link for Navigator, then choose to have Navigator start with either a blank page, a home page, or the last page you visited before exiting Navigator.

If you want a certain Web page displayed every time you click the Home button or use the CTRL-N keystroke combination, enter the web site location for that page in the Location field. You can also click the Use Current Page button to use the currently displayed page as your home page.

Once configured, if you don't remember the URL of your home page, simply move your cursor over the Home button and the URL will appear.

? How do I get a <u>digital certificate</u>?

When you need a digital certificate to verify who you are, click the Security toolbar button, then select Yours under the Certificates section. Next, click the Get A Certificate button. Click Continue, and Communicator will launch a browser window with a VeriSign link. Click the link, click Continue, and then click the link for the Digital ID center. From there, simply follow the instructions to fill out the information on the form. Once completed, your ID should appear in your personal certificates listing.

? Can I use a <u>direct IP address</u> with Conference?

If you want to enter an IP address in the "E-mail address" field from the main Conference screen, you must enclose it in parentheses, as in (204.149.99.41). If you are entering an IP address under Call | Direct Call, you do not need the parentheses.

? Is there a way to control how much <u>disk space</u> is used for my e-mail and discussion group messages?

Yes, you can control the amount of disk space your e-mail and newsgroup messages take up through the Edit | Preferences option. To set the amount of disk space, follow these steps:

1. Select Edit | Preferences, then expand the Advanced option in the Preferences window.
2. From the expanded list, select Disk Space.
3. Click "Do not download any messages larger than..." and supply the number of kilobytes you want to allow for downloading messages as shown in Figure 4-8. A good range is between 50K and 1024K.
4. Click OK to save the changes.

? Can I search the list of users on a <u>DLS server</u>?

Yes. First click the Web Phonebook button in Netscape Conference | Communicator. This will bring up the interface to the DLS server. In the Search field, enter the name of the person you are looking for; this will filter all the lists that match your criteria and display the filtered results in the list. If there are too many users listed, you can filter your results.

Note The default phone book is located at *http://home.netscape.com/ comprod/products/communicator/conference/phonebook/.*

? I need to get out of e-mail, but I want to finish writing this message later. How do I save a <u>draft version</u>?

If you don't want to send a message right away, you can select the File | Save Draft option from the main menu while you're composing the message. After you save the draft version, you can go back to that message at any time by opening up the Drafts folder and clicking on the saved message.

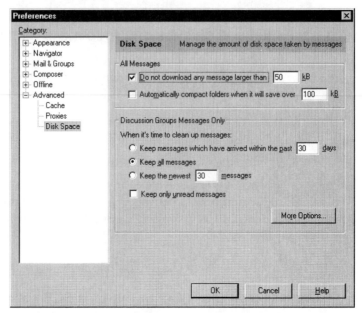

Figure 4-8.   Setting the amount of disk space your messages occupy

❓ How do I <u>expand a toolbar</u> I've accidentally hidden?

Each toolbar has a small vertical tab on the left edge. This vertical tab is like a light switch; click it once, and the toolbar shows. Click it again, and the toolbar collapses, leaving the vertical tab showing.

If you want to hide a toolbar completely, select Hide X Toolbar from Navigator's View menu. To show the toolbar again, simply select Show X Toolbar from the View menu. If you want to rearrange the order of the toolbars, simply click in an empty spot on a toolbar and move it up or down.

❓ Is there a way to automatically <u>filter e-mail messages</u> into specific folders?

You can set up filters to act on any message, based on who the sender is, what the subject of the message is, what the body of the message is, the date of the message, the priority, the status, or who is included on the cc list.

To auto-filter your messages, follow these steps:

1. Select Edit | Mail Filters.

2. Click the New button. You'll see the Filter Rules dialog box, shown here:

3. Enter a name for the filter you're creating in the Filter name: field.

 Note   *Every filter must have a name.*

4. Select the field for the filter to use in the "If the" field.

5. Select the operand in the "of the message" field, then supply the variable for the filter to look for. For example, if you wanted to check each message's subject field for the word "Navigator," you would type **navigator** in the variable field.

6. Select the type of action you want to perform on the message from the drop-down list next to the "then" field. If you want the filter to work on the priority of a message, select the message priority level from the second drop-down field.

7. Enter a description for your filter. Describe it so that a month from now, you'll remember exactly what the filter does and exactly what kinds of messages the filter will work on.

8. Next, activate the filter by clicking the On radio button.

9. Click OK to save the settings and activate the filter.

? What kind of <u>hardware</u> do I need to run Conference?

You need at least a 486/33MHz PC with at least 16MB of RAM and 10MB of free hard disk space. You should have at least a 28.8Kbps modem and a sound card, with a set of speakers and a microphone.

The faster the PC, the faster the response; the faster the modem, the clearer the voice quality.

 *Note   If you have an IBM MWave modem, currently Conference does not work with the MWave chipset technology. Check Netscape's tech support Web site at **http://help.netscape.com** for more information on when the MWave technology will work with Conference.*

I don't like the <u>HTML tags</u> used in Messenger. How do I turn that feature off?

The HTML tags are used to display Web-like e-mail messages.

1. Select Edit | Preferences.
2. Select the plus sign for the Mail & Groups category to expand the list.
3. Select Messages.
4. Click the checkbox labeled "By default, send HTML messages," if it is checked.
5. Click OK.

How do I include <u>images in my e-mail messages</u>?

You can drag and drop any image into an e-mail message you are composing. For example, if you find a graphic you like on a Web page and you want to include it in your message, press CTRL-M. This will open the Messenger Composition window, and you can then drag and drop the image into the new message.

 Note   You can also use the same drag-and-drop technique for any links you want to include in e-mail messages, assuming you have the default set to send HTML formatted e-mail messages in the Edit | Preferences | Mail & Groups option.

Can I use Conference to call people who are using other Internet telephone programs?

You can, as long as the other Internet telephone program is compatible with ITU's H.323 protocol. This includes NetMeeting, Intel Video Phone, and VocalTec's Internet Phone, to name a few. However, you have to make sure the program is using the same audio codecs, or sound compression options. Conference includes several high-quality modem-speed codecs, such as RT24, RT29, and Lucent 8300.

? Is there some way to <u>list all the Web pages I've just visited</u> so I can go back to a particular one?

Yes, just click and hold the Navigation toolbar's Back button. This will bring up a drop-down list of pages you've recently visited. Simply select the one you want, and Navigator will take you directly there.

? How do I mark a <u>newsgroup as "read"</u>?

First click on Messages in the menu bar, then select Mark. From the drop-down menu, choose "Mark as read."

? Doesn't Messenger <u>notify me when new mail is received</u>? I don't seem to see any indication I've received new mail.

Messenger displays a green arrow pointing to your inbox icon on your docked or floating Component bar to notify you when you have new mail. Clicking on the inbox icon will bring up your Messenger window, and you can retrieve your e-mail by clicking the Get Mail button in the Messenger window.

Note   *You can also launch the Netscape Mail Notification icon found in your Communicator directory. When you launch the Mail Notification application, Messenger will monitor your e-mail connection for new incoming mail and display the icon in the Taskbar Tray located next to the date. You can configure the Mail Notification application to alert you with just the green arrow icon, or you can choose from a variety of sounds to go with it.*

? I've been using Conference with my <u>Packard Bell computer</u>. Sometimes it works and sometimes it doesn't. What could be the problem?

First check your microphone to make sure it's working properly. If the microphone works properly, to record sound files, you may need to update your sound card drivers. Check Packard Bell's Web site at http://www.packardbell.com or Microsoft's Web site at http://www.microsoft.com for the latest sound drivers.

❓ How do I know what <u>plug-ins have been installed</u> once I install Communicator?

Communicator Preview Release 4 is shipped with a full complement of plug-ins, but you must select the Full Package when downloading your copy. The Typical package does not include plug-ins. If you are installing additional plug-ins, you must exit, then restart, Communicator before any newly installed plug-ins will work.

To check which plug-ins are installed, select Help | About Plug-ins (see Figure 4-9). A Web page displays, listing the plug-ins installed along with the file types they recognize and whether the plug-in is enabled on your system. Currently, there are 135 plug-ins you can install on your system. To find out what's available, click the "click here" link in the About Plug-ins page.

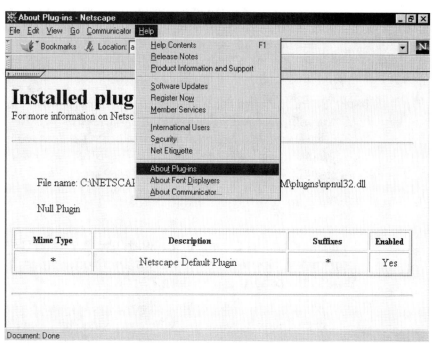

Figure 4-9.   Checking for plug-ins

? **I'm having <u>problems with my e-mail messages</u>. They either don't show up or show up garbled. How do I fix this?**

Most likely your mailbox has become corrupted. To fix this problem, you will have to rebuild your mailbox by following these steps:

1. Exit Communicator.

2. Open the C:/Program Files/Netscape/Users/ directory.

3. Open the folder with your username, then double-click to open the Mail folder stored inside your username folder.

4. Select all the files that end in .snm, then press the DEL key.

5. Restart Communicator and check your mailbox.

? **How do I <u>publish a Web page</u> using Page Composer?**

First, save your file using the File | Save option in Page Composer. Next, select File | Publish and select the option to send only the page you're editing along with all the graphics associated with that page. Next, enter the address where you want the page to be uploaded. The syntax of the location should be **ftp://ftp.isp.com/your folder/**. Supply your username and password in the appropriate fields. Finally, click OK, and the files will be uploaded to your server in the directory you've specified, with the filename you gave the page when you saved it.

? **What's a <u>quick way to send a message</u> to someone listed in my address book?**

You can highlight any name in your address list and then press CTRL-M to quickly send a message to the person or company highlighted.

? **I lost my Internet connection right in the middle of downloading a file! Is there a way to <u>resume the download</u>?**

Yes, this is a built-in feature of Communicator because the program caches all files being downloaded. All you need to do is return to the original link of the file you were downloading and resume the download from where it stopped.

• • • • • • • • • • •

Conference Whiteboard Tips

The Whiteboard lets you and other conference attendees exchange image files and information pasted from the clipboard. A quick way to share information displayed on your screen with others is to capture the current window. To do this, choose Capture Window from the Capture menu. A cross-hair pointer appears. Using this pointer, click and drag around the area of the screen you want to capture. An outline of the area should appear on your Whiteboard. If you want to preview the captured area, hold down the SHIFT key as you move across the outline.

If you don't want the Whiteboard to interfere with capturing a screen—say, a picture of your desktop—select Hide on Capture. The Whiteboard will disappear while you capture what's on your desktop.

❓ What's a quick way to search for somebody's address when I don't have it stored in my address book?

The address book not only keeps track of your coworkers', clients', relatives', and friends' e-mail addresses, but also can help you search the major e-mail search engines, such as Four11 and BigFoot. It can even help you track FedEx packages, assuming you have the FedEx tracking number. To quickly search any of these directories, type the name of the person you are looking for (or the FedEx tracking number) in the "Type in the name you are looking for:" field. Next, click the drop-down list to choose the search engine you want to use in the Search in: field. Click the Search button, and the results will be listed below the initial address listing.

❓ Are there any shortcuts I should know about for using Composer?

Yes, there are plenty, and they are context-sensitive. Just try right-clicking while performing any task. The shortcut menu will change depending on what function you are using.

? **Can I <u>start Communicator</u> without being connected to the Internet?**

Yes you can, but you will have to edit a few things. First go to Edit | Preferences, then click the Offline menu item. Select Offline Work Mode, then click the OK button to save the changes. Exit Communicator, then restart the program. Communicator should start without automatically connecting to the Internet.

Note   *Communicator will store all your outgoing messages, both newsgroup postings and e-mail messages, in the OutBox folder until you take the initiative to send them. To do that, start Messenger, and choose File | Send Messages after you've connected to the Internet.*

? **Does Conference <u>support video</u>?**

Yes, Conference supports H.323 video.

? **Why don't the <u>tags for Internet Explorer</u> work with Communicator?**

Currently, Communicator recognizes 3.0 and 3.2 HTML tags. If the page has been designed with tags specifically for Internet Explorer and those tags are not 3.0 or 3.2 compliant, Communicator will not be able to interpret them.

? **Can Conference be used to call <u>traditional phones</u>?**

The H.323 specification allows third-party hardware vendors to create special gateway devices that will provide the capability for any H.323 endpoint to connect with the traditional phone system. Conference's support for the H.323 architecture will allow use with such third-party gateways.

? **Can I <u>undelete e-mail messages</u> I've deleted?**

First, try going to the Edit menu and selecting Undo. The message you've deleted should reappear in your inbox. However, the Undo option works relative to the current window you have open. So, if you've moved to another option since you deleted a message, you will have to open the Trash folder from the Netscape Messenger Inbox folder and drag the message you want to undelete to the Inbox folder.

? How can I turn off underlining of hyperlinks?

Follow these steps if you want to turn off underlining of hyperlinks:

1. Choose Edit | Preferences, then select Colors under the Appearance heading (see Figure 4-10).

2. Uncheck the "Underline links" option, then click OK.

3. Click the Reload button to see the changes take effect.

? I've compressed the column headers in e-mail, but now I can't see what the text says. Is there a way to view the text without having to expand the column?

If you have compressed the column view of a column header so much that you can't read what's in the column, move your cursor over the

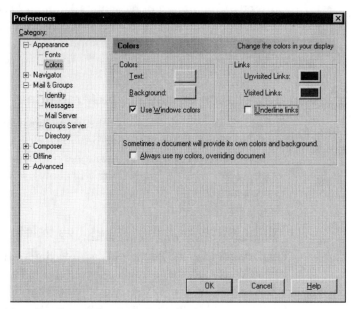

Figure 4-10.   Turning off the underlining option

text and hold your mouse button there until a box pops up with the complete text.

? **I get <u>Winsock error 10061</u> when I start Conference. What's up?**

This means Conference was unable to register with the DLS server. You could have a firewall blocking your connection, or the DLS server may be down or unavailable. Either try using another DLS server or check with your network administrator.

Cruising the Web with Internet Explorer

Answer Topics!

Internet Explorer @ a Glance

⇨   **Internet Explorer 3.0** offers easy access to just about any Web page on the Internet. Internet Explorer 3.0 was the first full-featured browser Microsoft released that offered access to the Web, newsgroups, e-mail, and online voice conferencing. Internet service providers around the globe, including America Online, offer Explorer 3.0 as their standard browser.

⇨   Microsoft isn't a sleeping giant by any means. By releasing **Internet Explorer 4.0**, with its many refinements and enhancements to 3.0, Microsoft is keeping up with other browsers on the market by offering advanced features such as offline browsing, an integrated desktop that mixes the Web with your own personal computer, and better e-mail and newsgroup capabilities. Explorer 4.0 can actually turn your browser into your desktop, making all your files accessible through a Web page and allowing you to add buttons to the Explorer toolbar that launch applications. It is truly a new kind of Internet application, offering full integration between the Internet and your desktop.

FREQUENTLY ASKED QUESTIONS ABOUT INTERNET EXPLORER

❓ I can't seem to get Explorer to work with my America Online account. What could be the problem?

If you can't browse the Web using Internet Explorer after connecting to America Online, you could be using version 3.0 for Windows instead of for Windows 95. If you want to find out what version you're using, select Help | About AOL from the main AOL menu. AOL 3.0 for Windows uses the 16-bit version of the Winsock.dll file, and the 32-bit Internet Explorer 3.0 won't work with this version.

❓ When I bring up Internet Explorer, the AutoDial option doesn't work even though I have it enabled. What gives?

You may have switched from using a proxy server to using the AutoDial feature. If this is the case, make sure you have the Dial-Up

Networking option selected. To do this select Start | Programs | Accessories, then choose Dial-Up Networking. Double-click to select the connection you use. Then restart Internet Explorer and try connecting to a Web site (see Figure 5-1).

❓ How do I use the Automatic Search function?

To use the Automatic Search function, go to the URL field and type **Find** followed by a search topic. For example, if you wanted to find Alaska, type **FIND ALASKA** and Internet Explorer will automatically search the Yahoo database or default search engine site for Web sites that match your search query.

❓ How do I customize AutoSearch so I can point to any search site I want?

The answer to this question involves running the Registry editor. Make sure you have a backup of your Registration database and

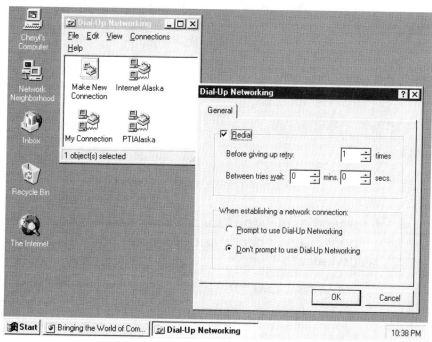

Figure 5-1.   Setting proxy options in the Dial-Up Networking program

have exited Explorer and all other programs before following these instructions:

1. Select Start | Run, then type **Regedit** in the Run dialog box and hit ENTER.

2. Find the following key entry and select it: HKEY_CURRENT_USER\Software\Microsoft\Internet Explorer\SearchUrl

3. Double-click the Default value under Toolbar.

4. Type in the text that corresponds to your search site. Use one of the following choices to specify the search engine you want AutoSearch to bring up:

AltaVista	www.altavista.digital.com/cgi-bin/query?pg=q&q=%s
Excite	www.excite.com/search.gw?search=%s
InfoSeek	guide-p.infoseek.com/Titles?qt=%s
Lycos	www.lycos.com/cgi-bin/pursuit?query=%s
Magellan	searcher.mckinley.com/searcher.cgi?query=%s
Default MSIE autosearch	home.microsoft.com/access/autosearch.asp?p=%s
Yahoo (plain search)	search.yahoo.com/bin/search?p=%s
Yahoo (IE autosearch)	msie.yahoo.com/autosearch?p=%s

4. Hit F5 to refresh your entries to make sure the changes are reflected in the Registry database.

5. Exit the Registry editor, launch Explorer, and check to see if your AutoSearch options have changed.

? Sometimes when I try to connect to a site I see a blank page. Can I specify another page when Explorer can't connect to a site?

You can set the default system.htm file to display any page you want. But you'll need to use the Windows Registry editor to make that change. Select Start | Run and type **Regedit**. Next search for the following key, then select it:

HKEY_CURRENT_USER\SOFTWARE\MICROSOFT\INTERNET EXPLORER\MAIN

Double-click the LOCAL PAGE entry, then type the full pathname to the HTML page you want to use as a default. You can either use a local file or a remote file.

? I recently installed a disk-utility program on my computer and now I have a problem with Internet Explorer 3.01. When I access a Web site that's password-protected, the browser freezes after I enter my user ID and password. What's wrong?

You may be experiencing a conflict with the utility program you installed or a shared file may have become corrupted during installation of the utility program. First, disable the utility program, then try running Internet Explorer. If the utility program automatically launches when you start your Windows 95 machine, disable it by either removing it from your Startup program group or from the load line found in the win.ini file, then reboot. If that still doesn't work, you may have conflicts with other programs that are loading. You might try disabling them one at a time, trying Internet Explorer as you go. If you discover that the freezes don't occur with one particular utility disabled, you've found the conflict.

? How do I change the colors of the links or text used on Web pages?

First, choose View | Options | General, then click on the Color tab. You should see the color scheme Internet Explorer is currently using. To change those colors, click each choice and select another color, then click OK to close the Options window and save the changes (see Figure 5-2).

? I get an error message saying the "Content Advisor configuration information is missing." What does that mean and how can I fix it?

This error message happens when the rating system has been enabled but the ratings.pol file is missing or damaged. What you need to do is create a new ratings.pol file. Close Internet Explorer and delete the ratings.pol file from the C:\Windows\system folder.

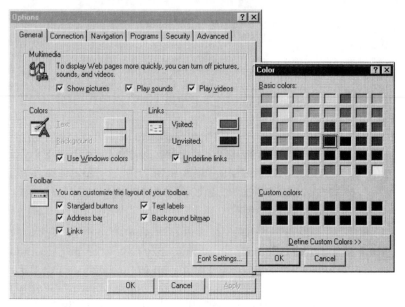

Figure 5-2.   Changing the color of the links

Next, start Internet Explorer then choose View | Options. Click the Security tab, then click the Settings button in the Content Advisor section. If protected, supply the Supervisor password then click OK. Finally, select the Ratings options that meet your needs then click the OK button. You'll need to restart Internet Explorer for the new changes to take effect (see Figure 5-3).

? Can I copy a hyperlink directly to a floppy drive?

You can send a hyperlink to any type of device or location available from the Send To shortcut menu. Simply choose File | Send To. From there you can elect to use this feature to send URLs to your e-mail account, a floppy disk, your briefcase, or a fax.

? Can I copy a Web page without having to go directly to that page?

You can copy any page by just clicking a link that points to that page. First right-click on the link, then choose Save Target As from the shortcut menu. This will copy the page along with all the links.

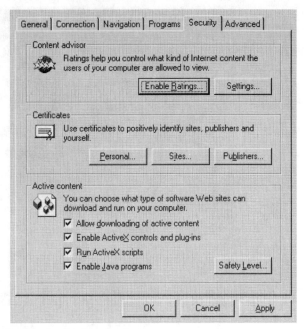

Figure 5-3.   Setting the Ratings options

Warning   *When you copy a page this way, no background graphics, pictures, or sounds will be included. If you want all these options go directly to the page, and use the File | Save option.*

How do I make Internet Explorer the default browser instead of Netscape?

First, understand that when you make Internet Explorer your default browser, your shortcuts saved on the desktop will be loaded by Explorer when you double-click them. To make Explorer your default browser select View | Options | Programs, then check the "Internet Explorer should check to see whether it is the default browser" checkbox. Click the OK button to save the changes.

How do I change the default color scheme of Explorer?

Try going to View | Options | General and uncheck the Use Windows Colors option, then use the Colors option to select the color scheme you want. Click OK to save the changes (see Figure 5-4).

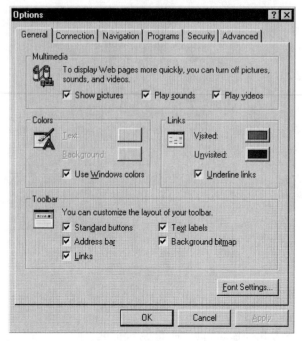

Figure 5-4.   Changing the default color schemes

❓ How do I change the **default mail client** in Internet Explorer?

To change the default mail client in Internet Explorer, follow these steps:

1. Select View | Options, then the Programs tab.

2. In the Mail and News section, use the Mail box option to select the program you would rather use as your mail client.

3. Click Apply, then click OK to save your changes and have them immediately available.

❓ Can I change the **default search page** Explorer brings up?

Yes, you can. First go to the search engine you want to use, for example, AltaVista at **http://www.altavista.digital.com**. Next select View | Options, then the Navigation tab and choose the search page from the list box. Click the Use Current button, then click OK.

Tip   You can use this same procedure to change the QuickLinks button. Just choose the QuickLinks from the page list, then make your changes and click OK.

Can I take an image I see on a Web page and use it as desktop wallpaper?

If you come upon a graphic image you'd like to turn into desktop wallpaper, simply right-click the image and select Set as Wallpaper from the shortcut menu.

Caution   You may find that your graphic doesn't look good as wallpaper, because it will have been converted from a GIF or JPEG to a BMP format.

How do I change the amount of disk space Explorer uses for the cache?

First, select View | Options. Click the Advanced tab, shown in Figure 5-5. In the Temporary Internet Files section, click the Settings button. This will open the Settings window showing you the amount of disk space designated for the cache. The size of the cache is shown in relationship to the percentage of free space on your drive. You can increase or decrease this percentage by clicking the slider and moving it left or right while holding down the mouse button. When you've changed the settings to reduce the size of the cache, make sure you click OK to save the changes.

Is there some way to display a Web page more quickly without turning off the graphics entirely?

You can have Internet Explorer load a Web page quicker if you press a key, such as the SPACEBAR. This makes Internet Explorer jump to Fast Text mode, display the text immediately, and work on loading the graphics later.

Do I have to wait for a file to download before continuing to surf other pages?

No, you can continue to surf while a page is downloading. That's the beauty of the later versions of Internet Explorer (versions 3.01 or

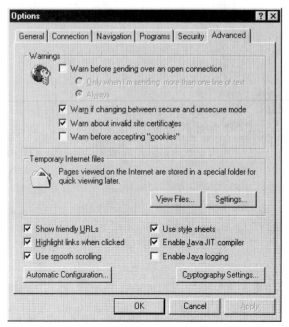

Figure 5-5.   Changing the disk cache settings

above) and the capabilities of the TCP/IP protocol. Together, they allow you to do more than one thing at a time, such as download a file and surf a Web page. Simply open another window or minimize the download dialog window to continue your surfing.

❓ Can I specify another drive to store cache files?

You can as long as the drive is always available when using Explorer. To change the default cache drive, click View | Options | Advanced, then click the Settings button. Next click the Move Folder button, and select a new drive (and/or directory) for your cache.

❓ When I try to load a Web page, Explorer just freezes. What could be the problem?

Your disk cache may be full. You should empty the cache by selecting View | Options | Advanced, clicking the Settings button, and emptying the folder. When the dialog box pops up, make sure you choose the Yes button. Then try exiting and restarting Explorer.

? **How do I keep my <u>Favorites on my desktop in synch with my laptop</u>? I want to make sure when I travel I have my Favorites handy.**

You can use the Briefcase option to keep your Favorites in synch. First make sure your two machines are connected through the network, or insert a floppy disk into your desktop computer to save your files to disk so they can quickly be transferred to your laptop. From Internet Explorer, choose Favorites | Organize Favorites on your desktop computer. Right-click the background of the file list and choose New | Briefcase. Drag the briefcase icon to the Favorites folder of your laptop.

When you select Add to Favorites and click the Create In option, make sure you select the briefcase and click OK. Now as you add Favorites, you will synchronize them with your desktop.

? **Can Explorer help me <u>find a site</u> even if I don't know the URL?**

Sure. For example, if you want to find the site for WalMart but you have no idea what the URL might be, type **Walmart** in the Location field and Explorer will search the Yahoo database for a listing of URLs that refer to Walmart.

? **Can I increase the <u>font size</u> used in Web pages?**

To increase the font size, first try the ALT-V-N keystroke combination, then press R for largest, L for larger, S for smaller, or A for the smallest font.

? **What are all these files in this <u>History folder</u>?**

Internet Explorer saves files and graphics of the Web sites you've visited in the c:\windows\history folder. Specify the number of days you want kept in the History folder by selecting View | Options | Navigation (see Figure 5-6). For the number of days you choose, a history of the sites you have visited will be kept in the History folder.

? **Can I use the <u>History folder</u> to return to sites I've visited previously?**

Yes. Select Go | Open History Folder and find the site you want to view again, then double-click the title to open it up.

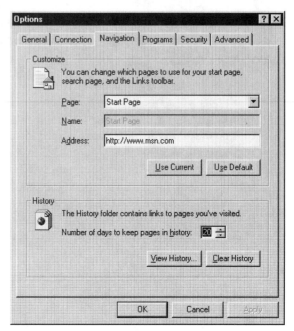

Figure 5-6.   Setting the expiration date of history files

    Tip   *If you want to make the chore of finding a particular site in your History folder easier, list the folder either alphabetically, by groups, or by the date you visited the site. Click a column header, such as Title, Internet Address, or Last Visited and Explorer will automatically sort the sites by whatever column you click.*

? How do I clear out the <u>History listing</u>?

Choose View | Options and then click the Navigation tab. You can empty the History list by clicking the Clear History button. Clicking this button will also remove all items from the drop-down list in your address bar.

? How do I set the <u>home page</u> for Internet Explorer to something other than the default?

First, go to the site or page you want to use as your home page. Next, select View | Options | Navigation (see Figure 5-7). Start Page should be displayed in the drop-down menu—if it isn't, select it from the

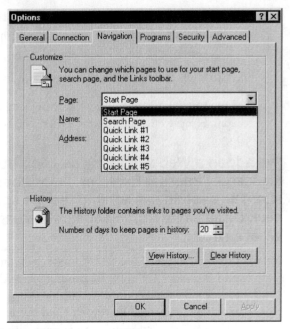

Figure 5-7.   Setting the home page URL

drop-down list. Click Use Current, and the page you're viewing will become your start page.

Is there a place I can go to learn how to use Internet Explorer?

Amazingly, you can go directly to Microsoft's Web site and have the site take you step-by-step through the features of Internet Explorer. Check out **http://www.microsoft.com/ie/**. Click Learn About Internet Explorer on the drop-down menu, and then click the Go button. You will be taken on a guided tour of all the features of Internet Explorer.

Can I add a button to my toolbar to launch my HTML editor?

Definitely. Just follow these steps:

1. Select View | Options, then the Program tab.

2. Click the File Types option.

3. Select Internet Document (HTML) from the list Verified, then click the Edit button to view the Properties.

4. Next click the New button under the list of actions.

5. Give your Editor button a name, such as "Edit" or "Editor," then add the path that points to the location of your HTML editor program.

6. Click OK to save the changes and exit Internet Explorer.

The next time you launch Explorer, an Edit button will appear on your toolbar. Simply click this button when you want to edit a page.

? I've added a Web site to my desktop but I get the following message, "Internet Explorer cannot open the Internet site. The system cannot find the file specified." When I click OK, a white frame appears instead of the Web site. What's wrong?

It's likely that you have added the Web site to your desktop but forgot to add the "http://" at the beginning of the URL. To fix this problem, right-click on the desktop and choose Properties from the shortcut menu. Next click the Desktop tab and in the Active Desktop objects list, click the Web site you added. Next click Edit, then type **http://** at the beginning of the URL.

? I'm trying to access a site that includes a tilde (~) in the URL, but Internet Explorer hangs and I have to restart my computer. What's wrong?

Most likely you're using Internet Explorer version 3.0 and you will probably encounter problems any time you try to view a Web page with a tilde in the URL. Internet Explorer 3.0 turns the tilde into the gibberish %7E, which in turn causes the software to hang. The only way to cure this problem is to upgrade to version 3.01 or above.

? Can I modify or change that Internet Explorer logo, possibly using another graphic instead?

If you want to change the logo in the upper-right corner of your Internet Explorer browser, you will have to do some Registry editing. But first, exit out of Explorer and create a BMP image that measures 32 by 32 pixels wide.

Next, run the Registry Editor by selecting Start | Run and typing **Regedit**. Click the HKEY_CURRENT_USER. Expand the listing down to Software | Microsoft | Internet Explorer | Toolbar. Find the entry called BrandBitmap and double-click it. This will open the options for BrandBitmap. Supply the full pathname of the BMP file you created, then close the Registry Editor to save your changes.

? I'd like to view a page written in <u>Japanese</u>. What do I need to do so Explorer can display the proper character set?

You'll first need to download the proper character sets for the languages you'd like to view. You can find them on Microsoft's Web site at **http://www.microsoft.com/ie/default.asp**. After you download and properly install the character sets according to the installation instructions provided, when you want to use another character set, click the flag icon in the lower right-hand corner of the Explorer browsing window and the characters will display properly.

? Is there a way to increase <u>Java performance</u>?

If you use the JIT Compiler, you'll be able to increase the performance of any Java applets. To turn on the JIT Compiler select View | Options | Advanced and select Enable JIT Compiler. Click OK to save, and then try loading a Java-enhanced page to see if there is any increase in speed.

? Is there a quick way to <u>jump from frame to frame</u> on a framed Web site?

You can use the CTRL-TAB key combination to jump forward from frame to frame, or you can hold down CTRL-SHIFT-TAB to move you backward through the frames.

? Are there any <u>keystroke shortcuts available in Kiosk mode</u>?

The same keystroke shortcuts that work in Explorer running under normal mode work under Kiosk. Here are a few more shortcuts you'll find handy, however, if you elect to use Kiosk mode:

Key Combination	Function
ALT-F4	Close
ALT-LEFT ARROW	Back
ALT-RIGHT ARROW	Forward

Key Combination	Function
CTRL-A	Select all (editing)
CTRL-B	Organize favorites
CTRL-C	Copy (editing)
CTRL-F	Find (on current page)
CTRL-H	View History folder
CTRL-L	Open Location dialog box
CTRL-N	New window (opens in non-Kiosk mode)
CTRL-O	Open Location dialog box (same as CTRL-L)
CTRL-P	Print
CTRL-R	Refresh
CTRL-S	Save
CTRL-V	Paste (editing)
CTRL-W	Close (same as ALT-F4)
CTRL-X	Cut (editing)
ESC	Stop
F5	Refresh

? Are there any keystroke shortcuts I can use to go backwards and forwards?

You can hit the BACKSPACE key to go backwards or SHIFT-BACKSPACE to go forward.

? Is there a quick way to open a link in a new window, leaving the previous page opened as well?

If you hold down the SHIFT key when you click the link for a site, Explorer will automatically open that link in a new window.

? Is there a quick way to add a link to my Favorites menu?

The quickest way is to select Favorites | Organize Favorites while viewing the site you want to add to your list of Favorites. This will add that link to the Favorites menu as shown in Figure 5-8.

? Is there a quick way to identify which links are active on a Web page?

You can use the TAB key to highlight active links. Pressing the TAB key also works on imagemaps. If you want to open a link you've tabbed to,

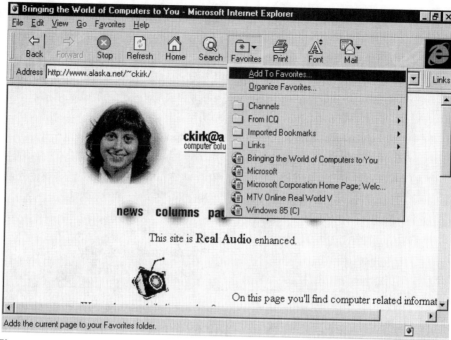

Figure 5-8.   Adding a favorite link to your Favorites menu

simply press the ENTER key. If the link is a button, press the SPACEBAR.
To view the shortcut menu options for the link try pressing SHIFT-F10.

If the Web page you're viewing is framed, you can jump between
frames by using CTRL-TAB to go forward or CTRL-SHIFT-TAB to go
backwards within the framed site.

❓ How do I add a new Web page to my list of Favorites?

The quickest way to add to your Favorites list is to right-click on a
blank area of the Web page you want to add. Next select Add to
Favorites from the shortcuts menu.

❓ Is there a way to view a list of Web pages I've visited?

You can view the last few hundred Web pages you've visited by
viewing the history file stored in the c:\windows\history folder. The
number of pages stored depends on the number of days worth of
browsing history set in the View | Options | Navigation tab.

Keyboard Shortcuts

If you have used Netscape Navigator, you'll notice that all of your favorite keyboard shortcuts also work in Internet Explorer 3.0. Here are a few of those shortcuts:

ALT-LEFT ARROW	Goes back to the previous page
ALT-RIGHT ARROW	Goes forward to the next page
CTRL-B	Opens the Organize Favorites window
CTRL-D	Adds to the Favorites listing
CTRL-H	Opens the History folder
CTRL-N	Opens a new browser window
CTRL-R	Reloads the current page
CTRL-W	Closes the active Internet Explorer window

? Can I mail a Web page to someone else?

Of course. If you select File | Send, then supply an e-mail address, the current page will be sent.

? Can I use Explorer to view my Microsoft Office documents?

You can drag and drop any Office document into an open Internet Explorer window to view the document without having to launch Office to view it. If the Office software has been installed on your system, all the editing options such as Zoom, Font and Font sizes, along with the Edit menu features, will work within Explorer.

? Can I open more than one Web page window at a time?

If you want to open another window so you can browse multiple windows, select File | New Window or right-click on a URL and choose Open in New Window from the shortcut menu.

? How can I add Netscape bookmarks to Internet Explorer Favorites?

There's a freeware program that lets you convert all your Netscape bookmarks to Internet Explorer Favorites in one simple step. You can download the program directly from **http://www.microsoft.com/kb/softlib/mslfiles/winbm2fv.exe**.

After you've downloaded and extracted the program, double-click the executable and locate your Netscape bookmark file by clicking the Browse button. Then click the Convert Bookmarks button. A dialog box will display alerting you that your bookmark files have been converted.

Note   *It might be a good idea to save a copy of your Bookmarks file first before you convert to Favorites.*

How do I print just a frame?

You can choose which frame to print. To print all the frames on a page select File | Print, then click the "Print documents in all frames" checkbox. If you want to print a single frame, click your mouse anywhere in the frame you want to print, then select File | Print, then select "Print document in selected frame," then click OK.

Is there a way to print a Web page from a link without going directly to that page?

Yes. Right-click on the link you want to print, then choose Print Target from the shortcut pop-up menu. By selecting this option, Explorer will print the page without you having to go to the page first.

How do I print a Web page without printing the URL or date?

Choose File | Page Setup. In the Header and Footer sections, click to deselect those items you don't want printed, such as the Date Printed or Document Location (URL), then click OK to save the changes. Finally, select File | Print to print the page.

How can I change the URLs that are on the QuickLinks buttons?

You can set your QuickLinks buttons to point to any five Web sites you like. Select View | Options, then the Navigation tab and select the drop-down list to set each QuickLink button. You can also change the Name field of each QuickLink button to anything you choose. You can even specify a QuickLink button to launch any program or executable file from your hard disk or network. All you have to do is type the full path in the Address field for the QuickLink button to point to a program file (.exe) or shortcut.

? How do I quit Explorer from Kiosk mode? There are no menus!

To quit Internet Explorer when it is running in Kiosk mode, use the ALT-F4 key combination. If you want the menus to reappear, you must launch Explorer normally.

? Do I need to download the RealAudio player in order to hear RealAudio files?

Since version 2.0, Internet Explorer has supported RealAudio file formats. That means you don't need to download the RealAudio Player. RealAudio files should automatically play when you click either RealAudio files or streaming links.

Note   *If you want to use the latest version of RealAudio, you will still need to download it or check the Microsoft Internet Explorer site for updates. You can find the Microsoft Internet Explorer site at* **http://www.microsoft.com/ie.**

? How do I reload a page?

You can click the Refresh button on the Explorer toolbar or hit the F5 button. Either will reload the page from the server instead of from your cached Temporary Internet Files folder.

? How do I resize the toolbars?

First, drag the bottom edge of the toolbar you want to resize until it is the size you want. Then release the mouse button and the toolbar will be resized.

? When I scroll down a Web page the screen refreshes really slowly. What's the problem?

Most likely your system has a relatively slow-drawing graphics card. When you use Smooth Scrolling, this will cause the screen to refresh at an agonizingly slow rate. The solution? Turn off Smooth Scrolling in the View | Options | Advanced option.

? How do I specify a different <u>search page</u> for the Search icon on the button bar?

Go to the search site you want to use and select View | Options | Navigation. Under the Page box, select Search Page and click the Use Current button. Clicking the Search icon will now take you directly to your new search page.

? How can I keep my <u>search results listed in an active window</u> while I view the results?

Clicking New Window on the File menu is a great way to keep your search results list active in one window while you navigate in another. Note that when you click the New Window command, the new window will point to the same Web page as the old window. The new window also remembers where you've been, so the Back and Forward buttons will work just as they did in the old window.

? How do I know what kind of <u>security</u> a Web page offers?

You can right-click anywhere on the background of a page, then select Properties | Security. This will display a window identifying exactly what level of security the site offers.

 Tip Want to search the Web quickly? Just type **GO**, followed by your search term in the URL address field. Press ENTER, and Explorer will use your default search site to locate pages that contain exactly what you're looking for. If you're looking for information on a person, you can omit the GO and just type the full name. The results will display in a Web page.

? I've heard there are problems with the <u>security of Internet Explorer</u> but I'm confused about what version I should use to prevent security intrusions to my computer. Which is it?

You should be using version 3.02. If you are running Internet Explorer 3.0, 3.01, or any other version of Internet Explorer 3.x for Windows 95 or NT 4.0, Microsoft recommends that you download Internet Explorer 3.02 from their site located at **http://www.microsoft.com/ie/ security/update.htm**. If you're using America Online, you don't have to worry about downloading this version since AOL will automatically update your software when you log on.

? How do I create a shortcut and place it on my desktop to a Web page?

Simply drag the URL to your desktop and a shortcut will be created. Double-clicking on the shortcut opens the page. You can also drag and drop any link to Microsoft Office to include that link in your Office documents. They become clickable links in your document.

? Is there a shortcut for going to a particular site?

Explorer has a feature called Completions that lets you type the beginning of an address and have Explorer try to figure out the rest. To use the Completions options, type the beginning of an address, and Explorer will display the rest of the URL in the Location field. You can then use your right mouse button to highlight the address and select the Completions option to click the actual address you want to go to. Explorer will fill in the rest, such as the http:// and the .com, if necessary. If you already know the site's URL, you can type just the site's domain, such as alaska.net, again, entirely leaving out the http:// and the www.

? How can I speed up Internet Explorer?

There are several things you can do. You can elect not to have pictures, sounds, videos, or other multimedia files displayed in your Web pages. You do this by selecting View | Options, the General tab, and then clicking on one or more of the following checkboxes in the Multimedia area to clear them:

⇨ Show Pictures

⇨ Play Sounds

⇨ Play Videos

Next, click on the Security tab and clear the following checkboxes:

⇨ Allow downloading of active content

⇨ Enable ActiveX controls and plug-ins

⇨ Run ActiveX scripts

⇨ Enable Java programs

Finally, click OK to save your changes. These options will not be loaded and response time should increase.

Can I change my mind and <u>stop a page from loading</u>?

You can use the ESC key to stop any Web page from loading. Use ESC to cancel any dialog box or close out any window. You can also use the DOWN ARROW key to scroll down through a page (which will interrupt the graphics on the page from loading).

I just noticed a folder called "Temporary Internet Files." It's full of graphics and files. Can I delete these files? I need to reclaim some disk space.

Internet Explorer automatically caches the graphics and Web pages you have visited in a temporary folder so the next time you view a page, it will load quicker. Unfortunately, this folder can fill up and take up a great deal of space on your hard drive. To empty this folder, open the C:\Windows\Temporary Internet Files folder, then press CTRL-A. Once all the files are selected, simply hit the DEL key on your keyboard, and the files will be placed in the Recycle Bin.

Remember   *Make sure you empty the Recycle Bin to make sure you reclaim all the space occupied by the cache files.*

Can I find <u>text within a Web page</u>?

Use the Find option in the Edit menu or the CTRL-F keystroke combination. Type in the keyword or phrase you are looking for in the text field available in the standard Search dialog box, as shown here:

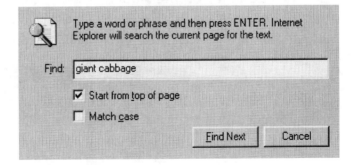

Click the Search button and if found, Explorer will highlight the word or phrase you are looking for.

Can I hide (or view) whatever toolbar I want?

You can hide or view the Address, Links, and Standard buttons on the toolbars collectively or individually. Select View | Options | General and toggle the appropriate checkboxes under the Toolbar section for the toolbar you want to show or hide. You can also rearrange these toolbars in any order you like by dragging them to your preferred location.

Is there a way to know what a URL offers before clicking the link?

You can right-click the URL and choose Properties from the shortcut menu. From the Properties window, you can view the Internet address, the date you visited the link, and the date it is scheduled to disappear from the History file.

Tip   *For a good place to send virtual gifts, check out* ***http://www.virtualgifts.com*** *or* ***http://www.virtualflowers.com***.

Can I use Explorer like the Windows Explorer?

You sure can. If you want to take a quick look at the contents of your hard drive, simply type **C:** in the URL address field of Explorer and you'll see the contents of your hard drive within an Internet Explorer page.

INTERNET EXPLORER 4.0

How do I turn off the Active Desktop?

To turn off the Active Desktop, right-click on the Windows desktop and uncheck the View as Web Page option, as shown here:

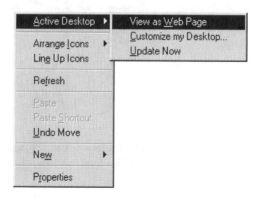

This will turn off the Active Desktop, freeing your computer for other things.

? Can I add URLs to my Start menu?

You sure can, and it's relatively easy to do. Simply drag any URL, Web page, or graphic to your Start button and they will automatically be added to the Start menu.

 Tip   *Did you know that after Explorer has been installed, you can rearrange the items on your Start menu by simply dragging them to a new location?*

? How do I customize my Subscriptions? Can I customize each one or do they all have to be the same?

You can customize any Subscription you want. Each can have its own unique set of Properties allowing you to customize exactly when, where, and what the Subscriptions do. To customize the settings of a Subscription, select Favorites | Subscriptions, then select Manage Subscriptions. Right-click to select the page you want to subscribe to, then select the Properties option from the pop-up menu.

Select either the Subscription, Receiving, or Schedule tab to make changes to the settings of the currently selected subscription. The Subscription tab lets you unsubscribe or change the login name and password for a particular site. The Schedule tab allows you to specify exactly when the page will be updated and what network option you use. The Receiving tab, shown in Figure 5-9, lets you specify whether you want to be notified by e-mail or gleaming icon when a site has changed, and lets you specify whether you want to download the site for viewing offline.

? How do I set a default e-mail application other than Outlook Express?

To change the default e-mail application, select View | Options, then click Programs. Click the drop-down arrow next to the Mail field. Click the DOWN ARROW to select another e-mail application to use as the default e-mail application.

? Can I drag and drop a document and have Explorer open it up in a Web page?

Sure. Drag the document onto an open Web page in Explorer and Explorer will display the contents of the file in a new Web page.

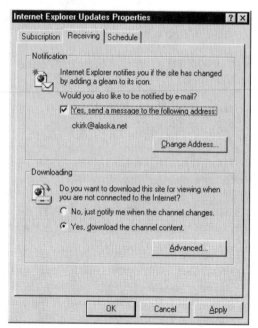

Figure 5-9.   The Receiving options for informing you of updated pages

? **Can I drag and drop a file from an FTP server to my computer when I'm connected to an FTP server using the Windows Explorer option?**

While you can use the Start | Programs | Windows Explorer option to download files, unfortunately you can't just drag and drop files from one location to another. To fetch a file from an FTP server, you have to first click the link for the file, then Explorer will open the File Download Wizard. Select whether you want to save the file or open it, then supply the folder you want to save the file in and click OK to start the file transfer process.

? **How do I get rid of that annoying Explorer logo?**

Right-click on an empty spot of your Windows desktop, then select Properties from the pop-up menu. Click the Settings tab, then check the option "Disable all Web-related content in my desktop."

? **Can I find people on the Internet without having to start Explorer?**

Yes, you can. Internet Explorer installs a Find option within the Start menu. Simply choose Start | Find | People, then click to select the database you want to search. Enter the name or e-mail of the person you are trying to find, as shown here:

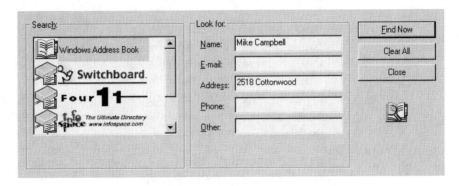

In a few minutes, Explorer will return with a list of results. You can then click to select and add them to your address book, or click the Properties button to find out more information about the person behind the e-mail address.

How do I clear the **History file** in Explorer 4.0?

Select View I Options, then click the General tab. Next click the Clear History button to clear the History file. All links listed in the History directory will be deleted and will no longer show when you click the History button on the toolbar.

How do I change the **home page**?

First, locate the page you want to make as your home page. Then, select View I Options and click the General tab. Click the Use Current button to use the currently viewed Web page as your home page. If you would rather type the address, click in the Address field in the General tab window and type the complete URL.

Can I change settings so I don't get so many **open windows** every time I open up a folder on my hard drive?

First, click Start I Programs I Windows Explorer. Next, choose View I Options I Folder and check the "Browse folders by using a single window" option, then click OK. From this point on, when you open a folder, it will appear in the same window instead of opening up a separate window.

? Can I override the settings on a Web page, such as the background or the color of the text?

You can change the settings by selecting View | Options | Colors. You can also view a Web page, then use the color scheme from that Web page as a style sheet. Display the Web page with the settings you want to copy and save it. Next select View | Options | Accessibility and click all Formatting options, then click the option "Format documents using my style sheet." Finally, click the Browse button and locate the Web page you've just saved. The settings used on this Web page will be used for all pages you view.

? Is there some way I can get a quick overview of all my favorites, like in a Print Preview?

First select Favorites | Organize Favorites from the main Explorer menu, then select the folder of the favorites you want to preview. Next, right-click inside the folder window to select the folder and check the "Enable thumbnail view" in the General tab, as shown here:

General	
	Favorites
Type:	File Folder
Location:	C:\WINDOWS
Size:	303KB (311,188 bytes), 26,116,096 bytes used
Contains:	791 Files, 67 Folders
MS-DOS name:	FAVORI~1
Created:	Thursday, August 15, 1996 1:21:00 PM
Attributes:	□ Read-only □ Hidden
	□ Archive ☑ System
	☑ Enable thumbnail view

You should see miniature pictures of each page. If these pages aren't in your cache, Explorer will connect to the Internet to display them, which may cause somewhat of a delay.

? **How do I know a site is <u>secure</u> when I'm using Internet Explorer 4.0?**

If you are connected to a secure site you will see a little lock in the status bar at the bottom of the Web page. Double-click this icon and you'll see the exact type of security used.

? **What are <u>subscriptions</u> and how do I use them?**

Subscriptions allow one to download a Web page or an entire site in one fell swoop, at a particular scheduled time. With a subscription, you can instruct your computer to connect to the Internet automatically while you're asleep, or when the Internet isn't so busy, and download the information you need; you can then read that same information offline at your leisure.

You can subscribe to sites several ways. The easiest way is to right-click a page, then select Add to Favorites. Check the Subscribe checkbox and follow the Subscription Wizard guidelines. Once subscribed, Explorer will connect to the page and search to see if changes have been made to the page since the last download. If you leave the defaults set, this will be done between midnight and 5 A.M. If the page has changed, the icon on the System Tray will display a red asterisk or you will be notified by e-mail, depending upon the options you selected when you first subscribed to the site

? **What are <u>Tooltips</u> and what do they do?**

Windows Tooltips are special pop-ups that supply you with detailed information about a site or its graphics. You'll notice that Tooltips pop up when you move your pointer over the Back and Forward buttons, telling you the names of the sites each button would take you to. They also appear over any picture you move your cursor across in a Web page, showing you the alternate text name given to the graphic.

? **Is there anything I can do to make <u>Web pages load faster</u> in Explorer 4.0?**

One way is to turn off the multimedia options. Select View | Options, then click the Advanced tab. Locate the Multimedia section and uncheck the following options: "Show pictures," "Play animations," "Play videos," "Play sounds," and "Smart Image dithering." With these options off, only the text of a Web page will load. You can then individually load the graphics by right-clicking on the graphic and selecting Show Picture.

File Transferring

Answer Topics!

File Transferring @ a Glance

⇨   The Internet is one huge global network connecting all sorts of computers scattered all over the world. People want to not only communicate but also send and receive files. Whereas e-mail allows for limited file transfer capabilities, dedicated file servers offer many more features for unattended transmission of every type of computer file imaginable. The special file transfer server software that runs on computers set up as FTP servers controls the basic functions needed to transfer computer files to and from users. Some of these functions include the ability to move, delete, or rename files and/or directories and the option for controlling who has access to the server. Authorized users log on to the FTP server using what is called *client FTP software*. This client software lets the user issue special **FTP commands** that control which functions the server will perform, such as downloading files to the user's computer or uploading files from the user's computer to the FTP server. The first step in learning how to control FTP servers is to examine a few basic commands and what they do.

⇨   You can use a variety of client **FTP programs** to download files from virtually any file server you please. Programs such as CuteFTP or WS_FTP for Windows 95 computers let you do everything from uploading and downloading files to moving entire directories of files to different file servers. Many of these programs offer interfaces resembling the File Manager in Windows or offer you the ability to drag and drop files from your desktop directly to the FTP server you've connected to. All of these specialized client FTP programs offer a variety of settings that allow you to configure the software for use with public and private FTP servers. You can also use the programs behind and in front of corporate firewalls.

⇨   Many people prefer **using a Web browser** for transferring files rather than having to use a separate FTP application. Using the same program to download files as you do to browse the Web can make it easier, especially if all you want to do is download a few files here and there. Browsers such as Netscape's Communicator and Microsoft's Internet Explorer let you list and download files from an FTP server without having to launch a separate application, although they offer limited FTP functionality.

⇨   Most files stored on FTP servers are compressed so they take up less space and transfer faster (over slower phone lines) to your computer. Once you've downloaded a file you may need to **uncompress** it using one of several compression programs such as WinZip, Stuffit, or PKUnzip. These uncompression programs work with a variety of computers and can be found on many of the popular public-oriented file servers such as shareware.com (**http://www.shareware.com**).

⇨ Of course, not everything will work properly all the time. There will be times when you will get all sorts of **error messages and problems** when trying to transfer files. Some error messages relate directly to the program you're using, while others may in fact be coming from the file server you are connecting to. There may also be problems related to your Internet connection itself.

⇨ Files are not the only things you might download to your system. **Viruses** can also lurk on the Internet cleverly disguised as programs, macros, and even text files. Because a plethora of viruses pop up on the Internet on an almost daily basis, it is very important for any regular FTPer to know which protection programs to use.

⇨ Whether you are looking for the latest virus-checking program or the most recent release of SimCity, **finding FTP sites** can be relatively easy and painless. You can use a variety of Web-based search engines or fall back on older standards such as *Archie*, a combination client software and FTP index. Regardless of the method, you can transfer literally thousands of programs and files—as well as clip art, games, movies, and music—to your computer, whether you use a Mac or a Windows-based computer.

FTP COMMANDS

? Allright. I know how to download files in batch mode. Now how do I <u>batch upload</u> files?

To download files you use the mget command. So it shouldn't be any big surprise that to batch upload files you use the mput command. As with mget, you can specify groups of files, using wildcards to upload like files, such as those with the .gif three-letter extension or those starting with the letter *m*.

Note   *When you use batch file transfer commands such as mget and mput, the default is to have the FTP client stop on each file, then ask if you really want to transfer the file. Having to enter the letter* Y *with each file can be time consuming. To stop the FTP client from prompting you for each file, type* **prompt** *at the ftp> prompt. Like the hash and bell command,* **prompt** *is an on/off command. Issuing it once will turn off interactive prompting; issuing it again will turn it on.*

❔ Does it matter how I type these commands in? Are the commands <u>case-sensitive</u>?

Yes, indeed. It does matter what case you use to type commands, because most operating systems' FTP servers run on UNIX, which is very case-sensitive (unlike DOS). You should always use lowercase letters when issuing the most common FTP commands.

❔ What's the command to <u>change directories</u>?

Surprisingly, it's an easy one. Just type **cd** and the name of the directory, then hit the ENTER key. For example, if you wanted to change from the root directory to the files directory you would type **cd files**.

Note   *If you type just the command, your FTP server should respond by prompting you for any additional information the command needs.*

❔ What do I do when I want to <u>close an FTP session</u>?

You can close a session in several ways. You can use the disconnect command to disconnect from the current FTP server. Or you can use the Quit command to quit the FTP client application and close out the session. You can also double-click the left-hand corner of the FTP client application window.

❔ How do I know what the <u>current directory</u> is?

You can use either the ls or dir command, but if you just want to know what the current directory is without listing its contents, use the pwd command.

Remember   *You can use the cd command to change to another directory or the cd.. command to move back up to the parent directory.*

❔ I don't have a clue as to what this directory listing is showing me. What do the results of the <u>dir command</u> mean?

If you're accustomed to the DOS directory command, what you'll find is that UNIX FTP directory results actually display the information almost backwards. For example, the last column of information shown in Figure 6-1 is actually the filename, and the first column, where the DOS dir command would normally appear, indicates whether the information listed is a directory by specifying the letter *d*, or a file, along with read/write permissions.

Once I'm connected to the file server, how do I <u>display a listing</u> of files in the current directory?

There are two commands you can use: ls and dir. The DOS dir command provides other information about the files and directories, such as their size, date, and read/write permissions status. The ls command also provides other information about the files and directories such as size, date, and read/write permissions of the files and directories. The ls command, however, only lists file and subdirectory names.

Note If you want to stop the scrolling of the directory being displayed, try using the following UNIX command: ls–al | more. This command will only work with systems that have this option turned on. Not all UNIX systems do.

```
MS ftp                                                            _ 8 X
  Auto    ▼  ⬚ 🗋 🖺  🖾  📰📑  A
-rw-r--r--    1 ckirk     all         6841 Aug 10 00:36 .pine-debug4
-rw-r--r--    1 ckirk     all        12002 Jul 19 11:51 .pine-interrupted-mail
-rw-r--r--    1 ckirk     all        10355 Aug 11 12:57 .pinerc
-rwxr-xr-x    1 ckirk     all          213 Dec 21  1994 .plan
-rwxr--r--    1 ckirk     all          481 Jun 22  1994 .profile
-rw-------    1 ckirk     all         3142 Aug 11 12:58 .sh_history
-rw-rw-r--    1 ckirk     all            0 May 21 11:35 .vacation.dir
-rw-rw-r--    1 ckirk     all          129 May 21 11:36 .vacation.msg
-rw-rw-r--    1 ckirk     all         1024 May 21 11:36 .vacation.pag
-rw-rw-rw-    1 ckirk     all          619 Sep  4  1996 Office.html
-rw-------    1 ckirk     all          330 Aug  8 14:36 dead.letter
drwxrwxrwx    2 ckirk     all          512 Feb 13 13:40 icphone
-rw-rw-rw-    1 ckirk     all         3603 Sep  1  1996 index.html
drwx------    2 ckirk     all          512 Aug 11 12:56 mail
-rw-r--r--    1 ckirk     all            0 Apr 23 11:31 pinerca14846
-rw-r--r--    1 ckirk     all            0 Apr 23 11:34 pinerca15985
-rw-r--r--    1 ckirk     all            0 Apr 23 09:52 pinercb03351
-rw-r--r--    1 ckirk     all            0 Apr 23 11:33 pinercb14846
drwxrwxr-x    2 ckirk     all          512 Jul 29 12:01 radio
-rw-rw-rw-    1 ckirk     all         1089 Aug 31  1996 radio.gif
-rw-rw-r--    1 ckirk     all          677 Feb 16 21:27 weblink.txt
drwx-----x   20 ckirk     all         1024 Jul 24 11:22 www
226 Transfer complete.
2117 bytes received in 0.77 seconds (2.75 Kbytes/sec)
ftp>
```

Figure 6-1.   Information displayed when the dir command is invoked looks a little different in FTP.

How do I <u>download a file</u> to my Windows 95 computer using the Windows 95 FTP command?

Simple. Just use the get command. First log on to your server, change to the directory where the file you want to download is located, then issue this command:

get *filename*

The file will then be copied to the local working directory on your Windows 95 computer. You know the file has been transferred successfully if the file server responds by displaying the prompt "226 Transfer completed."

Remember   *Commands and filenames are case-sensitive. If you keep getting "File not found" error messages, check to make sure that the filename you are specifying is actually stored on the file server with the same name, and that you are typing it in correctly. The filename WinZip is different from the filename winzip.*

Can I <u>download multiple files</u> with a single command?

By using the mget command you can download multiple files. You can use wildcards, or you can specify each file individually. To download all files with the .htm extension, you would type the following at the ftp> prompt:

mget *.htm

Or, if you want to download three files—index.html, form.html, and banner.gif—you would type the following:

mget index.html form.html banner.gif

Note   *Generally, UNIX-based FTP servers and the Windows 95 FTP client program do not have graphic representations like a moving thermometer to display the number of bytes already transferred. But you can turn on the special "hash" command for your current FTP session. This will then display a number for every 1024 to 4096 bytes transferred depending upon the settings in your FTP client application. To invoke the command, simply type **hash** at the ftp> prompt. You can also have your computer beep every time an FTP command has successfully completed by typing **bell** at the ftp> prompt. Both "hash" and "bell" are on/off switches. You issue them once to turn them on, then issue the same command again to turn off the feature.*

? **Since I'm already in a DOS window, can I <u>exit to DOS</u> while still in FTP?**

You certainly can. You can exit to DOS while still in the FTP program by issuing the ! command. The ! command will maintain the connection to the FTP server you are currently connected to, and at the same time allow you to exit to DOS and issue any DOS commands you please. To return to the FTP client, simply type the word **exit** at the DOS prompt. If your connection has not timed out, you should be able to continue issuing FTP commands.

? **Is there an <u>FTP client</u> included with Windows 95?**

As a matter of fact, there is, although unlike many of the Windows 95 accessories, the Windows FTP client is not a graphically oriented application. Instead, it's strictly command-line driven, requiring you to know FTP commands to control the flow of files to and from your system.

To start the Windows FTP client, follow these steps:

1. Click the Start button on the task bar.
2. Select Run, then type **FTP** in the Run dialog box.
3. Click OK.

The command-line FTP client will open to an ftp> prompt in its own DOS window. From this point you type your FTP commands, hitting ENTER at the end of each command.

? **Is there a quick way to <u>list all the commands</u> I can use with the Windows FTP program?**

Yes; simply type the word **help** at the ftp> prompt. Windows FTP will respond by showing you a list of commands that can be used, as shown in Figure 6-2. If you want specific help for any of the individual commands, type **help** *command*. For example, if you wanted to know what the pwd is used for, you would type **help pwd**.

? **My <u>local working directory</u> seems to already have been set. Can I change it?**

The local working directory is the default directory on your Windows 95 computer where the files you download will be stored. To set the local working directory you use the lcd command. For example, to set

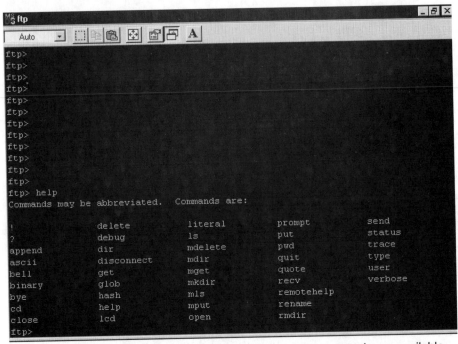

Figure 6-2. Windows FTP will quickly remind you what commands are available and what they do.

the default directory for all downloaded files to be stored in the c:\windows\download directory you would type the following at the ftp> prompt:

lcd c:\windows\download

Caution   *Make sure you use the full pathname when you specify where you want your downloaded files to be stored, and do not include a slash at the end of the pathname. Otherwise, you'll receive an error message and the default directory will not change.*

❓ How do I open a connection to an FTP server using the command-line FTP client with Windows 95?

Once you've launched the Windows FTP client, follow these steps at the command prompt:

1. Establish a connection to the Internet as you normally would, either through your dial-up network connection or by logging on to your company's network.

2. Start the FTP program by clicking the Start button, selecting Run, and typing **ftp** in the Run dialog box.

3. Type **open** at the ftp> prompt, then hit ENTER.

4. Type in the name of the FTP server at the (to)> prompt. For example, if the FTP server's name is ftp.alaska.net, you would type **ftp.alaska.net**.

5. Press ENTER.

 Note   *You can also include the server name after the open command, such as open [servername].*

If the server name you specified is a valid FTP server, you will be connected, then asked to enter your username. Enter your username or the word "anonymous" if the server only allows anonymous FTP connections. Make sure you hit ENTER after entering your username.

If the server requires a password, enter it at the password prompt. If the username and password were entered successfully, the server should respond by indicating you are now currently logged in to the file server.

FTP PROGRAMS

? When CuteFTP starts to load a directory listing, I get a General Protection Fault followed by the error message "Can't establish data socket error." What's the problem?

Most likely you are trying to use CuteFTP from behind a firewall. You need to configure CuteFTP to work behind your firewall by going to the Options dialog box, then clicking on the Firewall section. In the Firewall Type section, choose PASV Mode, then check the Enable Firewall checkbox.

? When I use WS_FTP I can connect to a server, but it won't return a complete file list. What's wrong?

Most likely you are using Trumpet Winsock version 2.1d. Make sure you upgrade to version 2.1e or above. You can find the latest version of Winsock at **http://www.winsock.com**.

? I've tried downloading files, but they always end up corrupted. Why?

You are probably using the wrong mode when transferring files. If you plan to transfer text files, make sure you set the file mode to ASCII (or text). All other files should be set to binary so that the information is retained properly when the file is transferred. You set those options by clicking the Radio button for the appropriate option below the list of files in the main WS_FTP screen.

? Why can't I transfer more than 2048K using CuteFTP and America Online?

You may have two problems, one being that CuteFTP is having problems utilizing the Winsock DLL provided with the America Online software. Try downloading the latest Winsock DLL from America Online by using the keyword WINSOCK and following the instructions found in the Winsock area. Another problem may be that the AOL network node is overloaded. Try using America Online again during a less busy time of day.

? How do I download from more than one site at a time?

First, go to the Session menu, then choose Spawn Session. This will bring up another session of CuteFTP, logged in to the same server. You can then choose to change sites, or you can continue on downloading multiple files from the same site.

? Can I drag and drop files into the remote listing box?

Only with the Professional version of WS_FTP. If you have the Professional version, click the Options button. Next, select the Pro tab in the Properties window, and check the "Enable drag and drop between windows" option.

? How do I edit, add, or delete folders within the FTP site main window?

First, move your pointer over the Folders List box located on the right-hand side of the main window. Next, right-click the mouse button, and the Folders Management menu should appear, allowing you to add, delete, or edit the current listed folders.

? **Using CuteFTP, I can connect to the server, but no <u>files or</u> <u>directories</u> appear. Is something configured wrong?**

First, try going to the Site Manager, then bring up the editing screen for the site you are connected to. Next, disable the Resolve Links option, making sure you save your changes. Then try reconnecting to the site.

? **I've tried using WF_FTP at work, but can't seem to connect to anything. Someone mentioned something about our corporate firewall. How do I configure WS_FTP to work behind a <u>firewall</u>?**

First, you will need to get the settings for your company's firewall configuration from your network administrator or help desk. You should find out the following information:

⇨ The host name or IP address of your firewall

⇨ The user ID for the firewall

 Note *This is not your user ID, but the ID for the firewall itself. Your company may or may not use this option.*

⇨ The firewall port number

⇨ The firewall type, such as Proxy, User with no logon, User with logon id, or Site Hostname

Once you've gathered that information, click the Connect button in WS_FTP's main screen, then click the Session Properties | Firewall tab and enter the information you've collected in the proper fields. Make sure you click the Apply, then OK buttons to save your settings.

? **I've connected to my file server, but the list of files for my server contains <u>garbled information</u>. What's wrong?**

Most likely you have the wrong setting options selected for the type of system you are connecting to. Try another setting by following these steps:

1. Select the Options button at the bottom of the screen.

2. Select a different Host Type, such as UNIX or WinQVT/Net.

3. Click OK, disconnect from the server, then reconnect.

? I connect to my file server fine using WS_FTP, but the <u>list box for the remote site</u> is blank. The last thing that displays in the status window is DoDirList returned 4. What's the problem?

You need to change the MTU settings in your network stack to 576. This requires adjusting your Windows Registry File. Check Chapter 2, "Connection Basics," for more information on changing the MTU settings.

? How can I select <u>multiple files</u> to download with WS_FTP?

Hold down the CTRL key while you select multiple files with your mouse. Once you've selected all the files you want to transfer, click the arrow to either upload or download the selected files.

? Why does my local FTP server ask me for my <u>password</u> every time I connect?

You just haven't clicked the Save PWD checkbox in the Session Properties | General tab.

Remember   *You must do this for each host you want to connect to. This option only applies for the host currently listed.*

? I can't seem to log on to several public sites; I keep getting a message that my <u>password is invalid</u>. What am I doing wrong?

You probably don't have the password field filled in correctly. It should include your full e-mail address, such as **ckirk@alaska.net**. If it's set to **mozilla@**, then you'll need to change it in the Session Properties | General Tab when you first click the Connect button for the session you plan to connect to.

? When I enter ftp://ftp.alaska.net in the <u>Site Manager address box</u>, I can't connect to the site. What am I doing wrong?

You don't need to enter the ftp:// protocol designator as part of the address when you want to connect to a remote site. CuteFTP already

supplies this, much like many browser programs supply the http://
protocol designator.

? How do I <u>sort the listing by date</u> instead of name?

Simply click on the Date heading once in the list of files. Click the
Name heading once to have it sort by name again.

? I've got several files with <u>special characters</u> in them, but I can't seem to get them to upload. Is there a problem with using nonstandard characters?

No, there's no problem, but you probably won't be able to select
them as you would standard filenames. To select files with special
characters or files that have been hidden by using Windows
Explorer's Hide command, you must specify the full pathname
along with the file by clicking the transfer arrow button when you
have no file selected. This will prompt you to enter the filename
you want to upload or download.

? The connection to my server keeps <u>timing out</u>. Can I change something in my connection settings to prevent this?

Check the Sessions Properties | Advanced Tab when you click the
Connect button for the host you want to connect to. Try changing the
Network Timeout option from the default of 65 seconds to something
higher.

? I downloaded WS_FTP but it <u>won't run</u> on my Windows 95 computer. Is something wrong with my system?

No. You most likely are using the 16-bit version of Trumpet Winsock
or some other 16-bit network stack. Either use the Microsoft TCP/IP
stack that comes with Windows 95 or download a 32-bit version from
a provider, such as Ipswitch, at **http://www.shareware.com**.

Note *You cannot run a 32-bit network application on a 16-bit network
stack on a 32-bit operating system. An example of such a configuration is if
you've upgraded from Windows 3.1 to Windows 95 but are still using your
old version of Trumpet Winsock.*

? **I've tried to get a directory listing from a server, but I keep getting a "write error" message. I connect to the server just fine, so what could be wrong?**

You probably don't have the TEMP environment variable set in your DOS system. To do this, open a DOS window, then type the following:

    MD C:\TEMP
    Set C:\TEMP

Another method is to include a line in your autoexec.bat file specifying the temporary directory you've created to store variables like remote directory listings.

? **What is WS_FTP?**

WS_FTP is one of the most widely used Windows-based FTP clients around. The FTP client program offers a graphical interface with many advanced features, such as multiple file transfers, directory and file renaming, and quick point-and-click access to files. It's much easier to use than the text-only Windows 95 FTP client.

Note   *You can get WS_FTP directly from WS_FTP's Web site at http://www.wsftp.com.*

USING A WEB BROWSER

? **Every time I try to connect to a file server using Netscape, I get an "Access Denied" message. Why can't I connect?**

Most likely you have not included your e-mail address in the Options | Mail and News Preferences settings. If you do not include an e-mail address, some anonymous FTP servers will not allow you to connect, because the password field commonly used is the e-mail address configured in your browser's settings.

? **Is there a way to avoid having my e-mail address used as an anonymous login password?**

In versions of Netscape Navigator 1.*x*, Navigator uses your e-mail address as an anonymous login password. However, starting with version 2.*x*, the default configuration is to send the address **mozilla@domainname**. Starting with version 3.*x*, you can elect to use either *mozilla@* or your actual e-mail address by selecting the Network Preferences | Protocols tab, then simply click the Send E-mail Address as Anonymous FTP Password checkbox.

? I'm trying to download with Navigator. Why am I ending up with so many <u>corrupted files</u>?

If you are getting corrupted or unusable files, you may not have the file extension listed in the Helper Applications section of Netscape Preferences. Navigator looks in the MIME Type table for the extension of the file you are trying to download. If it doesn't find the file extension, then Navigator will download your file in ASCII mode, whereby carriage returns and linefeeds in the file will be converted to whatever's natural for your computer system. This will cause all sorts of havoc with binary files.

To correct this problem, select the "application/octet-stream" entry in the MIME Types list, then add the three-letter file extension you are trying to download in the Extensions field. Save the settings and try downloading the file again. If you still get a corrupted file, contact the administrator of the file server and ask if their system is configured for understanding that type of file system. It could be a problem with the configuration of the File Transfer Protocol server itself.

? When I click on a link to download a file it <u>displays the contents of the file</u> instead of downloading it. Why?

You have that particular file type configured as a MIME type, which Netscape can display. For example, Netscape can display HTML, GIF, TEXT, and JPG files. If you want to download rather than see the actual contents of these files, use your right mouse button and select from the Save Link As.drop-down menu.

? What does <u>"Error–57"</u> mean?

It simply means the FTP server is too busy to handle your request at the moment. Try connecting again at a later time during the day when the server is less likely to be busy, such as very early in the morning, during the lunch hour, or very late at night.

❓ I can't download any <u>files with spaces</u> in their filenames using Explorer 3.0. What gives?

Unfortunately, Internet Explorer cannot parse file lists properly, meaning that it cannot display file lists with long filenames or spaces included in the name. Your only option at this time is to use another FTP program to download such files.

❓ What <u>FTP capabilities</u> does my Web browser offer me?

Both Netscape and Internet Explorer let you upload and download files; however, they do not offer the full FTP capabilities that dedicated FTP programs allow. With Navigator and Explorer, version 2.0 or above, you can download a file by clicking the link and holding down the mouse button on the file (if you are using a Mac), or right-clicking (if you have a PC). You will see a dialog box asking where you want to store the file. Here is a list of things you can do:

⇨ Upload files by simply dragging and dropping the file from your desktop or directory into the open FTP window.

⇨ Upload files by specifying which file to upload using the File | Upload File menu option.

⇨ Specify your login name and password, plus the directory and/or file, in the URL location field.

⇨ Change directories by following directory child and parent links.

❓ It seems that certain <u>FTP commands are not available</u> when I'm using my Web browser. What's going on?

Unlike full FTP clients such as Fetch and WS_FTP, there are many FTP commands Web browsers cannot perform. The main FTP features integrated into Web browsers are primarily for downloading files, not for moving files, working with groups of files, or deleting files. Here is a list of things you cannot do with most common Web browsers:

⇨ If the file transfer is interrupted, you cannot resume the aborted download where it left off before being interrupted unless you're using the latest version of Netscape Communicator.

⇨ You cannot issue remote commands, such as those for moving directories or batch-transferring files.

⇨ You cannot remove files from the server.

⇨ You cannot rename or otherwise modify files on the server.

? **I keep getting the error message "Internet Explorer cannot open the Internet site." What's wrong? I've double-checked the link for the FTP server.**

The settings for your proxy server probably are not configured correctly. To double-check those settings, follow these steps:

1. Click View | Options.

2. Click the Connection tab.

3. Click Settings, then make sure the correct proxy server is entered in the FTP field in the Server area. If the FTP proxy server is the same as the HTTP server sites, click the "Use the same proxy server for all protocols" check box.

Note   If you only have the HTTP proxy field entry supplied, you will only be able to connect to HTTP servers. You must either have an FTP server entered or select to use the same server for all protocols.

? **Can I automatically enter my login name and password when specifying the URL of the FTP server?**

Yes. Enter the following URL in the location field of your browser:

ftp://*username:password/serversite.com/path/file*

In this way you can specify not only the FTP server but also the user login name, password, pathname, and file you want to download:

⇨ *username* is your FTP login username

⇨ *password* is your login password

⇨ *serversite.com* is the name of the FTP server you want to connect to

⇨ *path* is the directory path you want to go directly to

⇨ *file* is the file you want to download or upload

? **When I connect to an FTP server using Internet Explorer on my Mac, no files are displayed. This doesn't happen when I'm using Explorer 3.0 on my PC. What's going on?**

Most likely you are connecting to a file server that is configured to send directory listings in an MS-DOS format. Check Microsoft's Web site for an upgrade to the Mac version of Explorer, or continue using Explorer 3.0 on your PC to retrieve your files.

? Using Microsoft's Internet Explorer on my Mac, I get no prompt for a location in which to save files. How do I fix this?

The default is to save files in the location specified in the Internet Config settings. If you want Explorer to prompt you for a location, you must first hold down the OPTION key while you hold down the mouse button on the link for the file you want to transfer. You will then be prompted for a location in which to save the file.

? The FTP server I want to connect to has a nonstandard FTP port number. How do I connect to this server?

You can enter the port number in the URL. For example, if the port number is 40, the URL should look something like this:

ftp://ftp.*mysite*.com:40

? I can't seem to open a connection to an FTP server located outside my firewall using Netscape Navigator. What's up?

You may need to configure your firewall to allow outgoing connections on high-numbered ports. Netscape uses passive FTP protocol for connecting to file servers, and this means it handles data transfers differently than standard FTP clients do.

? When I log on to an FTP site using Internet Explorer, it says "password was not allowed." Do I really need a password?

Internet Explorer version 3.0 for Windows does not support the ability to prompt the user for a password. This means when you connect to an FTP server requiring a password, the server denies the connection since no response would be given. If you have to connect to an FTP site using a password, include the password in the URL instead. For example, if your password were "snoogie," you would enter it like this:

ftp://*username*:snoogie@alaska.net

? I've been trying to upload a file by connecting to the FTP server through a <u>proxy server</u>. However, the Upload File menu option is not available. Why not?

You need to put a slash at the end of your FTP's URL, which tells Navigator that this is a proxied FTP page and that the listing is a directory listing. Because some proxy servers will not return a / at the end of an FTP URL, you may have to include the last slash manually.

? I'm trying to upload a file to a <u>secured server</u>, but it keeps crashing. How can I prevent this?

Navigator 3.*x* running under Windows 3.*x* has problems connecting to secured file servers, especially when trying to upload large files. When transferring large files, the Secured Socket Layer buffer ends up becoming larger than 64K, making Windows 3.*x* unstable. This causes the system to crash. Netscape suggests you upgrade to Netscape Communicator to fix this problem since there are no fixes to this problem for version 3.*x* of Navigator.

? With Netscape and my <u>SLIP connection</u>, the transfer stops after a certain number of bytes are transferred. Why?

You should first try decreasing the MTU value in your SLIP software from 1500 to 1006. You should also check your SLIP settings to make sure they match your service provider's settings.

 Remember   *Check Chapter 2, "Connection Basics," for more information on adjusting the MTU value.*

? Which Web browsers can <u>transfer files</u>?

Virtually every new version of the most popular Web browsers supports downloading of files. That includes Netscape Navigator versions 2.0 and 3.0, Netscape Navigator Gold, Netscape Communicator, and Internet Explorer versions 3.0 and 4.0. However, not all FTP commands are supported through Web browsers. If you need to do more extensive file transfer options, such as creating directories or moving groups of files, you'll need to use a true FTP client.

? **Why is the <u>Upload File</u> option ghosted in Netscape's File menu?**

A ghosted File option means you are either not connected to a file server or you are trying to connect to an FTP site outside a firewall using a proxy server. Either connect to a file server or, if trying to access the site outside your firewall, add a slash at the end of your FTP URL. For example, if you are connecting to Netscape's site, outside of your firewall, type **ftp://ftp.netscape.com/**. The added slash tells the proxy server you are requesting an FTP service, not an HTTP service.

UNCOMPRESSING FILES

? **What do the various <u>file types</u> stand for and what programs do I need in order to use them?**

There are really only two types of files—*ASCII*, or text-based, and *binary*. Binary files are executable programs that retain the settings for the type of computer they should operate on. However, there are many different file extensions that indicate exactly what type of file you are downloading. Because virtually every computer can be used on the Internet, there are a wide variety of file extensions for different computers. Table 6-1 provides a quick rundown of the most common file types.

Table 6-1.   Common File Extensions

File Extension	Storage Type	Type of File
.arc	Bin	Archive, not widely used anymore.
.arj	Bin	Archived file used mainly for MS-DOS-based computers.
.gif	Bin	Graphics Interchange Format, the main graphic file format used on the Internet. GIFs can have multilayers that display at predetermined intervals. These multilayered GIF files are called *animated GIFs*. GIFs can be downloaded to virtually any Internet-connected computer. GIF files can only display up to 256 colors.

Table 6-1.   Common File Extensions (*continued*)

File Extension	Storage Type	Type of File
.gz	Bin	GNU Zip is a combination of .tar files normally used on UNIX-based systems.
.hqx	ASCII	The Macintosh equivalent of uuencode; these are basically text files that, once uuencoded, can be translated back into Macintosh-specific files. Because many UNIX file transfer servers cannot store Macintosh files in their native format, .hqx provides a convenient way to translate Macintosh files into text files that can then be stored on different file servers.
.jpg	Bin	Joint Photographics Experts Graphic format, a file format used universally on the Internet; mainly used to display photographic images and those images that require more than 256 colors.
.lzh	Bin	
.shar	ASCII	Shell Archive files used on UNIX platforms.
.sit	Bin	Macintosh files that have been compressed with the program Stuffit.
.tar	Bin	Tape Archive files, a file format used on UNIX computers.
.uu or .uue	ASCII	Uuencoded/uudecoded files, text files that retain information specific to the operating system from which the files came.
.Z	Bin	UNIX compressed files most commmonly used with .tar or .tar.z files.
.zip	Bin	MS-DOS, Windows, or Windows 95 files that have been compressed with the compression programs PKZip or WinZip.
.exe	Bin	MS-DOS-, Windows-, or Windows 95-based self-extracting file type or computer program.
.com	Bin	MS-DOS, Windows, or Windows 95 applications.
.pdf	Bin	Adobe Portable Document Format. Can be used on a variety of computers including Mac and PC.

Table 6-1.   Common File Extensions (*continued*)
....

File Extension	Storage Type	Type of File
.ps	Bin	Postscript source file that can be used on a wide variety of systems provided the system offers some form of Postscript interpreter.
.mpg	Bin	MPEG compressed video mainly used on Windows and Windows 95 platforms.
.avi	Bin	Movie file format that can also contain audio. Used mainly on Windows and Windows 95 platforms.

? I'm getting general protection faults when I try to unstuff a file on my PC. What's wrong?

If you're getting a General Protection Fault when trying to unstuff a file, that usually means you have an invalid field in the file header within the archive itself. The file has probably been damaged in some way. Try re-downloading the file. If you still have no luck, the problem could lie in the way in which the archive was created.

? What are MacBinary and BinHex?

A MacBinary file is created when the 8-bit Resource and Data forks of a file are combined into a single 8-bit data file. This file format allows Mac files to be transferred to non-Mac file servers. The information about the file is retained so that when it's downloaded to a Mac system it can then be decoded into the original file.

A BinHex file is much like a MacBinary. The 8-bit Resource and Data forks of a file are attached end-to-end into a single 7-bit-wide data file turning it into basically a text file. This enables BinHexed files to be sent through 7-bit-wide gateways without damage.

? How do self-extracting files work?

Self-extracting files, or *archived files,* are electronic packages of data that contain multiple files and can be extracted by simply double-clicking them. Self-extracting files end in .sea for the Mac and .exe for the PC. Self-extracting files can also be made for the PC using the .sea extension, but require Stuffit Expander for Windows in order to open them.

? **<u>Stuffit Expander</u> won't expand files on my Mac. What's the problem?**

You could have several problems. First, check to see if you are having conflicts with INITs or Extensions that are loaded into memory every time you boot your Mac. Try turning off as many INITs as you can with the Extension Manager or removing the INITs from your System Folder | Extensions folder. Also check to make sure the file has not been encrypted or optimized in some way. Encrypted and optimized files cannot be opened with Stuffit Expander.

? **Can I <u>uncompress an .exe file</u> on my Mac?**

.exe files are usually self-extracting, PC-based PKZip archived files that are intended for use on a PC. However, you can use programs such as Stuffit Expander with DropStuff installed to open up .exe files on your Mac. If you use SoftWindows, you might consider purchasing Stuffit Expander and downloading the shareware DropStuff program from Aladdin Systems, maker of both programs. Their Web site can be found at **http://www.aladdinsys.com**.

? **What other programs are available for <u>uncompressing files</u>?**

You can use WinZip or PKUnzip on Windows-based systems or Stuffit on the Macintosh platform. In Windows, most compressed files are either stored as self-extracting files, which do not require special uncompression programs, or are stored in .zip file format, requiring PKUnzip or WinZip. On the Mac, compressed files are stored as .sea for self-extracting files or .sit for files requiring Stuffit for extraction.

ERROR MESSAGES AND PROBLEMS

? **I'm not getting a full <u>28.8Kbps transfer rate</u>. I'm getting much less. What's wrong?**

It could be a variety of things. First of all, never expect to get the full speed of your modem when transferring files, since your modem must transfer not just raw data but also acknowledgments that the information is being sent and received. This overhead will take away from the total amount you can transfer at any one time.

If you are getting very low transfer rates, it could be for one of the following reasons:

⇨ Noise on your phone line

⇨ The wrong modem INIT string

⇨ The wrong dial-up software settings

⇨ A server with a slow link or a busy server with lots of users transferring files at the same time

? Why do I get an "Access Denied" message when I try to connect to my file server?

You are either trying to log in to an FTP server as Anonymous, and that server doesn't allow for anonymous logins, or the name or password you supplied is incorrect. It could also mean you have specified a particular directory to connect to, but you don't have the proper authorization to read or upload to that directory. Or, it could mean that too many users are currently connected to the file server.

? I've uploaded my Web page to my own personal directory on my service provider's computer, but all I see is an index of my files—I still can't see my Web page! What should I do?

In order to see your Web page automatically you may have to name the first page of your Web site either index.html, index.htm, default.htm, or default.html. Most Web servers use a default name for the first Web page in your directory that you want people to see. So if a user simply types the URL of your directory, he or she will get that first Web page. Usually those default names are either "index" or "default" with some variation of either .htm or .html. Check with your service provider to find out which you should use for your server.

? When I first start transferring files, everything goes fine, but soon my file transfer program slows to a crawl. Finally, the connection to my service provider drops altogether. What's wrong?

Your dial-up software is either configured improperly or has the wrong settings for the type of server being used. It may also contain the wrong IP addresses for the server in the configuration or the wrong network settings. Consult your service provider for the correct configuration for the version of the software you are using.

? After downloading a program, then trying to run it, the program <u>freezes my PC</u>. What's wrong?

Most likely you forgot to use binary mode when you downloaded the file, and this has corrupted the file. Or, it could be that Helper Applications in your Web browser is not configured for the type of file you have downloaded. Go back and make sure you download in binary mode first, then check the three-letter file extension and compare it to the list of MIME types in your Helper Applications preferences.

? I've tried connecting to a file server using the file server name, but the screen says <u>"host unknown."</u> What am I doing wrong?

You either have the name of the FTP server wrong or the server has moved. If the server name is something like ftp.alaska.net and you are issuing the command **ftp://ftp.alaska.net**, try dropping the second FTP. For example, try this instead: **ftp://alaska.net**. Or do the reverse; add FTP to the name of the server. Or try using the IP number instead of the aliased server name.

? I get the message <u>"Program too large for memory"</u> when I try to install a file I just downloaded. I have 32MB of RAM, so I know I have enough memory. What could be wrong?

Possibly the file is corrupted, or maybe you didn't use binary transfer mode when downloading the file, thus also corrupting the file. Go back and make sure you select "binary transfer mode" in your FTP client. If the file still comes over corrupted, check with the administrator of the file server. They may have a corrupted file.

? I keep getting the message <u>"Server returned extended information."</u> What does that mean?

You'll most likely see this message when you are trying to connect to an FTP server with Internet Explorer. It simply means Explorer wasn't able to understand why the connection failed. There are probably too many people using that site.

VIRUSES

? **If I use a well-known commercial service like <u>America Online or CompuServe</u>, won't I be immune to viruses?**

No. Because America Online and CompuServe both provide links to the outside world, you are still as susceptible as any user to virus attacks from downloading files if you don't protect yourself.

? **Recently I downloaded some files on my Mac. The next time I started up the computer my screen had turned to <u>black and white, with a system date of 8/27/56</u>. Have I been infected?**

No. There is a lithium battery in your computer that helps retain the settings for such things as screen appearance and date; this battery has probably run down. You simply need to change it.

? **How do viruses <u>infect my system</u>?**

Viruses only infect systems when they are executed or when a disk containing a virus is used to boot the computer. Macro viruses can infect application software—such as Microsoft Word or Excel—when the macro is opened or run. If you are unsure whether a file contains a virus, run virus-checking software against it before you execute the program or open the macro. Viruses spread by attaching themselves to other programs, then executing when the infected program is run.

? **Can a <u>Mac virus infect a PC</u>, or vice versa?**

Because the way in which files are constructed on the Mac is different than on the PC, it's relatively certain you cannot infect a PC with a Mac virus or vice versa. However, macro viruses that infect Microsoft Word and Excel files can be run on either platform. Be careful when downloading spreadsheets and Word documents. Make sure you have turned on Macro Virus checking in the Tools | Options | General tab settings of Word and Excel.

? **Where can I go for <u>more information about viruses</u>, virus hoaxes, and Trojan Horses?**

There are a ton of places that offer information about viruses. Table 6-2 lists some of the more popular places to go to find out about viruses, virus checking programs, and virus hoaxes.

Table 6-2.   Sites Offering Information on Viruses

Resource	Location
AOL VIRUS Keyword	America Online
Symantec, makers of antivirus software for PC and Mac	http://www.symantec.com
McAfee Associates, makers of antivirus software for the PC	http://www.mcafee.com
Computer Knowledge; provides Tutor.com, an interactive tutorial all about computer viruses	http://www.cknow.com/
Stiller Research; provides a lengthy explanation of how viruses work and how to protect your PC	http://www.stiller.com
Computer Virus Myths	http://www.kumite.com/myths

? What's the best way to prevent my system from being infected with a virus?

There are a number of things you can do. Here is a quick rundown of how you can protect yourself:

⇨ Install a virus-checking program.

⇨ Stay current on the regular updates; new viruses pop up all the time. The old version of a virus-checking program does no good on new strains of viruses.

⇨ Download files from reputable sources.

⇨ Never download files sent to you via e-mail unless you know who sent the file and why.

⇨ Always have backups of your hard disk files on tape or other media.

⇨ Don't panic. It may not be a virus. It may be a problem with your system software or hardware. Run your virus-checking software first, but also investigate whether you have software or hardware incompatibilities.

? What is a Trojan Horse?

A Trojan Horse is not a virus. It is a program masquerading as something else, but intended to do some sort of harm or mischief. The most recent Trojan Horse to hit the electronic airwaves was a file called AOL4Free, a program intended not to give the user free time on America Online but rather to delete files from hard drives. Trojan Horses may or may not be identifiable through virus-checking software since they do not alter any boot sectors or programs or attach themselves to other program files.

FINDING FTP SITES

? How does <u>Archie</u> relate to FTP?

Archie, a name derived from the word "archive," is basically a tool used to search for files stored on anonymous FTP file servers. You tell Archie the name or part of the name of the file you want to find and Archie goes off to find it in the list of Archie databases. You can use graphical Archie clients to search the Internet for files that match your needs; however, more and more sites are turning to search engines that are accessible through World Wide Web browsers rather than third-party Archie clients.

Tip   *You can find Archie by searching Shareware.com's site, located at http://www.shareware.com.*

? Where can I <u>find files to download</u>?

There are literally thousands of FTP sites scattered across the globe. Universities, commercial services, even local ISPs usually have a large collection of files for you to download. Table 6-3 offers a list of some of the more popular FTP sites and FTP search sites available on the World Wide Web.

? What is a <u>mirrored site</u>?

A mirrored site is simply an alternate location for a file repository. Many busy sites on the Internet mirror their file collections at another (usually distant) location. This allows more users to view and get files from the same collection and allows faster access by providing alternate sites closer to a user's physical geographic location.

Table 6-3.   Popular Shareware Ssites

Name of Site	Location	Systems Supported
Shareware.com	http://www.shareware.com	Apple, IBM, Macintosh, Amiga, DOS, all flavors of Windows, Atari.
Download.com Note: Mainly a site with demos of commercial products	http://www.download.com	Macintosh and all flavors of Windows.
Windows95.com	http://www.windows95.com	Windows 95 and some Windows NT files.
Tile.net	http://www.tile.net	Users looking for files. Offers a search engine that lists links to FTP sites catering to your specific needs.
WinSite	http://www.winsite.com	Offering an entire collection of shareware and trialware software. All versions of Windows software are available.
TuCows	http://www.tucows.com	All flavors of Windows, plus Macintosh software, arranged by category.
CDRom from Walnut Creek CDRom	http://www.cdrom.com	Users looking for demos and shareware that can also be ordered on CD-ROM.
ZiffNet	http://www.ziffnet.com	A large selection of all platforms of Windows software.

Where can I find files on a **public FTP server**?

Look for a directory called "pub" or "public." This is where most FTP server administrators store files for public consumption. If there isn't a public directory, look for a file called "readme" or "index." You should be able to use your browser to instantly display the contents of these files so you can see how the files are arranged.

Newsgroups

Answer Topics!

Newsgroups @ a Glance

⇨   Newsgroups are essentially gigantic, constantly circulating and changing, worldwide electronic bulletin boards. Looking for computer advice? Thinking of selling your boat? Have questions about love and romance? You can read messages from people all over the world about all kinds of topics just by finding the right newsgroup. Granted, when you first start cruising newsgroups, you'll have some **basic newsgroup questions**, since the whole newsgroup concept can be somewhat daunting.

⇨   If you are **using Navigator or Internet Explorer to read newsgroups**, you probably have questions about setting up your software to access your server. Maybe you want to know how to forward, post, or reply to messages. Each application has a plethora of features to make handling newsgroup messages easier.

⇨   Reading **newsgroups on commercial and Web-based services** has some additional quirks. If you are using America Online (AOL) or CompuServe, accessing newsgroups can be slightly different from using a standard Internet service provider. And, in an effort to differentiate themselves from other services, the commercial services have some features for reading newsgroups that differ from Netscape Navigator or Internet Explorer. Web-based newsgroup services offer you the ability to search for archived postings, newsgroups that meet your particular needs, and postings by particular individuals.

BASIC NEWSGROUP QUESTIONS

 Can I cancel a message I just posted?

> Yes, but you have to do it before it's too late. Don't wait three or four days; delete it as soon as you can. To cancel a posting, click the newsgroup, then the message, and select Edit | Cancel Message. Click OK to verify the cancellation of the message.

? **Why didn't I get a reply from the person who posted a message? I replied to his posting.**

If you want to ensure that your reply is read by the original poster of a message, you should reply via e-mail as well as posting a reply to the newsgroup. Often, people post messages but forget to check back with the newsgroup for replies. Sending a reply to the poster's e-mail address means you're more likely to get a reply from the poster, if that's what you're looking for.

? **How does the Internet prevent a posting from being displayed twice?**

First, the Path line in the header shows the path the posting has traveled. If the next server to receive the post appearing in the Path line is the same as the current server, the sending server will not send the article to that server. The Message-ID header line also contains an identifying code unique to each posting. Before a post is sent from one server to another, it checks to see if the receiving server has received that unique message header. If the receiving server does not have the message, the server requests the message.

? **What is newsgroup etiquette?**

Although just about anything goes on the Internet these days, it's a good idea to follow newsgroup posting etiquette. Here are some of the major things to remember and consider:

⇨ Make sure you post your question to the proper newsgroup. For example, don't post a question about your Macintosh to the alt.sex newsgroup.

⇨ Make sure you supply a descriptive header in the subject line of your posting. Most people search by subject headers instead of by the text of the posting, so the more descriptive the better.

⇨ If you are posting a message about a particular computer, make sure you supply enough descriptive information about your operating system, the version, the type of computer equipment, the amount of memory, the amount of hard disk space, and so forth.

⇨ Consider whether the posting should be sent out to the world or directly to a particular poster. If you are replying to the entire Internet world, make sure your post is written for the entire Internet audience to read.

⇨ Try to hold back on posting personal flames, dumb jokes, or advertising. Don't post chain letters or information that could be construed as libelous. Don't respond to flames. Just let them drop unless you have something worthwhile to say. Forget about replying to people who post advertising to a newsgroup. Most of the time it's futile, and if you have problems with posters, reply directly to their postmaster rather than filling up the newsgroup with a bunch of inane messages about how lame advertising is.

❓ Where can I find all the FAQs for all the newsgroups?

There are several places you can go to read the FAQs for each newsgroup on the Internet. One place is at the University of Ohio, located on the Web at **http://www.cis.ohio-state.edu/hypertext/faq/usenet/FAQ-List.html**. You can also grab the FAQs off an FTP file server at MIT, either through the Web or through an FTP client. The location for the FTP file is **ftp://rtfm.mit.edu/pub/usenet-by-group**.

❓ What file formats can I save newsgroup postings in?

You can save them as HTML formatted postings or as text files. HTML formatted postings will retain any clickable links, pictures, and graphics. Text files will only contain the text of the posting. Most newsgroup reader programs offer the ability to save a posting under the File menu.

❓ How do I write a good newsgroup message that will get noticed and get answered?

First, make sure you are posting to the right newsgroup. Second, make sure your posting is one of a global nature. Third, make sure your posting includes all the necessary details but is no longer than one screen length—two at the most. Include your e-mail address and whether you would like replies sent to the newsgroup or directly to you. Use good grammar and spelling, and above all be concise.

? **When I replied to a posting via e-mail and to the newsgroup, my e-mail message bounced back with the error message "Host or Username not found." What's wrong?**

Many times people use fictitious e-mail addresses to post messages to newsgroups because they want to remain anonymous or do not want to have their e-mail mailboxes filled with unsolicited replies or flames. There's not much you can do other than post a reply to the newsgroup and hope the poster sees your message.

? **Where do I get a list of all current newsgroups?**

The official list of all the newsgroups can be found in any of these newsgroups:

> news.lists
>
> news.groups
>
> news.announce.newsgroups
>
> news.answers
>
> news.newusers.questions

You can also find a list of active newsgroups at the Usenet Launch Pad, located at **http://www.cis.ohio-state.edu/hypertext/faq/usenet/ top.html**. Or you can read through the list of active newsgroups found at **http://www.cis.ohio-state.edu/hypertext/faq/usenet/ active-newsgroups/top.html**.

? **How long do messages stay posted on a newsgroup?**

Usually news servers remove old postings every day because of the volume of messages sent and received on a daily basis. Each server sets its own expiration time for newsgroup postings. Some set postings to be cleared out daily, while others may allow postings to remain on their server for up to two weeks. Your posting may have expired on your server, but you may still receive replies because other servers haven't removed the posting.

Remember   If you don't see your posting, it may be due to the fact that your newsreader software is hiding all the messages you've already read. Try using the Show All option to see all messages, including those you have already read, if you are searching for a particular posting.

? **What's the difference between posting a reply to <u>News or</u> <u>to Mail</u>?**

If you post a reply to Mail, you are essentially sending the poster of the message a reply through e-mail, and your posting will not be seen by other people throughout the Usenet community. If you post a reply to News, you are posting a public message to the newsgroup for all the world to see. If you decide to use the Both option to post a reply, your message is sent both to the individual poster's e-mail address and to the newsgroup. Post a message to both the newsgroup and poster if you want a reply from both the poster and others who are reading the newsgroup.

? **Why do I get the error message "<u>News Error—Timeout</u>" when I'm checking my newsgroups?**

This just means the connection to your newsgroup server has timed out and dropped the connection. Simply click on the name of the newsgroup again, and you should reconnect and see all the articles.

? **Are <u>newsgroup postings copyrighted</u>? Can I use something from a posting in a report or presentation?**

Although newsgroup postings are in the public domain, the person who posted the original message holds the copyright of that message and is covered under U.S. copyright laws. You can use up to 25 words of a posting for "reporting" purposes, but you should first double-check with the poster if you plan to include material from a posting in a presentation, book, manual, or other publication. Never include graphics, sounds, or movie files in a presentation without first seeking authorization from the creator of the work. Someone may have posted a message containing copyrighted material from another source, so make sure the original poster is the actual copyright holder and has authorization to allow you to use the work before including it in anything you may use.

? **How do administrators know which <u>newsgroups to place</u> on the server?**

Newsmasters make their own decisions on what newsgroups they want to carry. Some Internet service providers elect not to carry sexually explicit newsgroup servers, for example, while others may be limited in the number of newsgroups they carry by the amount of newsgroup file server space they have. Essentially, the admin server will send out a request for what newsgroups the service wants to receive. You can ask your administrator to carry a particular newsgroup if your provider doesn't offer it. Check with your service provider to find out exactly what e-mail address to send requests to.

? What is the <u>order of postings</u> in newsgroups?

Since most postings are sent from server to server, there is no real order. If a server is down, the newsgroup sending the original post will simply send the message to the next server. Depending upon when the message arrives, replies to the original message may actually arrive to before the original message does.

? I posted a question in a newsgroup a day ago, and the posting still hasn't appeared. What's wrong?

The newsgroup may be moderated. In that case, there will be a delay while your article is mailed to the moderator. Or the server you're using may not have received that message just yet. It could be that you may not have posted to a newsgroup; if you were replying to a post, you may have inadvertently replied directly to the poster instead. Finally, something may be wrong with your service's newsgroup server. Check with your administrator if you think your server is not receiving your postings.

? Why are my newsgroup <u>postings listed with the wrong time</u>?

You probably don't have the clock set properly on your computer. To make sure you do, follow these steps:

1. Double-click the time listed in the System Tray on the Windows toolbar.
2. Click the Time Zone tab, and make sure the right time zone is selected.
3. Check the time and date to make sure these options are set correctly.
4. Click OK to save your changes.

? How do I search for a newsgroup?

Most browsers, such as Navigator or Internet Explorer, currently don't have Find or Search features for locating newsgroups on a particular topic. You can, however, use a variety of Web-based search sites to find what you are looking for. Here is a brief listing of the more popular newsgroup search sites:

Search Site	Location
DejaNews	http://www.dejanews.com
Tile.Net	http://www.tile.net
Usenet Info Center Launch Pad	http://SUNSITE.UNC.EDU/usenet-i/home.html
Infinite Link - Finding Newsgroups	http://www.ii.com/internet/messaging/newsgroups/

? Can I search newsgroup postings?

Most newsgroup reader software allows you to search the current messages within a newsgroup itself. However, if you want to search multiple newsgroups, the quickest way is to use a Web-based newsgroup search engine such as DejaNews. You can search the text of messages using DejaNews, a Usenet News search engine available on the Web at **http://www.dejanews.com**. DejaNews allows you to search only the text, but it also allows you to search by author, date, newsgroup, or keyword in the title. Other popular search engines are AltaVista, located at **http://www.altavista.digital.com**; HotBot, located at **http://www.hotbot.com**; and Metacrawler, located at **http://www.metacrawler.com**.

? What newsgroup will tell me whether my software and configuration are working properly?

You can post to alt.test or misc.test to determine whether your posting worked and whether your newsgroup configuration is working properly. Both newsgroups are monitored by autoresponders—automated computer programs that send back an automatic message to reply to your posting.

? **I've heard there are three types of newsgroups. What are they?**

The three types of newsgroups are closed, moderated, and unmoderated. Closed newsgroups are not open to the public and require that you request access to the group from the newsgroup administrator. Moderated newsgroups are open to the public, but each message is sent to an administrator or to administration-type software for review. The administrator (moderator) or software posts only those messages relevant to the newsgroup or that have been filtered through the software. Unmoderated groups are open to anyone, and anything can be posted to the newsgroup.

? **Where does a message really go when I post it to a newsgroup?**

When you post a message, the information is first posted to your local news server. There is no central Usenet newsgroup server. Rather, assuming the newsgroup is unmoderated, each article propagates from one server to the next, starting with the original server where the post was made.

Postings to moderated newsgroups may first be forwarded to an e-mail address of the moderator, who approves all postings. Once the moderator has approved the posting, she or he will post the message to the newsgroup server, and the message will propagate much like an unmoderated message.

Eventually, your posting will travel to thousands of newsgroup servers—from university servers to Internet service provider servers. Within a few days, your posting will have made it across the world.

USING NAVIGATOR OR INTERNET EXPLORER TO READ NEWSGROUPS

? **Can I cancel the loading of messages if I don't want to wait for the listing of messages to display?**

Sure. Simply press ESC. This will cancel the loading of messages for both Navigator and Explorer.

Table 7-1.   Internet News 3.0 Keyboard Shortcuts

Function	Keyboard Shortcut
View the properties of a selected message	ALT-ENTER
Go to the previous message	CTRL-<, CTRL-SHIFT-<, ALT-LEFT ARROW
Go to the next message	CTRL->, CTRL-SHIFT->, ALT-RIGHT ARROW
Forward a message	CTRL-F
Post a reply	CTRL-G
Post a new message	CTRL-N
Open a selected message	CTRL-O or CTRL-ENTER
Print a message	CTRL-P
Reply directly to the author of the post	CTRL-R
Mark a message as read	CTRL-SPACEBAR
Go to a particular newsgroup	CTRL-W
Cycle through the message list and previous pane	TAB

? How do I change the newsgroup settings in Internet Explorer?

To change any of the settings in Internet Explorer's newsreader, follow these steps:

1. Click News | Options | Server.

2. Click Properties, then click the Add button to enter the newsgroup server information.

3. Click OK to save the settings, then OK again to close the Properties window.

? How do I decode a binary file in a newsgroup posting?

Binary files, such as graphic files like GIFs or JPEGs, posted to newsgroups display as garbled text. When you run across a binary file in a newsgroup posting, Netscape will take this garbled text, referred to as Uuencoded text and automatically decoded it, displaying it in the window of the message. Sometimes, however, because of the size of the file, the original sender may split the binary file up into several postings. When this happens, since Netscape doesn't know where the file begins or ends, Netscape simply displays the Uuencoded text, not the file. If you want to view the binary file you will have to find all the pieces in the various posts, then copy and paste the pieces of Uuencoded text into a text processor such as Notepad. Once gathered into a single file, you then need to use a program such as WinZip to decode the text, turning back into it's original binary file.

How do I delete News messages in Microsoft Outlook?

You can delete the News messages stored on your computer, but not on the newsgroup server you are posting to, unless you have *just* posted a message within the last few minutes. If what you want to do is delete those messages you've downloaded to your computer, follow these steps:

1. Click Tools | News Options.
2. Click the Advanced tab.
3. Click one of the following boxes to clear the messages: "Delete messages (<X>) days after being downloaded." "Don't keep read messages."
4. Click OK to save the changes.

Can I disable the reading of newsgroups in Navigator?

Probably the easiest way to prevent someone from reading newsgroups is simply to leave the settings for your newsgroup blank in the Options | Mail and News Preferences | Servers | News (NTTP) Server field, as shown in Figure 7-1.

Why do I only see a few newsgroups in the list?

When you first connect to a server, a list of the newsgroups available is shown. The newsgroup file that Netscape Navigator uses is stored in the News RC Directory entry in the Options | Mail and News | Servers option. If you only see a few newsgroups listed, but you have added more, this NewsRC file may be damaged. To fix this problem, delete the NewsRCfile stored in the directory specified in the Options | Mail and News | Servers window. Make sure you exit Navigator first, then restart it.

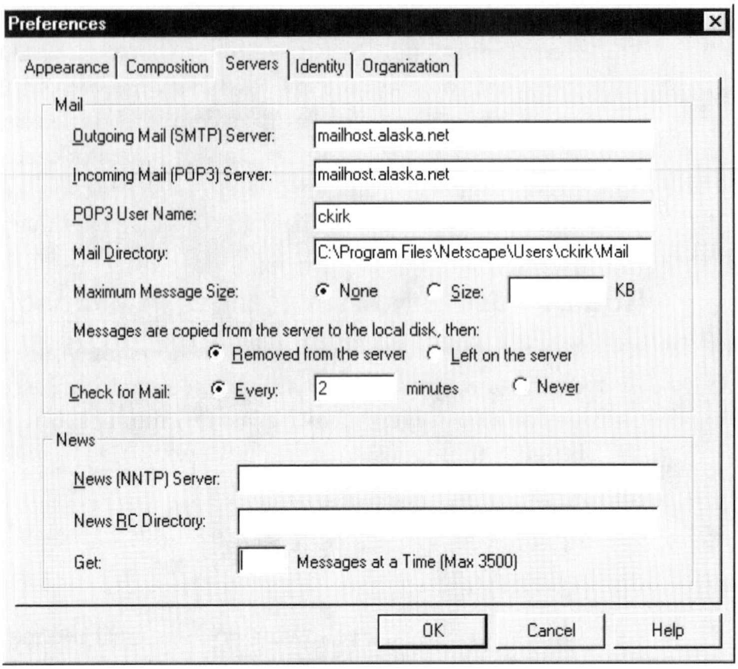

Figure 7-1.   Leaving the newsgroup settings blank

❓ Can I forward a newsgroup posting to someone's e-mail address?

Yes, just choose Forward from the Message menu, or click the Forward button, and the message will be sent to the e-mail address you specified.

❓ I can't seem to get rid of a newsgroup server after choosing the File | Remove Newsgroup Host option. What else can I do?

Netscape Navigator keeps a list of the news servers you've added in a file called Fat. If you can't remove the host by choosing Remove Newsgroup Host from the File menu, you can try one more solution. You can try manually editing the Fat file to remove all occurrences of the newsgroup server you want to remove. To edit the file, open the C:\Netscape\Program\News\ directory and double-click on the file labeled "Fat." Your system should ask what application you want to open this file with. Select WordPad, then click OK. Next, remove any mention of the newsgroup server you want to delete from the file. Save the file, then restart Navigator. Only those servers you left in the file will be listed.

? I don't seem to be getting all the messages a newsgroup should have. What could be the problem?

The maximum number of messages in your Options | Mail and News Preferences | Servers section could be set at a very low number, preventing you from loading all the messages at once.

? How do I go to a specific newsgroup if I know the name and it isn't listed in my subscribed newsgroup list?

Choose File | Add Newsgroup, then type the complete name of the newsgroup, as shown here:

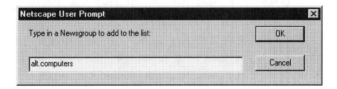

Click OK, and the newsgroup will appear in your list. You can then decide to subscribe to that newsgroup if you wish to see it listed the next time you bring up Navigator's News option.

? How do I hide newsgroup articles I've read?

If you're using Navigator, try selecting Options | Show Only Unread Messages. If you are using Communicator, try View | Messages option | View New Messages Only.

? Why can't I read articles from a particular news server in the Netscape Message Center?

Some older news servers don't support the XOVER command, which is Message Center's command for reading news postings. The Netscape Message Center requires XOVER support from the news server to display the message thread and the messages. Ask your

network administrator if the news server in use supports the
XOVER command.

When I quit Navigator, my newsgroups disappear. What's the matter?

This usually happens because you have specified an invalid
pathname to store your News RC file in the Options | Mail and News
Preferences | Server option. Double-check the entry in the News RC
Directory field to make sure the directory specified is actually a valid
directory on your system.

> **Note**   *In Communicator, you specify the News RC directory by choosing*
> *Edit | Preferences | Mail & Groups | Groups server | Discussion groups*
> *(news) folder.*

What's happening if my newsgroups suddenly disappear?

You may have changed the directory where the NewsRC file is
located. This file contains information about the newsgroups you've
subscribed to. You can open the Windows Registry file by selecting
Start | Run; then type **Rededit** in the Open field. Expand the :My
Computer\HKEY_CURRENT_USER\Software\Netscape\Netscape
Navigator\Main entry and look for a line with your NewsRC file.
That line should contain the directory where your Newsrc file is
stored. Make sure Navigator's Options | Mail and News Preferences
| Servers window contains the same directory in the New RC
Directory field. If the two directory entries are the same, the next thing
you should do is exit Navigator, and delete the NewsRC file in that
directory. Then restart Navigator, and the NewsRC file should be
re-created. Next, go to the Newsgroup option and resubscribe to
your newsgroups.

How do I get old newsgroup servers to stop displaying in my list?

First, click the newsgroup host server you want to remove. Next,
select File | Remove News Host, as shown here:

The newsgroup server should not be displayed the next time you launch Navigator.

How do I <u>open a newsgroup</u> from a Netscape Navigator window?

In the URL location field, if you know the name of the newsgroup you want to access, simply type **news:** and the name of the newsgroup. For example, if you are interested in opening the alt.hackers newsgroup, you would type **news:alt.hackers**. When you specify a newsgroup this way, Netscape will use the default newsgroup host setting you specified in the Options | Mail and News Preferences | Servers section.

What can I do to <u>prevent archiving</u> of my Usenet posts?

Simply add the following line to the header of your posting:

X-no-archive: yes

If your software does not allow this, make it the first line of the message, or include it in the last line of the message.

How do I know if I've <u>read a message</u>?

A green triangle next to the message means a message hasn't been read. All others have been read. You can also choose Options | Show All Messages if you want to see all the messages or Options | Show Only Unread Messages if you just want to concentrate on the unread ones.

❓ How do I remove a newsgroup from the list?

Click on the check mark next to the newsgroup you want to remove. When you uncheck the newsgroup, the next time you start Navigator News, the newsgroup will not be displayed.

❓ How do I search postings within a specific newsgroup in Navigator?

Make sure the newsgroup you want to search is selected, then choose Edit | Find. In the Find field, type the keyword you are looking for, making sure the option Messages Headers in this Folder option is selected.

 Note   *If you want to search within a message, select instead Body of this Message, and this will show you where the keyword you are looking for appears in the message.*

❓ How can I select a group of messages to read later?

You can flag them as you go through the list of messages. Then when you want to read the messages, simply choose Go | First Flagged (see Figure 7-2), and the first message you flagged will be highlighted. To continue to read the rest of the messages you've flagged, continue to choose Go | Next Flagged or Go | Previous Flagged.

❓ How do I set up Netscape Navigator so I can read newsgroups?

First, you must know the name of your newsgroup server. Your Internet service provider should be able to give you this information. Each provider names the newsgroup server differently, so there is no universal name. Some may be news.serviceprovider.com, and others may be nntp.serviceprovider.com.

In the Options | Mail and News Preferences | Servers window, type the name of your news server in the News (NNTP) Server field. Then select the number of news messages you want to receive at any one time, as shown in Figure 7-3.

Keep in mind that some newsgroups have thousands of messages, which would take some time to load all at once. After setting these options, click OK to save the changes. You should then be able to access or subscribe to any newsgroup your service provider carries.

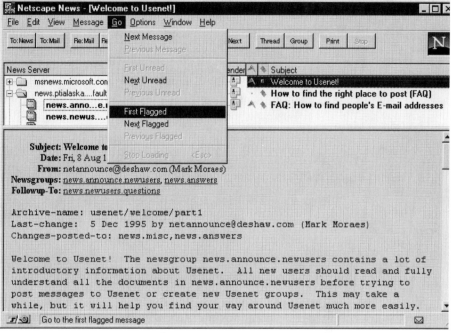

Figure 7-2.   Flagging messages

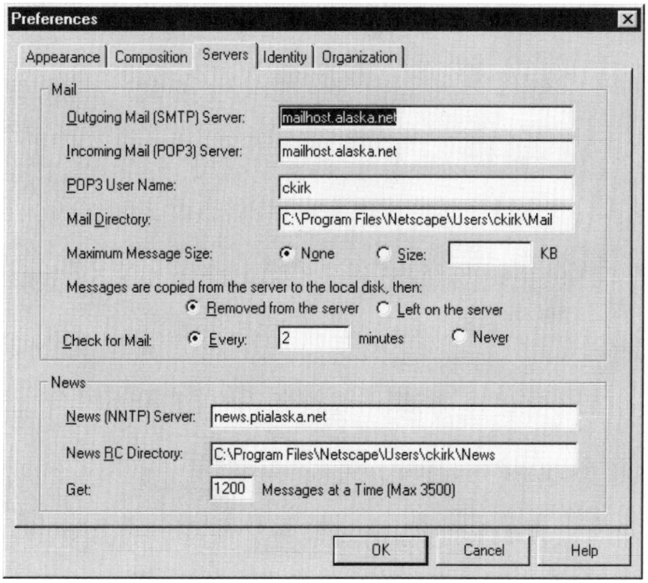

Figure 7-3.   Setting the newsgroup server and preferences

? What are the settings to connect to the MSN network's newsgroup?

You can use the following newsgroup servers if you are using Internet Explorer or Outlook to connect to the MSN network:

msnnews.msn.com

netnews.msn.com

? How do I sort messages in descending instead of ascending order in Navigator?

Select View | Sort, and select the subject you want to sort by first. Next, select View | Sort | Ascending to sort in ascending order, then select it again to sort in descending order.

? How do I sort messages by sender instead of date?

The quickest way to sort a message by Sender is to click the Sender header. This automatically sorts all messages alphabetically by the Sender's name. Click any other field header such as Subject or Date and the messages will resort by that category.

? How do I subscribe to a newsgroup in Netscape?

You can subscribe to a newsgroup by clicking the empty checkbox to the right of the name of the newsgroup, as shown in Figure 7-4. If you do not see any boxes, click the divider, and slide it to the right to extend the newsgroup listing pane. When you subscribe to a newsgroup, you are simply telling your newsreader you want to list

Table 7-2.   Navigator News Keyboard Shortcuts

Function	Keyboard Shortcut
Forward a message	CTRL-F
Find text within a message or within a newsgroup	CTRL-L
Print message	CTRL-P
Reply to a message	CTRL-R
Select a thread	CTRL-SHIFT-A
Stop loading newsgroup messages	ESC

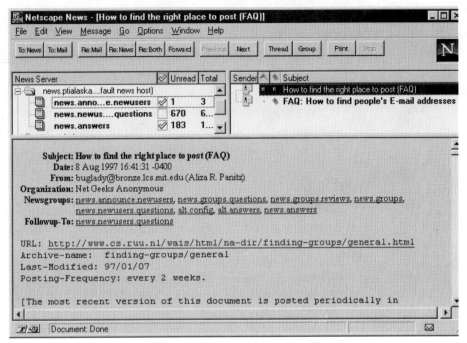

Figure 7-4.   Subscribing and unsubscribing to newsgroups

that particular newsgroup every time you start the newsreader program. To unsubscribe from a newsgroup, simply uncheck the box.

How do I uninstall Internet News so I can use another newsreader program?

To uninstall Internet Mail and News, follow these steps:

1. Click Start | Control Panel, and double-click the Add/Remove Programs icon.

2. Click the Install/Uninstall tab.

3. Scroll through the list to find and select Internet Mail and News.

4. Click the Remove button to remove the software. This will remove all portions of the program.

Tip   Write down your settings for connecting to your newsgroup server so you will have them handy when you install the new software.

When I select Options | Show Active Newsgroups, the number of <u>unread messages</u> doesn't seem to be in sync with the number of postings I've actually read. What's up?

You could have problems with the News RC file being out of sync with the newsgroup server you connect to. If the newsgroup server you use has crashed or been reset, you can find some problems and discrepancies between the number of postings Navigator thinks are unread and what actually are unread.

What is <u>Usenet?</u>

Usenet, or Usenet News, is a global community bulletin board system for the Internet. When someone posts an article to Usenet, that article is sent out worldwide for other people to read. Usenet is organized into thousands of topic areas, called newsgroups, that discuss anything from recipes to politics to sex to computers. Over 250,000 articles are posted to Usenet each day. Millions of people around the world read Usenet News.

Newsgroups categorize articles on Usenet to help organize it. There are 15,000 newsgroups organized according to their specific areas of concentration. The groups are organized in a tree structure with seven major categories:

⇨ *Comp* contains topics of interest to both computer professionals and hobbyists, including computer science, software sources, and information on hardware and software systems.

⇨ *Rec* contains groups oriented toward hobbies and recreational activities.

⇨ *Sci* contains discussions marked by special knowledge relating to research in or application of the established sciences.

⇨ *Soc* contains groups primarily addressing social issues and socializing. Included are discussions related to many different world cultures.

⇨ *Talk* contains groups largely debate-oriented and tending to feature long discussions without resolution and without appreciable amounts of generally useful information.

⇨ *News* contains groups concerned with the news network, group maintenance, and software.

⇨ *Misc* contains groups addressing themes not easily classified into any of the other headings or that incorporate themes from multiple categories. Subjects include fitness, job hunting, law, and investments.

There are also dozens of other areas that are not part of the "big seven"; the most famous is the *alt* hierarchy, created by people who wanted to bypass the "Usenet cabal" who control the big seven groups.

Other areas are controlled by individual organizations; for example, *clari* groups are controlled by Clarinet, Inc., and *ucb* groups are controlled by the University of California, Berkeley. Articles can be anything people want to share with others. They are normally simple e-mails but can also be encoded pictures, sounds, or binary programs. Articles are posted to Usenet News, which sends them out worldwide for other people to read.

? How do I know what newsgroups are available on the server I've set as a default in Netscape?

First, select Options | Show All Newsgroups. This should show all the newsgroups available to you from the server you have currently configured in your Options | Mail and News Preferences | Server settings. If you select Options | Show Active Newsgroups instead, you will see only the newsgroups to which you are currently subscribed.

? I'm using Netscape Navigator. Is there a way to find out who posted a message or where it came from?

You can view all the headers of the posting, and they may give you some idea of who and where the message came from. To do this, choose Options | Show Headers | All. A sample header is shown in Figure 7-5.

Remember   *Anonymous reposter software is widely used, and it's simple to change the e-mail address and name of the poster.*

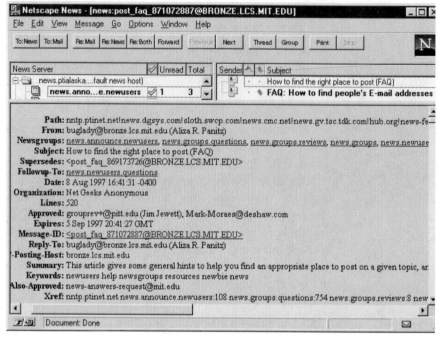

Figure 7-5.   A sample header

NEWSGROUPS ON COMMERCIAL SERVICES AND WEB-BASED SERVICES

? How do I add a newsgroup to my list of newsgroups in AOL?

AOL gives you three options for adding different newsgroups. To read any newsgroup, no matter how you select it from the options listed here, go to the main Newsgroup window and click on the Read My Newsgroups button.

Follow these steps if you don't know the newsgroup but only the topic:

1. From the main Newsgroup window, click the Add Newsgroups button. You will see a list of different types of hierarchies—categories of newsgroup names such as "rec" for recreation-related groups, "biz" for business-related groups,

"comp" for computer-related groups, "soc" for social-type groups, and so on. The hierarchy becomes more specific from left to right. For example, rec.rowing could encompass any information about the sport of rowing, but rec.rowing.college would be specific to collegiate rowing. Selecting a hierarchy gives you a list of lower level hierarchies (subcategories) and, finally, a list of actual newsgroups.

2. Once you narrow your selection, you can add a particular newsgroup to the Read My Newsgroups list by selecting it and clicking on the Add button.

Note   Remember when viewing this list that the initial settings do not show you the full listing of Usenet newsgroups that AOL carries. The abbreviated list does not include newsgroups with sexually explicit names or groups missing an English-style name (also called a descriptive title; AOL adds newsgroups to the list as they add an English-style name for them). Groups with sexually explicit names will never appear in the shortened list. Read the Parental Controls document to find out how to view the full list or get access to unlisted newsgroups.

If you know the topic and don't want to browse, but instead, search more quickly for a specific newsgroup, follow these steps:

1. From the Newsgroup window, click the Search All Newsgroups button and search for a particular word that may appear in the Internet-style name of a newsgroup.

2. From the search results, select a newsgroup and click the Add button. For example, a search for "multimedia" turns up many newsgroups, including comp.multimedia and comp.publish.cdrom.multimedia.

Follow these steps if you know the exact name of the newsgroup you want to find:

1. From the Newsgroup window, click Expert Add.

2. In the Internet Name field, type the newsgroup's name—for example, **alt.best.of.internet**—and click Add. A message confirms that the newsgroup has been added to the list of your newsgroups (Read My Newsgroups), or tells you that the name you entered was invalid (because it was misspelled or because the newsgroup does not exist).

? How do I add a signature to my newsgroup posting?

Signatures are text files that are attached to all of your posts. A signature file can contain your name, Web address, business information, quotations, links to other Web pages, or anything you want to add. To add a signature follow these steps:

1. From the Newsgroup window, click the Set Preferences button.

2. Type your signature in the signature box.

3. Click OK to save your signature.

From this point on, every posting you make will automatically have your signature file attached to the bottom of the post.

Note   *A long signature file is frowned upon, so keep it short. Also, do not include any personal information you wouldn't want a complete stranger to know. Don't include your home phone number or address, for example.*

? What is an Author Profile in DejaNews?

An Author Profile displays statistical information about the person who has posted to a particular newsgroup. Clicking the author's name or the Author Profile icon at the top of an article will display articles originating from this particular e-mail address. From there, you can gain better insight into what this person's interests are and where he or she has posted messages.

? How do I work with binary files stored in AOL?

Such files contain special nontext characters that cannot be reliably transmitted through some Usenet computers. For these files to go through the Internet, they must be translated into plain text and then posted as regular messages. The translation process most commonly used is called *uuencoding*, or *binary encoding*.

Encoding a binary file makes it larger, so it's often necessary to break the encoded file into a series of smaller, more manageable parts. In the past, this has frustrated people who wanted to retrieve the encoded file, because they had to save each encoded chunk separately, combine them into one file, and then decode the file. AOL's FileGrabber feature eliminates this complicated process.

When you read a newsgroup posting that contains encoded data, a window pops up alerting you to that fact. You then have three options: to download the decoded file and automatically decode it (Download File), to download only that encoded chunk as a text file so you can manually decode it (Download Article), or to quit (Cancel).

Note   *To protect new users and children from encountering certain images or files, the ability to download binaries is blocked for new users (even on master accounts). The master account holder can change this setting in the Parental Controls section.*

Where are the <u>Clarinet newsgroups</u>, and how do I access them?

The Clarinet newsgroups (clari.*) are mainly news service wire feeds of late breaking and daily news from news organizations such as Reuters and the Associated Press. Since Clarinet charges for these feeds, some services such as AOL elect not to carry them because they already receive news from a variety of sources and repackage that news into their own specialized online news sections. So you won't find them on America Online and you may not find them as part of your Internet Service Provider's package either.

If you are using AOL, you can't access the clari.* newsgroups. Instead you can get news updates by using the keyword NEWS to check out the latest news. If you want to set up your own news filtering agent, use the keyword NEWSAGENT to create a unique news filtering profile.

If you are using an Internet Service Provider try adding the Newsgroup clari.web.biz.briefs. If that Newsgroup does not display or you get an error message, your ISP may not subscribe to ClariNet news. Either contact your provider, or check out ClariNet on the web at **http://www.clari.net** to search for another provider in your area that does.

Can I <u>cross-post messages</u> to more than one newsgroup on AOL?

Cross-posting—posting the same message to several newsgroups at one time—is often considered poor netiquette and should be avoided. The AOL newsgroup reader does not permit cross-posting. If you want to cross-post a message, you will have to do it manually, adding the message individually to each newsgroup.

How far back does the DejaNews archive go?

As of now, the DejaNews archive extends back to March 1995. The entire list of Usenet articles can go back as far as 1979. Eventually, services such as DejaNews will provide full archives of all the postings.

Can I delete a newsgroup posting once I've posted it?

If you want to delete a newsgroup posting you've created, send an e-mail message to **NewsMaster@aol.com** with the following information:

⇨   The date the article was posted

⇨   The subject of the article

⇨   The Message-ID of the article

Note   *The AOL newsmaster can cancel a newsgroup article up to four days after it was originally posted. However, since postings start moving from one newsgroup server to another rather quickly, the sooner you request the cancellation, the better. If it's more than 24 hours after the post, there is no guarantee the message won't have already made its way to another newsgroup server.*

Can I download binary files with DejaNews?

Because of the size and difficulty in indexing binaries, DejaNews removes binary files, such as GIFs, that are longer than four lines. DejaNews is considering offering another separate library complete with binary file attachments. If you want to see binary files, you should try connecting to an ISP's newsgroup server.

Why do I get duplicates in some of my searches?

People sometimes repost the same thing more than once. In these cases, it's not really the same post, although the content may be the same. By checking the Message-ID in the article headers, you can make sure the posting is not the same.

? **I get error messages when I try to add a newsgroup. What's wrong?**

You could have problems adding newsgroups for a variety of reasons:

⇨ The newsgroup's name could be invalid. Check the spelling, and make sure you are using the periods in all the right places.

⇨ You may have the spelling right and the group may be valid, but AOL may not have added it to their servers yet. You can contact the newsmaster to find out when the newsgroup will be available, or you can wait patiently until it is.

⇨ The newsgroup may be valid and included in the newsgroup servers, but it may be blocked by the Parental Controls invoked on the master account. You'll need to log off, then log back on using the master account to change these settings.

⇨ The newsgroup may be blocked by an AOL administrative block that has been invoked on your screen name. You can contact the newsmaster to find out how this block can be removed from your account.

? **Are standard DejaNews searches "fuzzy"?**

No. Unlike other search engines such as AltaVista, DejaNews searches for all the keywords you submit and returns articles that match all of these words. You can use the Power Search page to specify any keywords matched, and DejaNews will display the results, ranking them from the highest to the lowest scored results.

? **How many newsgroups does DejaNews archive?**

Currently DejaNews archives approximately 15,000 newsgroups, including alt.*, soc.*, and talk.*. They also carry a wide variety of local newsgroups, such as uk.* (United Kingdom-related newsgroups) and relcom.* (Russian language newsgroups). Use the Search option to search for the newsgroup of your choice.

? **Should I include a line break in my messages when using AOL to post a message?**

The AOL software will automatically include line breaks for you. You only need to add a line break if you want to increase the line spacing in the text you're typing.

? How often is the listing of <u>new newsgroups updated</u> on AOL?

Every two weeks a list of all the newsgroups is posted to a file called "List of Active Newsgroups" in the new.lists newsgroup. Currently there are over 20,000 newsgroups listed, so it will take a while for this file to display.

? How do you get a list of <u>newly added AOL newsgroups</u>?

To get a list of newsgroups added to AOL, follow these steps:

1. Open the Newsgroup window, then click the Expert Add button.
2. Click the Latest Newsgroup button.
3. When the listing is displayed, you can select any newsgroup and click the Add button to add it to your Personal List.

? What <u>newsgroups are carried on AOL</u>?

America Online automatically carries all newsgroups created for the global Usenet audience. This means some 20,000+ newsgroups are available. (Some local newsgroups may not be carried on AOL.) If you don't find a newsgroup, but you know it exists, check to make sure the Parental Controls option set for the main account allows for access to such groups.

If you would like to see a particular newsgroup available through AOL, send a message to **NewsMaster@aol.com** and specify the name and the audience that this newsgroup would serve. If applicable, the newsmaster may add that newsgroup.

? How do you get rid of the <u>newsgroup headers</u> with the AOL reader?

From the main Newsgroup window, click the Preferences button. In the Header section, select whether you want headers to show or not to show. If you want them to show, you can select whether they appear at the top or bottom.

? Why do some posts say <u>"No longer available"</u>?

A newsgroup window may indicate that a certain number of messages are unread, but some of them may no longer be available because they have expired or been automatically deleted to make room for new postings. You have complete control over the number of days before a posting will expire. Currently the default for postings stored on America Online is 14 days, but you can extend that up to 30 days. To change the number of days, use the keyword NEWSGROUPS to go to the Newsgroup window. Next, select any of the newsgroups you currently subscribe to, and then click the Preferences button. Make changes to the expiration date, then click OK to save the changes.

Note   *The Preferences button in the window of the subscribed newsgroup is not the same as the Preferences button on the main Newsgroup window. The former allows you to set the expiration for posts; the latter allows you to set naming, order, and signature preferences.*

Why are some postings broken into segments on DejaNews?

If the posting of a message is over 4K, it will be broken into segments. You can click to see the rest of the post using the Next or Previous link. You can also retrieve the entire article. You may have to wait a few minutes if the posting is lengthy. Postings with attachments will only display the text of the message, not the attachment, unless the attachment has been UUencoded.

Can I read newsgroups offline with AOL?

To read newsgroups offline, you will need to create a Flashsession. Follow these steps:

1. In the Newsgroup window, click the Read Offline button. The list of newsgroups you subscribe to should appear. If you have any newsgroups already listed, they should appear in the Read My Newsgroup list.

2. In the Subscribed Newsgroups list, highlight the newsgroup you want to read offline, then click the Add button. Or choose Add All to add all your subscribed newsgroups to the offline reading list.

3. Click OK to save the changes, then invoke your Flashsession by selecting Mail | Activate Flashsession Now. Once the FlashSession has completed, the postings to the various newsgroups should download to your system for reading offline at a later time.

How do I <u>search all the newsgroups</u>, not just the ones I'm subscribed to?

To search all newsgroups, click on the Search All Newsgroups button, and in the text field, type the text you want AOL to search for in the newsgroups.

 Note   When you invoke this type of search, AOL will only look at the Internet names, not the English names AOL uses to help describe the newsgroup. For example, if you search for "interactive," the comp.multimedia newsgroup won't be listed.

Can I <u>search newsgroup postings</u> through AOL?

You can search the subject line but not the text of each posting. To search the subject line, open any newsgroup window by clicking the Read My Newsgroups button. Next, select any of the groups you are currently subscribed to and choose Edit | Find. In the Find field, type the phrase you want to find in the subject lines of the postings, then click OK. A list of messages matching your criteria will appear.

Can I view an entire <u>thread of Usenet articles</u> on DejaNews?

First, search for a particular posting by keyword, then click an individual post. Click the Thread Search icon, or click the subject of the article. You should then see the entire thread pertaining to that article. This should include the original posting along with any follow-up articles posted.

With AOL's newsgroup reader, how can I <u>unmark messages</u> so they appear as unread?

First, click the Read My Newsgroups button and select the newsgroup where the messages you want to unmark reside. Next, click the List All button, and all the messages will appear, unmarked.

How many <u>Usenet articles</u> does DejaNews have?

Currently, DejaNews archives about 100 million articles, which accounts for more than 175 gigabytes of disk space. More articles are posted every day, so that number changes daily.

chapter

8 **A**nswers!

Chat on the Internet

Answer Topics!

Chat on the Internet @ a Glance

⇨ The Internet is all about communicating, whether it is with someone you know or with people worlds away you've never met. And real-time text chat can be found on just about any commercial service, including America Online (AOL) and CompuServe. **Commercial services' conferences and chats** let you chat with other members of the same service or, in many cases, with celebrities, sports figures, and specialists in particular fields. To participate in these chats you must use the client software provided by the online service.

⇨ **Web-based chatting**, on the other hand, requires only a Web browser and a keyboard if you want to chat away. Web-based chatting is catching on like wildfire since the introduction of Java-based browsers, which afford immediate updates from a chat server to your Web page of the text other users have typed.

⇨ The granddaddy of them all, the **Internet Relay Chat** network, is still going strong, offering text-based chats through specialized IRC servers and channels. Thousands of people from all over the world are chatting on the IRC every minute of the day, talking about everything from baking bread to online dating to configuring computers.

CONFERENCES AND CHATS
OFFERED BY COMMERCIAL SERVICES

? How do I get to the AOL chat rooms?

You get to AOL's chat rooms either through the People connection or by using the Chat option available in any section of AOL, as shown in Figure 8-1.

? How can I block all incoming messages on AOL?

If you don't want Instant Messages sent to your account, follow these steps:

1. Select Members | Send an Instant Message.

2. In the To field, type **$im_off**, as shown here:

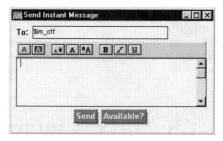

3. In the body of the Instant Message, type at least one character.

4. Click the Send button. You will be notified that you are now ignoring all Instant Messages.

5. Click the OK button to continue.

 Note   *When you turn off Instant Messages this way, they are only turned off for that particular logon session. They are not turned off permanently.*

? How do I keep my name off someone's Buddy List in AOL?

You can prevent others from monitoring your online activity by not allowing them to add your screen name to their Buddy Lists. To do that, follow these steps:

1. Select Members | Buddy Lists.

Figure 8-1. Entering a chat room while in an AOL area

2. Click the Preferences button.

3. Select Block All Members, or select Block Only These Members and supply the names of the members whose Buddy Lists you do not want to be on, as shown here:

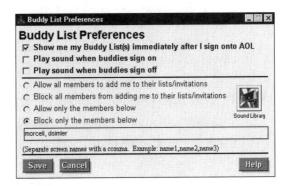

4. Click the Save button.

❓ Sometimes I can't get into my favorite chat room. Why not?

There are three main reasons you won't be able to get into a chat room. First, the chat room may have exceeded its limitations in terms of numbers of members it can accommodate. Second, the Parental Controls placed on the screen name through the master account may restrict your access to those particular chat rooms. Third, you may have been banned from a chat room for abusive or disruptive behavior.

? What's the difference between the CB Simulator and conference forums on CompuServe?

The CB Simulator offers real-time chat in an unstructured format. Conferences are held in particular forums on particular topics pertaining to that forum. Think of the conference forums as organized meetings on a particular topic and the CB Simulator as people milling about during a break, drinking coffee and socializing.

? How can I be notified of upcoming celebrity chats on AOL?

Subscribe to AOL's Live Guide. Use the keyword LIVE, then click the Intermission button. You should see a button for subscribing to the Live Guide. Once subscribed, every week you will automatically receive a listing of live events for that week in your AOL mailbox.

? Where can I go on AOL to chat with other people in my city?

One of the best places to go is Digital City. Use the keyword PLAZA, then click the Chat Channels button. Locate the City by City folder, and double-click to open it. This folder lists all the cities that offer city-to-city chats.

? Where can I go on CompuServe to chat with other users?

There are plenty of chat locations on CompuServe, but some of the major ones are listed here:

Forum Name	Keyword
CB Simulator	GO CB
General Chat Forum	GO CHATFORUM
Casual Adult Chat Forum	GO CHATAFORUM
Intimate Adult Chat Forum	GO ICHAT

? **Where can I find a <u>directory for all the chat rooms</u> on AOL?**

Just use the keyword LIVE, and you'll be taken to the Live area, which details chats that are currently in progress and those scheduled with various celebrities.

? **How do I <u>enter a conference</u> on CompuServe?**

First enter the forum that offers the conference you want to attend. Next click the Conference button on the toolbar. Click the Enter Room button. This will provide you with a list of all the rooms in the forum, as shown in Figure 8-2. Select the room you want to enter, and click the Enter button. You should start to see the text of the chat messages being sent back and forth, along with a list of participants off to the side.

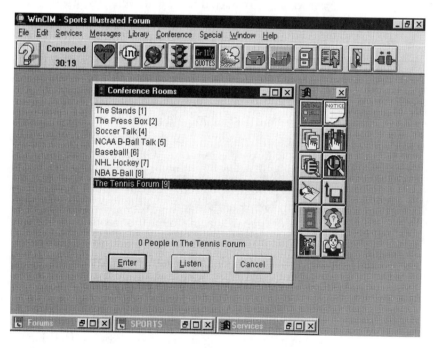

Figure 8-2.   Entering a conference room in CompuServe

? **How do I find people with similar interests on AOL or CompuServe?**

You can search the member directory by selecting the Members | Member Directory menu option on AOL or by using GO DIRECTORY on CompuServe. You can search by a wide variety of fields, such as Name, City, State, or Hobbies in the case of AOL. The service will return a list of members who meet your criteria.

? **How can I find out if one of my friends is on AOL and available to chat?**

You can do one of two things. Using the keywords BUDDY LIST, you can create your own Buddy List that will show you when your friends are online. Or, if you don't want to create a list, you can select Members | Locate a Member Online, and then type the member's screen name to see if she or he is signed on and in a particular chat room. If your friend is signed on, you can go directly to that chat room and talk to her or him, or you can send an Instant Message to chat privately.

? **What can I do about someone hassling me in an AOL chat room?**

The best thing to do is either click the Notify AOL button or use the keyword GUIDEPAGER and report the member's screen name to the America Online support guide, a live person who is online to help people with problems using AOL. You can also place a formal complaint in the Terms of Service area by using the keyword TOS. When reporting a problem, you can copy and paste the screen name and the context of the text the person sent you into the report form, or you can summon a guide to the chat room to view what is going on.

? **I can't hear the sounds other members are sending while they are chatting on AOL. How can I share in the fun?**

First, make sure your system can play sounds. You'll need a sound card and speakers in order to hear sounds. Second, make sure the volume is set so you can hear sounds by right-clicking the sound icon in the system tray and adjusting the sound levels. Third, you will need to enable sounds in AOL by selecting Preferences | Members, then clicking the Chat button. Next, check the "Enable chat room sounds" option and close the window.

Shortcuts for Common Phrases

LOL	Laughing Out Loud
ROTF	Rolling On The Floor (laughing)
AFK	Away From Keyboard
BAK	Back At Keyboard
BRB	Be Right Back
TTFN	Ta-Ta For Now!
WB	Welcome Back
GMTA	Great Minds Think Alike
BTW	By The Way
IMHO	In My Humble Opinion
WTG	Way To Go!

How many people can be in one AOL chat room at a time?

From 1 to 23 people can inhabit a single chat room. Conference rooms can hold up to 48, and the auditorium can hold as many as 16,000.

More Smileys

:)	smile
:D	smile/laughing/big grin
:*	kiss
;)	wink
:X	my lips are sealed
:P	sticking out tongue
{}	a hug
:(	frown
:'(	crying
O:)	angel
}:>	devil

❓ How do I ignore someone during a chat on CompuServe or AOL?

To ignore messages from certain people on CompuServe, click the Ignore button on the Conference toolbar, as shown in Figure 8-3. The Ignore button will then list all the members in the current forum's conference. If you want to ignore a member, click in the box next to the member's name. An X will be placed in the box, indicating you are ignoring any posts by that member. Click OK to continue. On AOL, the easiest way to ignore someone is to click the screen name in the list of participating members, then click the Ignore button. This will cause everything typed by that screen name to be ignored.

❓ How do I let other people know what my interests are?

Use the keywords MEMBER PROFILE, or select Members | Preferences, to fill out your member profile. A profile, shown in Figure 8-4, is available for each screen name you create.

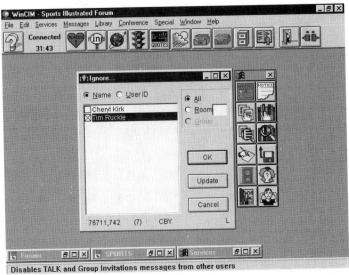

Figure 8-3.   Clicking the Ignore button to ignore another member on CompuServe

Edit Your Online Profile

To edit your profile, modify the category you would like to change and select
"Update." To continue without making any changes to your profile, select "Cancel."

Your Name:	C. Kirk
City, State, Country:	ANCHORAGE, AK USA
Birthday:	
Sex:	○ Male ○ Female ◉ No Response
Marital Status:	
Hobbies:	Computers, running, hiking, cross country skiing, writing, reading, DBM
Computers Used:	Macintosh & IBM
Occupation:	Computer Consultant/Writer
Personal Quote:	If you think you can, you can. But then again, now that I think about it...

Update   **Delete**   **Cancel**   **My AOL**   **Help & Info**

Figure 8-4.   Filling out a member profile

❓ After searching the member directory, how can I tell if someone is <u>online and available to chat</u>?

After searching the member directory, you will be shown a list of
members matching your criteria. Members with a little red pointer
next to their names are online. You can click their names and send
them an Instant Message, and they will immediately receive it on their
computer screens.

❓ How do I <u>play a sound</u> in a chat room?

In the text box where you normally send messages, type {S followed
by the name of the .wav file you want to play. The .wav file must be
stored in your \AOL directory. For example, if you have a .wav file
entitled hello stored in your \AOL directory, you would type {S **hello**
in the text message box, then click the Send button.

Note   *You don't need to include the .wav extension, and case is not
important. Also, in order for other members to hear this sound, they must
have the same file in their \AOL directory. You are simply signaling to their
computer to play the sound; you aren't sending this .wav file to them.*

? How do I record a CB Simulator conference?

First, select Special | Preferences | CB Simulator. Next, click the Record Channel or Record Group checkbox to record the conversation, and then click OK to save the changes. The conversation will be recorded in a text file stored in your \CIS directory.

? How do I save an AOL chat that's going on in a particular auditorium, conference, or chat room?

Select File | Log Manager. In the Chat Log section click the button labeled Open Log and provide a filename for this chat. Make sure you keep the chat window open, as shown here, if you decide to visit other areas of AOL. By doing so you will be able to record the text messages and still use other features.

When the chat is over, select File | Log Manager, and click the Close Log button.

? How can I save an Instant Message conversation on AOL?

You can save Instant Message conversations to a text file by following these steps:

1. Select File | Log Manager.

2. Click the Open Log button in the Session Log section and give the log file a name, then click Save.

3. Click the Log Instant Messages checkbox, then close the Log Manager window.

4. Continue conversing with your Instant Messages.

5. When you are finished and don't want to log any more messages, choose File | Log Manager, and click the Close Log button.

Note   *To read the transcript later, select File | Open and double-click the file you saved. The text of the messages should display in a separate window. However, if the file has grown to over 64K, it will not open, and you will have to use a word processing application to read the file.*

When I'm in an auditorium, if I send a message to someone in my row, will the entire audience see that message?

No. Only the people in your row will see your message. If you want to ask the emcee or the guest speaker a question, click the Interact with Host button for the auditorium, and type your question or message.

How do I start my own conference chat on CompuServe?

To start your own group conference, click the Invite button on the Conference toolbar. This will give you a list of all the members currently in that forum. To invite one of them, click an X next to the member's name, or click the All button to invite everyone, then click the Invite button. Soon members should be appearing in your conference window.

How do I talk to someone privately during a CompuServe chat?

Once you're in the forum's conference area, click Who's Here. This will show you a list of people currently participating in the conference. Click a name in the list to select the person you want to chat with. A little window will pop up with the person's name you've just selected. Type your private message in this window; no one else but you and the other member will see the message.

Where can I get a transcript of a chat I missed on AOL or CompuServe?

With AOL, use the keyword LIVE, then click the Intermission button or use the keyword INTERMISSION to go directly to the Intermission area. Click the Transcript button. From there you should be able to search for a particular transcript by day, topic, or speaker, or you can rummage through the Archives, which are sorted by date.

With CompuServe, check the forum's library where the conference was held, and either look for a transcript library or use a keyword to search for the name of the person who was in the conference you want the transcript for.

? **I've turned off Instant Messages on AOL. Now how do I turn incoming messages back on?**

To turn on Instant Messages once you've turned them off, follow these steps:

1. Select Members | Send an Instant Message.
2. In the To field type **$im_on**.
3. In the body of the Instant Message, type at least one character.
4. Click the Send button.

You will be notified that you are no longer ignoring all Instant Messages. Click the OK button to continue.

? **How do I whisper or send a private message in an AOL chat room?**

The easiest way is to send an Instant Message by selecting the Send Instant Message option from the Members menu and typing the name of the person you want to send the private message to.

Top Ten AOL Chats of All Time and the Number of Members Participating

Rosie O'Donnell	16,818
Michael Jackson	16,100
Pop Band Hanson	12,772
Spice Girls	6,172
Oprah Winfrey	5,702
Reba McEntire	5,166
No Doubt	4,119
Former LA Detective Mark Fuhrman	3,552
Michael Richards (Kramer on *Seinfeld*)	2,722
Former OJ Prosecutor Marcia Clark	2,646

? Can I use <u>wildcards and other search terms</u> when searching the member directory?

You can use the following wildcard characters if you are looking for members who meet certain criteria:

Wildcard	Purpose
* (asterisk)	Used to specify any number of characters to follow. For example, if you are looking for someone with a last name that starts with Harris, you would type **harris***. This would find all names with Harris in them, including Harris, Harrison, Harrisman, etc.
? (question mark)	Used as a wildcard for a single character. For example, if you don't know whether a person's name has an *I* or an *A* in it, you could use the ? wildcard, such as **H?RRIS**.
A single space	Used as an AND expression. For example, if you were looking for horse and riding, you would type **HORSE RIDING**
AND, OR, NOT (Boolean expressions)	Used to narrow searches. For example, if you were looking for someone who enjoyed snow skiing, but not water skiing, you would type **SKI NOT WATER**

WEB-BASED CHATTING

? How can I find out what all those <u>abbreviations and smileys</u> mean?

For a handy list, go to WBS.Net's Chatbook, located at **http://wbs.net/wbs3/flypaper/wbs/chat_book.html**. Here you can find out exactly what GTG, AYPI, CUIC, and LYLAB really mean.

? What are some of the <u>best Web-based chat sites</u>?

Thousands of chat sites are popping up everywhere, but the following table lists some of the more popular sites and their locations.

Site Name	Location
WBS.Net	http://www.wbs.net
The Palace	http://www.thepalace.com

Site Name	Location
ChatCom	http://www.chatcom.com
ChatBox	http://www.chatbox.com
ChatHouse	http://www.chathouse.com
Yahoo Chat	http://chat.yahoo.com
The Park	http://www.the-park.com
Café Utne	http://www.utne.com/cafe
World Without Borders	http://www.worldwithoutborders.com
Chat Soup	http://www.chatsoup.com
Chat Web	http://www.chatWeb.com
Chatalyst	http://www.chatalyst.com
Cool Chat	http://www.coolchat.com
Excite Chat	http://talk.excite.com
FreeTown	http://www.freetown.com
Keep Talking	http://talk.keeptalking.com

What's the difference between a bulletin board and a chat site?

Bulletin boards offer the ability to post messages that others can read at their leisure. A chat server displays text messages instantaneously as people type them; whereas with a bulletin board, you post a message and wait, sometimes days, sometimes weeks, for a reply. Also, most bulletin boards are not private, so everyone in the world will see your post. In other words, there is no way to have private conversations on public bulletin boards, whereas you can have private conversations on chat lines, as shown in Figure 8-5.

Why do colons appear in my posted reply?

The colons that appear in the message dialog box when you respond to someone else's message indicate that those lines are quoting the previous document.

Aren't the chat rooms really just for cybersex?

Many chat rooms are specifically for having cybersex or for chatting about dating and other relationship issues. However, cybersex is only a small portion of what goes on in chat rooms. Sites such as Electric

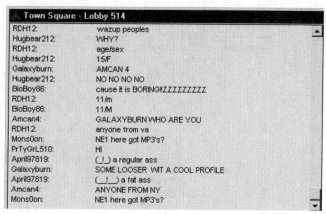

Figure 8-5.   A chat site with an ongoing real-time conversation

Minds, AOL, and CompuServe, along with WBS.Net, offer a variety of chat topics as well as celebrity chats.

? How do I find chat rooms and chat sites?

The best way to find a chat site is to use a directory search engine such as InfoSeek or Yahoo. Use the search term Chat, and you should be presented with a list of sites offering chat rooms and chat pages.

? What are some of the HTML tags I can use if a server offers such a feature?

Although you can use most standard HTML 2.0 tags with most chat servers that allow it, here are some of the more common tags you can use to emphasize your messages:

Format	Purpose	Tag
Bold	Emphasis. Formatted characters appear darker than other characters.	<B>*text*</B> Any text between the <B></B> appears as bold.
Italics	Often used to highlight a new term upon its introduction in the text. Also distinguishes quoted material or variable terms from surrounding text.	<I>*text*</I> Any text between the </I></I> appears as italics.

Format	Purpose	Tag
Font Size	Used to increase or decrease the size of the type being used	Two types of tags can be used—either Header tags or Font Size tags: <Font Size+1>*text*</FONT> increases the font size one size larger. <H1>*text*</H1> increases the font to a Level 1 heading. There are six heading styles available.
Blink	Makes the text blink on and off. Generally used for dramatic emphasis.	<BLINK>*text*</BLINK> Any text between the BLINK tags blinks on and off.

❓ What do I do if Internet Explorer doesn't work in some chat rooms and with some chat sites?

Internet Explorer 2.*x* and 3.*x* do not offer true "push" options that many chat servers use. Try using Internet Explorer 4.0, since that version offers the new push technology, or use Netscape Navigator version 2.*x* or above. Some sites also require Java, which is not an automatically installed plug-in for Internet Explorer 2.0. You'll need to download that plug-in to use Explorer 2.0 with Java-enabled chat sites. You can find the Java plug-in at **http://www.microsoft.com**.

❓ How do I put a link to a graphic on a Web-based chat site?

Usually it's just a matter of entering a World Wide Web URL, such as **http://www.Webserver.com/home/ckirk/dog.gif**. The URL must point to either a JPG or a GIF file.

❓ Is there a list of all the chat services on the Internet?

There are plenty of places that offer links to chat servers. One of the best is Emporium's Chat Links, located at **http://www.yepa.com/empo/empo.html**. You can also find a list of chat sites at Yahoo, located at **http://www.yahoo.com/Computers/World_Wide_Web/Communication/**.

? Why do I keep getting old messages when I enter a chat site?

Old messages may be part of an ongoing chat, or you may simply need to click the Chat button to see the new string of chat messages. Some sites you have previously visited may be retained in your browser's disk or memory cache. For example, in Netscape Navigator, to clear the disk and/or memory cache, follow these steps:

1. Select Options | Network Preferences.
2. Click the Cache tab.
3. Click Clear Disk Cache or Clear Memory Cache, as shown in Figure 8-6.
4. Click OK to continue, and if necessary, click the Reload button in your browser.

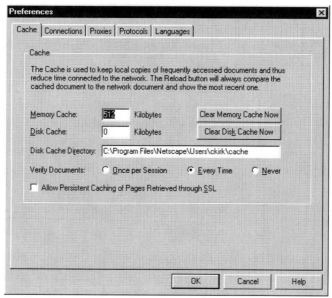

Figure 8-6.   Clearing the disk and memory caches

? Can I display <u>pictures</u> or use HTML tags in chat rooms?

It depends on the software used to serve up a chat room. Some chat servers allow for standard HTML tags. Those that offer HTML tags will also allow you to specify GIF or JPG files to include in your posting to the chat server.

? My <u>post doesn't show up</u>. What should I do?

Your post most likely did not show up because your browser did not reload the page; it simply pulled it out of cache. If you reload your browser, your post should appear.

? Do I have to <u>register</u> to start chatting?

Most services allow you to visit Web chat sites and read what others are saying. However, most will not allow you to post or interact with other members unless you are registered.

? How should I <u>set up my Netscape browser</u> so it works with most chat sites?

First you should probably clear both your disk cache and your memory cache by selecting Options | Network Preferences | Cache and clicking Clear Memory Cache and Clear Disk Cache. Also make sure you have the following options set in the Options | Network Preferences | Cache:

⇨   Verify Documents set to "Once per session"

⇨   Number of Connections in the Connections option set to 4

⇨   Network Buffer Size settings set to at least 50 Kilobytes

Also make sure the Options | Network Preferences | Languages option has both Enable Java and Enable JavaScript checked if you plan to use a Java-enabled chat room.

INTERNET RELAY CHAT

? What is a channel operator?

Channel operators maintain the channels they run. They can kick you out if they like, and they have great control over what and who goes on their channel. You can recognize channel operators by the @ symbol next to their nicknames.

? What channels always have conversations on them?

The two channels #hottub and #riskybus always have tons of people chatting up a storm, mostly about nothing in particular. #hottub is meant to simulate a hot tub, with people sitting around and kibbitzing. #riskybus is a nonstop game.

? Someone just told me to type a command I've never typed before. Can certain IRC commands damage my computer system?

Never type anything anyone tells you to without knowing what it is. Some programs, such as ircII allow someone else to gain control over the IRC client software with a few simple commands. Never type commands into an IRC client unless you know exactly what they will do and never allow someone else to control your IRC session remotely. Once they do, there is the potential for them to delete, copy or rename files on your computer.

? Why am I getting the message "Ghosts are not allowed on IRC"?

"Ghosts are not allowed on IRC" and a similar message,"You are not welcome on this server," mean that you are banned from using that server. This could happen for the following reasons:

⇨ You are banned specifically, possibly for inappropriate behavior, such as spamming, foul language, or for hassling other IRC users.

⇨   Your machine is banned, if you are using a university computer or a shared workstation at work, for example. This could happen if multiple users of the machine have been using the IRC channel inappropriately. Check with your system's administrator to find out who might have been using the equipment and if there can be a resolution to the ban.

⇨   Your whole site is banned. This could happen if there are flagrant abuses within your entire system.

❓ How does IRC work?

You, the user, use a "client" program to connect to a Web chat "server." The client connects to the IRC network via another server. Servers exist mainly to pass messages to and from users over the IRC network.

❓ Where can I go to get all the information about IRC?

The best place to go is the IRC Help site, located at **http://www.irchelp.org**. This site has the answers to just about any question regarding IRC, plus a listing of servers, software, and Frequently Asked Questions.

❓ Where can I find IRC client software for my computer?

You can find plenty of IRC clients at **ftp://ftp.undernet.org/pub/ undernet/clients/**. Or try some of the popular shareware repositories, such as Shareware.com, located at **http://www.shareware.com**; TuCows, located at **http://www.tucows.com**; or Windows95.com, located at **http://www.windows95.com**.

❓ What is an IRC operator?

IRC operators maintain the IRC network but are not channel operators, meaning they do not fix channel problems or kick people out of channels. They are mainly responsible for maintaining their end of the IRC network.

? How do I join a channel?

To join a channel simply type **/join #channelname**. Once you issue this command you should start to see the conversation taking place on this channel. Most likely you will be coming into the conversation somewhere in the middle. The best thing to do is to watch the conversation for a while. Don't just jump in and say, "Hi, what are you all talking about?" That not only wastes time but is annoying to those already involved in the conversation. You'll often find that most talk on certain channels has little to do with the actual subject name of the channel.

? How do I leave a channel?

When you want to leave a channel simply type **/part #channelname**. You will then be disconnected from the conversation of that channel.

? When I type the /list command, the screen scrolls by too fast. How can I slow it down?

In your client software there should be a "hold mode" or "scroll" option. To activate it, type **/set hold_mode on**. This will stop the screen from scrolling and allow you to press ENTER to view the next screen at your leisure.

? Is there a list of all the chat channels and what they have to offer?

There are plenty of lists, but the best one to check out is the Yahoo index of chat channels, located at **http://www.yahoo.com/ Computers_and_Internet/Internet/Chatting/IRC/Channels/**.

? Where can I see a list of IRC servers?

One of the best Web page listings available is NetPro Northwest IRC Servers and Channels, available at **http://www.sns-access.com/ ~netpro/irc_nets.htm**.

❓ Are there any IRC-related <u>newsgroups</u>?

There are plenty. Here is a list of the newsgroups and what they have to offer:

Newsgroup	What It Offers
alt.irc	General IRC questions, answers, comments and lots of flaming.
alt.irc.announce	Announcements of new IRC channels, servers, etc. Only a few postings will be listed.
alt.irc.bots	Information about IRC bots.
alt.irc.dalnet	Information about the DalNet IRC chat network.
alt.irc.games	Information pertaining to IRC-related games.
alt.irc.hottub	Specifically for the #hottub channel; discussions continue here when the chat is over.
alt.irc.opers	For IRC operators.This group may or may not be available to you through your ISP.
alt.irc.questions	If you have questions, this is the newsgroup to post to.
alt.irc.recovery	For all those IRC addicts who need help on the road to recovery.
alt.irc.undernet	Dedicated to answering questions about the Undernet, the alternative to the main IRC channels. The Undernet bypasses many of the rules and regulations of the main IRC channels.

❓ How do I use a <u>nickname</u> instead of my login name?

When you want to be known by a nickname instead of your login name, type **irc nickname**.

❓ How do I make sure I'm <u>notified</u> when someone I want to chat with logs on to an <u>IRC</u> server?

One way is to use the command **/notify** *nick*, where *nick* is the person's nickname. This will notify you the next time she or he logs on with that nickname.

? What do the **numbers before people's names** mean?

The numbers simply list the number of hops (servers) that person is from you. The larger the number, sometimes the longer the lag time before responses. Some IRC clients allow you to turn off this feature.

? What **port** should I use to connect to IRC?

In general, the port to use is 6667. Some IRC servers may be configured to listen to other ports, usually in the 6660-6670 range. If you are uncertain what port to use, simply use the default, port 6667.

? Which **server** should I connect my IRC client to?

The best server to connect to is one that is located within close geographic proximity. Once connected to a server, you can issue **switch to channel #irchelp**, which will give you a complete listing of currently available servers. To start, you might try one of the following:

Location	Server
United States	irc.bu.edu
	irc.colorado.edu
	piglet.cc.utexas.edu
Canada	irc.mcgill.ca
Europe	irc.funet.fi
	cismhp.univ-lyon1.fr edu
	irc.nada.kth.se
	sokrates.informatik.uni-kl.de

? How can I see what **servers are being used** between me and another user?

Use the command **/trace** *nick*, where *nick* is the nickname of the user. This will show you a list of all the servers between you and the other user.

? How do I start using IRC once I've downloaded the proper client software and started the program?

First be aware that all IRC commands start with a slash (/) and usually are only a single word long. When you first log on to a server, you might try typing **/help**. This will provide you with a list of commands along with their syntax. You can also type **/names** to get a list of channels available on that server. The word "Pub" next to a channel means public.

? Where can I find transcripts of IRC chat conferences?

On most commercial services you can find transcripts of most of the major chats they host. Several IRC chat conferences have been recorded in text-file transcripts. These include conferences on the 1994 San Francisco earthquake, the Gulf War, and the 1992 presidential election. You can find these chats archived at **http://urth.acsu.buffalo.edu/irc/ WWW/ircdocs.html** on the Web.

? What username and password do I use to connect to the IRC?

If you are being prompted for a username and password, most likely you are using Telnet. Telnet does not connect you to IRC servers. To connect to an IRC server, you need to use an IRC client.

? Someone is using my nickname. Can I do anything about it?

There are not enough unique nicknames for everyone on the IRC network to own his or her own name. If someone uses your nickname while you are not on IRC, you can ask the person using it to give it back. However, it is up to that person to give it back. Even channel or IRC operators cannot kill a nickname and give it to you.

? What is IRC?

The IRC is a network designed specifically for chatting and was originally created to replace the "talk" program available on Unix servers. With IRC you can talk to people all over the world in real time simply by typing messages back and forth. Originally created in 1988 by Jarkko Oikarinenin of Finland, it is among the oldest chat networks, with channels in over 60 countries. Other chat networks have since sprung up, such as Undernet, based in the United Kingdom.

New features of IRC have added the ability to write your messages in different colors, send sound files, and view GIF images of chatters, to name a few. IRC chats cover the gamut of breaking news events, such as earthquakes, political coups, and natural disasters, to simple time-wasting drivel.

? How do I keep my real name from showing up in parentheses when someone uses the /whois command?

The easiest way is to issue the command **setenv IRCNAME** *name*, where *name* is what you want to appear. If you don't want to type that every time you log in, put the line exactly as it appears here into your .cshrc file.

Interactivity, Multimedia Options, and Internet Telephones

Answer Topics!

Interactivity, Multimedia Options, and Internet Telephones @ a Glance

⇨   The quick and painless way to add a little multimedia interactivity to your browsing experience is to add **plug-ins** to your Web browser. Plug-ins are programs that embed themselves into your browser and are automatically invoked when the browser runs across a file the plug-in understands. For example, when a Web page that contains an embedded QuickTime movie file is accessed, if the QuickTime plug-in is installed, that QuickTime movie will automatically download, then play.

⇨   Besides using various plug-ins, another way to add some pizzazz to any Internet session is to try out the various **streaming audio and video** helper applications and plug-ins. Some of the more popular applications include RealAudio/Video, VDOLive, and Vivo. All you need is a multimedia PC to see and hear some pretty impressive sound and video clips and live audio and video broadcasts from around the world.

⇨   **Internet telephones** offer another fascinating multimedia adventure. The ability to talk into your computer's speakers and hear someone talk back is nothing less than amazing. And even more amazing than hearing is believing you can use this technology free of charge to talk to people anywhere around the world, as long as they are using the same or compatible software.

PLUG-INS

? **When I select the <u>About Plug-ins</u> menu option I get a blank page. I'm sure I must have some plug-ins installed. What's up?**

If you're using Netscape Navigator, first you need to make sure you have JavaScript enabled under the Options | Network Preferences | Languages tab, since the About Plug-ins option uses a JavaScript to display the plug-ins installed in your system. Once you have turned on JavaScript, as shown in Figure 9-1, try accessing the option again, or type **about:plug-ins** in the Location field.

? **Is there someplace I can go to find out what all the <u>acronyms</u> in browsers and plug-ins mean?**

Try the Acronym and Abbreviation list located at **http://www.ucc.ie/ acronyms/**. There you can type in the acronym, and the server will display what the acronym means.

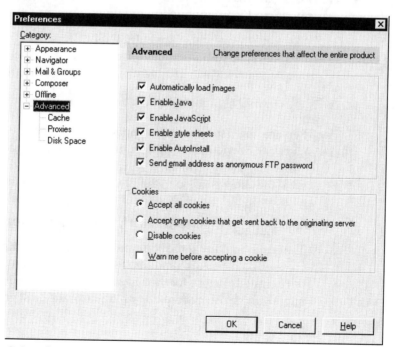

Figure 9-1.   Setting the Java options in your browser

? Why does this <u>Adobe.pdf</u> plug-in file not load?

This can happen when a .pdf file has not been optimized for slow downloads. This causes the Adobe Acrobat reader to time out before the file has had time to download. The first page may display, but subsequent pages may appear blank. You can opt to download the entire file to your hard disk, then use Adobe Acrobat to read the file offline later.

? When I try to install Internet Explorer I get the error message "Can't install plug-in if Netscape is not installed." What's the problem?

First check with the manufacturer of the plug-in to see if they have a plug-in especially created for Explorer, or available as what is called an ActiveX control. Or you can install Netscape Navigator as your default browser, then try installing the plug-in for Explorer. Some plug-ins require that you have Navigator installed and specified as the default browser.

? How do I <u>embed</u> a link to the location of a plug-in used on a Web page I've created?

You would want to use the PLUGINSPAGE parameter in your EMBED tag to tell users where they can go to get the plug-in, if they don't already have it. The tag would look much like this:

<EMBED PLUGINSPAGE="http://*servername*/*webpage*.html">

Replace **http://servername/webpage.html** with the location where users can download the plug-in. If the browser cannot find the plug-in within the user's browser, it will issue a warning and then let the user go to the URL specified in the PLUGINSPAGE parameter.

? How do I <u>find plug-ins</u> to work with my particular browser?

The best place to go is the home page for the manufacturer of the browser. Both Netscape and Microsoft provide links to companies that have created plug-ins for their browsers. The following sites specialize in offering links to just about every plug-in for the most popular browsers:

Site	Location
Internet Software and Browser Plug-Ins	http://www.bendnet.com/company/software.html
TuCows	http://www.tucows.com
Windows95	http://www.windows95.com
Shareware.com	http://www.shareware.com (search using the keyword PLUG-INS)
Plug-in Plaza	http://browserwatch.internet.com/plug-in.html
Windows 95 Plug-ins	http://members.aol.com/cbwin95/Webplugs.htm

Note   *You can also use the keyword PLUG-INS with your favorite search engine, or use the search string "title:plug-ins," which will display all the sites that have the word* plug-in *in the title of the page.*

What **hardware do I need** to run most of the common multimedia plug-ins, such as RealAudio, QuickTime or Netscape Conference?

You should have *at least* the following configuration in order to use multimedia plug-ins:

⇨ 486/66MHz computer (Pentium is always better)

⇨ 16MB of RAM (more is always better)

⇨ 2MB of hard disk space

⇨ Half-duplex sound card

⇨ Speaker and microphone (preferably noise reducing)

⇨ 28.8Kbps modem (the faster the better)

⇨ True 32-bit Winsock.dll Internet connection software

What's the difference between a **helper application** and a plug-in?

A helper application is a program that can understand and interpret files that your browser doesn't understand. It runs separately from your browser. Just about any program can be configured to run as a helper application. You configure helper applications to launch and execute when a certain type of file is encountered. When your browser is presented with an unknown file type identified in your configuration, the browser passes the file to the appropriate helper application, and the helper application is launched.

Plug-ins, on the other hand, can display or use the files they work with directly within the browser, acting as a kind of extension to your browser software. No new window is opened; instead, the file is opened directly in a browser window.

How many plug-ins are currently available for Netscape?

There are currently over 170 different plug-ins available, with more coming every day. Check the following Netscape Web page for a complete listing:

http://home.netscape.com/comprod/products/navigator/
version_2.0/plugins/index.html

What built-in plug-ins does Netscape Navigator contain?

With the new version of Communicator, the following plug-ins are installed:

File Types	File Extensions
Windows Video File formats, also now called LiveVideo	.avi
Sound file formats	aif, .aiff, .aifc, .wav, .au, .snd, .midi
QuickTime and Movie file formats	.qt, .mov
Virtual Reality Markup Language	Live3D

How do I use Navigator to find out what plug-ins are installed?

The easiest way to find what plug-ins are installed is to use the Help | Plug-ins option. This will display all the plug-ins currently installed, along with a link to the Netscape home page that will display other available plug-ins. You can also type **about:plugins** in the Location field of your Netscape browser to see the same page.

What are the most popular plug-ins?

There are literally hundreds of plug-ins you can get for your browser, whether you use Internet Explorer or Netscape Navigator. Here are the most popular plug-ins:

Plug-in	What It Offers	Where to Get It
QuickTime/QuickTime VR	Ability to play QuickTime movies and to view three-dimensional QuickTime virtual reality files.	http://quicktime.apple.com
RealAudio	Ability to play streaming and nonstreaming audio files. Many radio stations around the world have their live broadcasts connected to the Internet using RealAudio as the means of transmission.	http://www.real.com
ShockWave	Ability to play ShockWave files, which are basically animation files offering sound and interaction.	http://www.macromedia.com

? What does the puzzle-piece icon mean? I see it off and on when I view various Web pages.

That icon, which you can see here, represents a file that is not displayed because its associated plug-in is not currently installed in your browser.

Web sites will often outline exactly what you need to view pages within the site. Check the help page of the site, or try right-clicking on the puzzle-piece icon, to obtain more information about the needed plug-in.

? How can I reinstall plug-ins after I've deleted and reinstalled my browser software?

The best way to install plug-ins is to rerun the installation for that particular plug-in. If you'd rather chance it, you can copy the .dll file for that plug-in into the new directory where your browser resides, but you can't be sure this will invoke the entire plug-in.

? **Do I have to <u>restart</u> my system every time I install a new plug-in?**

No. All you have to do is type this in the URL location field:

javascript:navigator.plugins.refresh()

? **I've heard my <u>Sound Blaster</u> card is actually full-duplex. Could that be right?**

Yes. Older Sound Blaster cards were shipped full-duplex capable in the hardware, but with half-duplex drivers. To update your Sound Blaster driver software, check out the Creative Labs Web site at **http://www.creaf.com**.

? **My <u>system crashes</u> when I try to use multimedia options such as streaming video, audio, or Internet telephones. What could be the problem?**

It could be that your system has run out of system resources or memory. You should first make sure you run only the Internet connection and the multimedia application and that you don't launch any other programs that may be eating up system resources and memory. If you have to, restart your machine without any startup applications running; then connect to the Internet and launch the multimedia software.

If the multimedia application still crashes your computer, you could have a corrupted installation of that application. Fully remove the program, either through the uninstall application or through the Control Panel | Add/Remove Programs option, or by completely deleting the program and all its associated .dll files. If after a full clean installation you still have problems with your system crashing, there may be something wrong with your Windows 95 operating system. Defragment your hard drive, as shown in Figure 9-2, and run ScanDisk to see if that clears up problems. If it doesn't, reinstall a fresh copy of Windows 95 and make sure you have updated your system with the System Updates found on Microsoft's site at **http://www.microsoft.com**.

? **What kind of <u>video options</u> can I add?**

There are plenty, but the most widely used video options are listed here:

Plug-in	Company Web Site
RealAudio/Video	http://www.real.com
VDOLive	http://www.vdolive.com
CU-SeeMe (commercial version)	http://www.wpine.com
Streamworks	http://www.xingtech.com
QuickTime	http://quicktime.apple.com
Vivo Active	http://www.vivo.com

STREAMING AUDIO AND VIDEO

? **I'm getting the message "Error #40 Decoder type mismatch. Cannot load the requested decoder." What am I doing wrong?**

You probably have a previous version of RealAudio/Video installed. Although the installation process should have removed previous instances of RealAudio/Video, if your installation stopped in

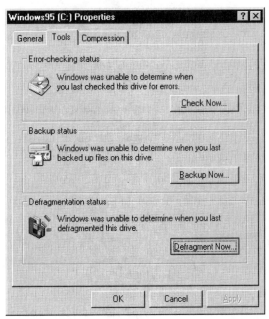

Figure 9-2.   Running the Disk Defragmenter

midstream, your system crashed, or you stopped the process manually, it may not have completed the deletion process of the older files. Now you will need to delete them manually and reinstall RealAudio/Video again. To do that locate the c:\windows\system directory and delete all the RealAudio/Video .dll files. Also delete the raplayer, if you are using Internet Explorer, and any files you find in the c:\raplayer directory.

? I have Internet Explorer and recently installed RealAudio, but I get all sorts of error messages when I try to listen to a RealAudio file. What's the problem?

RealAudio 2.*x* comes installed with Internet Explorer 3.*x*. If you want to upgrade to a newer version and avoid problems, you will first need to uninstall version 2.0 of RealAudio, then reinstall version 3.0. To fully remove RealAudio version 2.*x*, follow these steps:

1. Delete the raplayer from the c:\windows\system directory.

2. Next delete the following .dll files from the c:\windows\system directory:

   ra32.dll
   ra3214_4.dll
   ra3228_8.dll
   ra32dnet.dll
   ragui32.dll

3. Reinstall RealAudio 3.0 from the original compressed file.

4. Restart your system and reboot Explorer. RealAudio should work properly now.

? Why do I get "Error occurred while contacting Server" when I'm trying to use RealAudio? I'm using AOL or AT&T, CompuServe, or Netcom to connect to the Internet.

Usually, if the installation of RealAudio was successful, this error message means there is an incompatibility between the RealAudio or Video Player and the Internet dialer or Winsock file you are using. Most likely you are using a 16-bit Winsock with Windows 95. To fix this problem, either use the 16-bit version of RealAudio or Video for Windows 3.1, or upgrade your dialer or Winsock software to a 32-bit version.

? How do I configure RealAudio/Video if my network is behind a <u>firewall</u>?

First you should check with your network administrator to see if such data transmissions are allowed. If they are, RealAudio/Video 4.0 can automatically configure the settings for you if you follow these steps:

1. In your RealPlayer 4.0, click Preferences from the View menu.

2. In the Preferences window, click the Transport tab.

3. Click the Automatically Select Most Efficient Transport option.

4. Click the Auto-Configure button. The Automatic Transport Configuration window appears, as shown in Figure 9-3.

5. Click the OK button to run Auto-Configure.

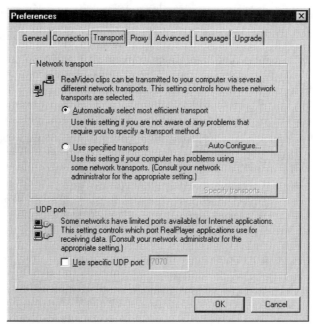

Figure 9-3.   The Automatic Transport Configuration window

Note   *If the Auto-Configure program finds an HTTP Proxy setup for Netscape Navigatior or Microsoft Internet Explorer, it uses that information to set up the HTTP Proxy information.*

What can I do to increase the transmission of streaming audio or video if I'm behind a firewall?

You should probably contact your network manager to see if there is a UDP port in your firewall that you can use to receive streaming audio and video and if there are any adjustments he or she can make to that port to allow for faster data transfer. You will need to include this UDP port number in the Setup, Settings, or Preferences of your streaming audio or video product.

How many frames per second can I expect to get with most streaming video?

It all depends on how fast your Internet connection is and how congested your ISP and server are. The following frames per second are assumed, based on a relatively uncongested network connection:

⇨   14.4Kbps modem can offer up to 2 to 3 frames per second

⇨   28.8Kbps modem can offer up to 8 to 12 frames per second

⇨   56Kbps modem can offer up to 10 to 15 frames per second

⇨   ISDN line can offer up to 20 frames per second

Where can I find a list of all the live RealAudio broadcasts going on right now?

There are several places you can go to find listings of live and recorded broadcasts for both RealAudio and RealVideo. Try the following locations:

Location	URL
TimeCast	http://www.timecast.com
AudioNet	http://www.audionet.com
Radio Tower	http://www.radiotower.com

? **I don't have the <u>minimum system requirements</u> for the latest RealAudio/Video player. Is there a version that will work with my computer?**

You can download previous versions from RealAudio's Archives, located at **http://www.real.com/products/player/blackjack**, or from their main site at **http://www.real.com**. Versions 1.0 and 2.0 didn't offer video, thus the system requirements were much less. You can try using these versions with older computers, but you must still have the following minimum requirements:

⇨ 486/66MHz computer

⇨ 16MB of RAM

⇨ 2MB of available hard disk space

⇨ Windows 3.1, 95, or NT

⇨ Sound card and speakers

⇨ 14.4Kbps modem

? **I'm getting a <u>"No Server"</u> error message when trying to use VDOLive. What's the problem?**

The server could be busy, or your Internet service provider may not support the UDP port option. Another reason you could encounter this problem is if you are using an incompatible Winsock.dll file. If you are using a dialer other than the Windows 95 Dial-Up network software, you should delete that dialer and use the Windows 95 dialer. Often, people use 16-bit Winsock.dll files with 32-bit Internet software, and this will always cause problems with applications such as VDOLive that rely heavily on the Winsock.dll file.

? **What can I do if the audio sounds like it is being <u>played too fast or too slow</u> on my Windows computer?**

If the audio sounds too fast or too slow, you will need to change the Advanced settings within RealVideo. To do that, select View | Preferences, then click the Advanced tab. Disable 16-bit sound or disable custom sampling rates.

? ## Where can I find a list of all the RealAudio error messages and what they mean?

You can find a list on the RealAudio support page, located at **http://www.real.com/help/errors/index.html**. If that location has changed, check the main site at **http://www.real.com** and look for a Service and Support link.

? ## When I try to play a RealAudio file, my browser downloads it instead of playing it. What gives?

You simply need to reconfigure your browser so it understands that you want to use the RealAudio or Video program instead of saving the .ra file to disk. You may have previously received a warning telling you there was a security risk and asking if you wanted to download the file instead of launch the application used to play the file. If this is the case, follow these steps to correct the problem:

1. Launch your Netscape browser.

2. Select Edit | Preferences and click on the Applications option under Navigator, as shown in Figure 9-4.

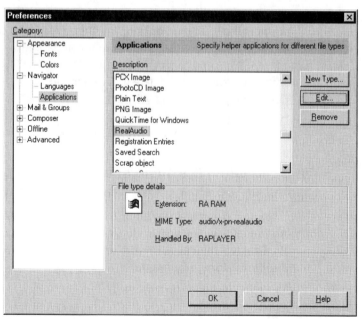

Figure 9-4.   Netscape's Preferences Application option

3. Locate Raplayer File in the Applications listing and click to select it.

4. Click the Edit button, then click the circle to the left of the Application category.

5. Click Browse to locate the raplayer.exe file in your computer's directory.

6. Uncheck the option "Always ask before opening."

7. Click OK, then OK again to save your changes, and try playing the RealAudio file again.

? I'm getting a message that my RealAudio/Video player has expired. Do I need to purchase a new one?

Most likely you've downloaded a trial version that needs to be upgraded to the most recent version. Unless you want to purchase the Player Plus, you don't need to buy a thing. Simply go to the RealAudio/Video site at **http://www.real.com** and download the latest player, not the Player Plus. The standard players are always free.

? When I start viewing a streaming video file, the reception rate drops dramatically. What's the problem?

There is no problem. It's just the way VDOLive makes the adjustments as it figures out the total amount of bandwidth your system can accommodate. VDO streams the data to a small buffer file on your computer. By doing this, VDO can allow the server to adjust the quality of the reception. In the meantime, the player begins to play the video file from the buffer, slowly deleting the buffer until it's completely empty. When this buffer file is emptied, the player will then adjust the actual bandwidth of the connection, scaling down the amount of bandwidth your connection will receive.

? Why does RealPlayer 4.0 continue to show it's rebuffering? I don't seem to hear a lot of loss in the audio coming over. It sounds pretty normal.

If you are experiencing rebuffering with RealPlayer 4.0, but you do not appear to be experiencing any packet loss, this may be due to low bit rates or a slow connection speed. You may also receive errors about poor system performance. You can check the difference between your connection speed and the requirements for the file you are playing. To determine your connection speed and the rate required for the clip, follow these steps:

1. Open RealPlayer 4.0.

2. Select Statistics from the View menu. You'll see a window that looks something like this one:

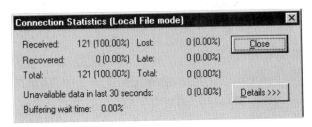

3. Click the Details button in the Statistics window. Under Bandwidth, the top option, Clip displays what bandwidth in bits per second (bps) the file requires, and Current displays what bandwidth or connection rate you are using to connect to your ISP.

The behavior you are experiencing is generally caused by thin bandwidth; thus the player cannot support the file you are trying to play.

I recommend you contact your ISP or system administrator regarding improving the quality of the connection in order to provide a consistent connection at a bandwidth capable of supporting the file format you expect to use. This should be based on the speed of the computer's CPU and the bit rate of the connection, such as a 28.8Kbps modem or a direct network connection such as a T1.

? Can I run other applications while I'm receiving streaming audio or video?

Yes you can, but the sound and video quality may suffer. Also, applications using the same Internet connection will compete with the streaming video/audio application, causing delays or glitches in the sound. Some applications, such as VDOLive, are set to play in the foreground, meaning they will pop up over other applications and cause you either to watch/listen to them or minimize their window so you can continue working with your computer. Be aware that such applications use the computer's processing power, causing applications to slow somewhat.

? I'm getting <u>"Server Busy"</u> or "Unable to Connect to Server" messages. What's wrong?

Most likely the server has maxed out the number of connections it can accommodate. You can try again later, or possibly try to find another station offering the same broadcast on a different server. If you consistently get this error message, contact the server administrator and report the error. The administrator may not be aware that others are having problems connecting and that the number of streams needs to be increased.

? How can I improve the <u>sound quality</u> of RealAudio/Video?

Several factors could cause problems with the quality of sound. First, the traffic on the Internet may be very busy, causing glitches and dropouts. The site or your Internet service provider may be the culprit. The best thing to do is try connecting to another RealAudio site. If you experience the same poor audio quality, contact your ISP and let them know you are having problems; your ISP may be overloaded with traffic or using a slow link to connect the network to the Internet. If the ISP cannot resolve the problem, look for another ISP. There are differences in speed of connections with ISPs.

Second, make sure you are not doing anything to interfere with the quality, such as downloading large files, browsing lots of Web pages, or taxing your computer's processing power by running processor-intensive applications. These sorts of things will also affect the quality of your sound.

Third, make sure your hard disk and software are in proper working order. Use ScanDisk, defragment your hard drive, and clear out your memory and disk caches on a regular basis. Finally, try upgrading the speed of your modem, if possible, and make sure the settings for your modem are correct.

? What are the neatest <u>streaming audio and video</u> applications I can buy?

By far that's got to be Onlive's Talker program. Dressed up as an avatar head, you enter a three-dimensional world and float around talking to other people in real-time voice. When you move away from someone, their voice gets fainter; move closer, and their voice booms over your speakers. It's truly an amazing program that is used to chitchat about Monday night football games during the season. Check out Onlive's Web site at **http://www.onlive.com** for more information or to download the software. The hardware requirements may limit some users from using the application.

❓ What are the average <u>system requirements</u> for using most streaming audio or video plug-ins or applications?

Although some products, such as Intel's Internet Video Phone, require at least a Pentium, most streaming audio and video products can work with the following minimum requirements:

- ⇨ 486/66MHz computer
- ⇨ 16MB of RAM
- ⇨ 2MB of free hard disk space
- ⇨ 14.4Kbps modem
- ⇨ Windows 3.1, 95, or NT operating system
- ⇨ Half-duplex sound card
- ⇨ Speakers

❓ <u>VDOLive doesn't work</u> with my Windows 3.1 computer. What's wrong?

Most likely you are using an older version of Trumpet Winsock. VDOLive only works with Trumpet 2.1 Rev. F. If you are using any other version of Trumpet Winsock, such as version Trumpet 2.0 Rev. B, a widely used freeware version, you need to upgrade to Trumpet 2.1 Rev. F.

❓ What can I do to improve the <u>video images</u> I get in RealVideo?

Besides having a fast Internet connection, there are a few other things you can do to improve the video quality:

- ⇨ Set your monitor to thousands or millions of colors.
- ⇨ Close all applications other than RealVideo and your Internet software running on your system.
- ⇨ Make sure the image is not zoomed in.

? Can I get a <u>virus</u> from using streaming audio or video products?

Probably not, unless you are using an Internet telephone product that allows you to transfer files from one Internet phone user to the next. Just the process of downloading a live or saved streaming audio or video file, however, cannot give you a virus.

INTERNET TELEPHONES

? Will a <u>56Kbps modem</u> give me better sound quality when using Internet phone or streaming audio or video programs?

Maybe. The 56Kbps modems send data back to you at 56Kbps but do not send data from your computer at the same speed. The data will come back from your service provider faster, but your speech will not go back to the server faster. So, although you will get better transmission with streaming audio if the server you are connected to offers high transfer rates, your Internet phone program probably won't give you substantially better quality than with 33.6Kbps modems.

? I'm getting the error message "<u>Another version of Internet Phone is probably running.</u>" I've checked and I'm only running one copy. What's wrong?

This error message can occur when you aren't connected to the Internet or when you are running a 16-bit Winsock version. It can also occur if you have moved the wsock32.dll file to a different location or if you have more than one wsock32.dll file. Double-check to make sure you have the proper version of Winsock installed and that it's in the right location.

? Can I use <u>AOL and CU-SeeMe</u> together?

Yes, but only if you have AOL version 3.0 for Windows 95 (or later). Previous versions of the AOL software did not offer compatibility with CU-SeeMe. You can find out what version you are using by selecting Help | About AOL, as shown in Figure 9-5.

Figure 9-5.   Finding out the version of AOL

**?   I keep hearing a buzzing sound when I'm using my
Internet phone program. What could be the problem?**

First, check to make sure the volume control on your speakers is not
turned up all the way. Second, make sure you don't have any
electromagnetic interference causing havoc with your modems. Some
large monitors may interfere with speakers, as can power cords and
some power supplies.

**?   With VocalTec's Internet Phone I keep getting a "can't
connect to a server" message. I know I'm connected to
the Internet, so what's wrong?**

VocalTec's Internet Phone uses the Global On-line directory to connect
you to Internet phone servers so you can see and talk to other users
around the world. If the first server it tries is busy or full of users, it
will continue down the list to connect to another server. If you
consistently have problems connecting, that probably means you
don't have the latest list of Internet phone servers in your Global
On-line directory. You should check VocalTec's Web site at
http://www.vocaltec.com for an updated list of servers you can
download and instructions on how to update your existing server list.

? **When I use my Internet phone program, people say they can't hear me, and I don't seem to be able to record any sounds. What's wrong?**

You could have a problem with your microphone, especially since you can't record any sounds. Here are a few things you should check to ensure the microphone is working:

⇨ Make sure the microphone is turned on if it has an on/off switch.

⇨ Make sure the microphone and speakers are securely plugged into their connections.

⇨ Make sure your speakers are turned on, or that the batteries are fully charged.

⇨ Make sure the volume is up for both the microphone and speakers.

⇨ Check that the mixer application that came with your sound card has been set to have the microphone turned on.

⇨ Make sure you have a sound card and microphone installed and listed in the Device Manager, located in the Start | Settings | Control Panel | System settings. If it is installed but simply isn't working properly, try reinstalling the sound card and microphone drivers.

? **I've tried to connect with one of these Internet phone programs, but I can't hear the other person. What's wrong?**

There could be a couple of things wrong. First, have you checked to make sure you can hear sound coming from your speakers? Try using your mixer application or the Control Panel | Sounds option to play sounds. If you hear sound from your speakers, the problem is probably on the other end. Try sending a message or e-mail message to the other party and ask her or him to check the following:

⇨ The VOX or automatic Talk trigger is set properly so it picks up the person's voice.

⇨ The microphone level is not set too low—so low it isn't picking up any sound.

⇨ The microphone has not been disabled by other sound applications. Also, just in case, check to make sure the microphone is turned on.

⇨ Use the Test Microphone feature of the Internet phone program to make sure the software is picking up the sound.

? **I can't seem to connect to anyone using my favorite Internet phone program. I'm trying to use it behind our company's firewall—could that have something to do with it?**

Most likely your network administrator does not allow those types of packets to be passed through the network. Contact your network administrator and tell him or her that Internet phone uses UDP port 22555 to enable calls.

? **When I'm using an Internet phone program, the voice coming over the other end sounds choppy. How can I fix that?**

First, you may just be experiencing problems with the Internet traffic. If possible, try contacting that individual at another time. If you think the connection is the problem, try reconnecting. If that still doesn't help, you might want to contact your ISP to find out if there are problems with their connections.

You can also try making sure the VOX level, or the level that picks up voice, is set correctly. If it's too high, Internet phone programs will often drop off sound. Also, if you are running other Windows applications, exit these applications. Many Internet telephone programs make big use of the computer, and the more applications taxing the CPU the more choppiness you'll hear.

If your Internet telephone software offers adjustable settings to compensate for dropouts, choose this option. This will cause delays, but you will hear more of the conversation.

? **When I'm using CU-SeeMe, why do I hear clicking and beeping sounds? It's really annoying.**

Nothing is wrong with your computer. You simply have the option turned on that notifies you when members join a conference. You can turn this option off by selecting Edit | Preferences | Conferencing and deselecting "Click when participants join."

? **What is a codec?**

A codec, which stands for compression/decompression, is a piece of software that compresses and then decompresses your voice. It's basically an algorithm that figures out the best way to compress and decompress the sound based on the type of machine and bandwidth used. One way to get better sound from any multimedia application or Internet phone application is to adjust what codecs are used based on the particular machine and setup.

How can I tell whether my connection is fast enough—and relatively noise-free?

There's a great Web site run by Onlive Technologies, the creators of Talker, an interactive audio chat program. You'll find the test site at **http://www.onlive.com/cgi-bin/nettest.cgi**. Just let the page do its work, then give you the averages of packet loss which gives you an indication if your connection is fast enough and free of noise, drop-outs and glitches. Information about the chart presented is listed at the bottom of the page.

I'm getting a "Connection Lost" error message when I use my Internet phone program. What could be the problem?

A "Connection Lost" message usually means the traffic between you, the other person, and/or the server is very heavy. This is called packet loss and can cause lost connections, glitches, and dropouts of conversations. The only remedy is to use the Internet when traffic is much lighter or investigate a new provider that offers faster network connections.

I'm using a Connectix QuickCam to talk to other people over Intel's Video Phone. Is there anything I can do to increase performance?

You will see a noticeable decrease in performance of your system because QuickCam uses the parallel port and your computer and hard drive to decode and display video and audio. Make sure you have the latest versions of the Connectix QuickCam drivers to ensure the fastest performance. You can find updated drivers at **http://www.connectix.com**.

Why do I get the error message "CUSEEM32 caused an exception 10H in module PMJPEG32.DLL at 0137:4000c954" when I try to use CU-SeeMe?

This means you are probably using an old M-JPEG driver and simply need to upgrade to the new driver. You can download the driver update/patch directly from this site: **http://support.cuseeme.com/ CU_docs/pmjpeg_patch.exe.**

❓ Can I use Internet phones to <u>dial someone's computer directly?</u>

Yes. Almost all Internet phone programs let you call another user directly if you know their Internet Protocol address—the number assigned to each computer once it connects to the Internet. Some software even lets you use an e-mail address to connect to the other user.

❓ I get the error message <u>"Directory server could not be found"</u> when I try to connect and make a NetMeeting call. <u>What's wrong?</u>

This may happen for several reasons. First, the directory server you are using may be down. Try connecting to another server. If you don't get any results, you may be using a 16-bit Winsock connection to your ISP. If you have been using previous versions of Trumpet Winsock with your Windows 95 software, you should install the Windows 95 TCP/IP software and remove the old 16-bit Trumpet Winsock software.

You might also get this error message if you are trying to connect to another NetMeeting user through a proxy server. Check with your network administrator to see if the proxy server is preventing you from sending and receiving NetMeeting data. One last reason could be that you've closed NetMeeting. Open it up again, and you should have no problem connecting.

❓ I'm talking along fine, then all of a sudden the other person stops talking. How can I tell if he or she has been <u>disconnected from the Internet?</u>

Most Internet phones will not alert you when the other party has lost the Internet connection. You will simply see an error message stating that he or she is no longer available. Look for these signs that the person has been disconnected:

⇨   There is no audio.

⇨ The activity indicator does not show any activity.

⇨ When using a video phone, the image of the other person remains frozen.

❓ When I talk to someone, I can hear my voice <u>echo</u>. What's the problem?

If you can hear your own echo as you talk, it usually means that the person you're talking to is using a full-duplex audio card. You might suggest they turn off the full-duplex option or lower the speaker volume setting. Ask them to keep the microphone away from the speakers and, if possible, to use the manual switch on the microphone or software. Using a headset also helps.

❓ What does <u>full-duplex</u> mean?

Full-duplex means you can listen and speak at the same time. Full-duplex sound cards allow you to have a conversation as you would on a telephone—you don't have to wait for the other person to stop talking before you talk, as you do on a speaker phone.

❓ How do I tell if my sound card is <u>full-duplex</u>?

Your sound card may be, but the software drivers that make the sound card work may not be. First, check with the manufacturer of the sound card to make sure you have the most up-to-date sound card drivers. Next, follow these steps to see if you can record and play sound at the same time:

1. Click Start | Programs | Accessories | Multimedia, and choose Sound Recorder.

2. Repeat step 1 to start a second Sound Recorder session.

3. In the first Sound Recorder session, try playing a sound or .wav file that lasts at least 30 seconds. There are plenty of sound file examples in the multimedia directory.

4. While the first session of Sound Recorder plays, switch to the second session of Sound Recorder and try recording a .wav file with your microphone.

If you successfully recorded and played two files at the same time, your sound card is full-duplex compatible. If not, you may not have the proper hardware or software.

❓ Is a <u>full-duplex sound card required</u> to use Internet phones?

No. All you need is a half-duplex sound card, speakers, microphone, and a computer capable of running the software. The only advantage of a full-duplex sound card is that you don't have to wait for the other person to stop speaking before you start speaking.

❓ Why doesn't my <u>full-duplex sound card work with NetMeeting</u>? I'm only getting half-duplex.

This could be caused by several things:

⇨ Your sound card was shipped with half-duplex drivers. Check the manufacturer's Web page for more information about updated sound card drivers.

⇨ You may not have enabled full-duplex in NetMeeting. Check Tools | Options, then click the Tab button. Make sure the Enable Full Duplex Audio checkbox is checked.

⇨ Background noise may be overloading the sound card, so that it has dropped down to half-duplex. Try adjusting your volume settings, or tell those noisy people to be quiet!

❓ Can you give me the names of some <u>good books</u> on Internet telephones?

Glad you asked. Without a doubt, the best one on the market is *The Internet Phone Connection*, by yours truly, Cheryl Kirk (Osborne/McGraw-Hill, 1997). Anything you'd ever want to know about Internet telephones, I've tried to include in this book—in a straightforward, non-techie style. It's a must-have if you plan to use Internet phones.

❓ Can you tell me what <u>hardware products are compatible with CU-SeeMe</u>?

You can find that list at the Cornell FAQ site, located at **http://support.cuseeme.com**. You can also check out White Pine's Web site, makers of the commercial version. Their site is located at **http://www.wpine.com**.

? How can I **improve the video** in NetMeeting?

There are several things you can do:

⇨ Make sure you are not running other programs in the background, including Internet Explorer.

⇨ Increase the camera lighting.

⇨ Try reducing the size of the video image. Smaller images mean better quality and faster send and receive rates. To change the size of your image, select Options | Tools and click the Video tab. Select Small in the Send Image Size area, then click OK.

⇨ Increase the amount of RAM you have in your computer.

⇨ Get a faster modem on both ends.

? Why did I receive the error message "An internal fatal error has occurred" when using Intel's Video Phone?

Intel's Internet Video Phone uses TCP/IP, which must be started first before running the Video Phone. If it is not, you might receive the message "An internal fatal error has occurred." If you have any question about whether TCP/IP is running, start your browser and view a page. If you can view a page, TCP/IP is running.

? How can I find out if one **Internet provider will be better** than another when using an Internet phone program?

You can ask your friends or request a network map from the prospective providers. You can also use a simple program called tracert to trace how many hops it takes to get from point A to point B. The more hops, or computing/networking devices, between two points, the more likely you will have delays, dropouts, and glitches in your Internet phone application. To check your connection follow these steps:

1. Select Start | Programs | MS-DOS Prompt.

2. In the MS-DOS Prompt window type **tracert** *domain name* and press ENTER.

3. Count the number of hops, as shown in Figure 9-6. (Your listing will look different.)

? How do I know what the IP address of my computer is?

To determine whether an IP address is assigned, type **winipcfg** in the Start | Run dialog box, as shown here, then click OK.

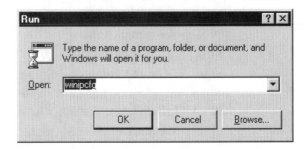

? Will I be able to run an Internet phone application if the winipcfg program says my IP address is 0.0.0.0?

An address of 0.0.0.0 means your system either is not connected to the Internet or the application you are using, such as early versions of

```
MS-DOS Prompt                                                    _ 5 X
  Auto    ▾  ☐ ▣ ▣ ▣ ▣ ▣ A

Microsoft(R) Windows 95
    (C)Copyright Microsoft Corp. 1981-1996.

C:\WINDOWS>tracert flex.net

Tracing route to flex.net [205.218.188.1]
over a maximum of 30 hops:

  1      *          *          *       Request timed out.
  2    117 ms     112 ms     122 ms   4700-1-e0.anchorage.ptialaska.net [198.70.245.25
4]
  3    262 ms     260 ms     211 ms   border6-serial3-0.Seattle.mci.net [204.70.205.69
]
  4      *          *        455 ms   core2-fddi-1.Seattle.mci.net [204.70.203.65]
  5    441 ms     403 ms     271 ms   core3.Memphis.mci.net [204.70.125.1]
  6    249 ms     276 ms     240 ms   core1-hssi-2.Houston.mci.net [204.70.1.33]
  7    276 ms     423 ms     243 ms   border4-fddi-0.Houston.mci.net [204.70.3.99]
  8    237 ms     270 ms     267 ms   flexnet-inc.Houston.mci.net [204.70.39.50]
  9    299 ms     267 ms     261 ms   flex.net [205.218.188.1]

Trace complete.

C:\WINDOWS>
```

Figure 9-6.   Checking the number of hops with tracert

AOL, does not truly connect your computer to the Internet. This usually means you cannot use an Internet phone, mainly because almost all Internet phone programs require you to use a true Internet connection that assigns an IP address once connected.

? Where can I find a list of all the Internet telephone products available on the Internet?

There are several, but you might check **http://www.alaska.net/~ckirk** or **http://www.von.com** for listings of most of the commercial products available.

? Do I have to pay long distance charges to use Internet telephones or programs like CU-SeeMe?

The only thing you have to pay for is your connection to the Internet. If, however, you dial a long distance number to reach your Internet service provider, normal toll charges apply.

? Can I control who lurks and who can be part of my CU-SeeMe conference?

You can elect not to answer a call, or you can disconnect the person from your conference if you are setting up your own conferences. However, if you are using a reflector to connect, only the person managing the reflector has that ability.

? My mouse seems to be really jumpy every time I use CU-SeeMe. What could be the problem?

The mouse pointer is actually part of the display. Some mice will jump more than others. First, make sure you have enough RAM; too little can cause a jumpy mouse. Second, make sure you have the updated mouse driver for your operating system. If those two things don't clear up the problem, investigate getting a better mouse.

? Why doesn't my name appear in the list of participants while I'm in a CU-SeeMe conference?

Many of the reflectors will not display your name in the list of active participants. As long as you can see and hear other participants, you are being seen and heard by them.

? How can I get NetMeeting to work on my AOL account?

You can use NetMeeting and AOL as long as you have the AOL version 3.0 software for Windows 95, *not* Windows 3.1. This version of AOL installs all the proper TCP/IP networking connections needed for NetMeeting and AOL to work. You can find out if you are using version 3.0 or above by selecting Help | About AOL from the AOL main menu.

? All I get is a black screen when I use NetMeeting's video. What's wrong?

Your video capture card may not be configured properly or may not support NetMeeting's video format. Your card may also be using the video overlay mode. Video overlay mode is not supported by Microsoft NetMeeting 2.0. You should configure the card to use one of the supported formats for NetMeeting. Those formats are RGB4, RGB8, RGB16, RGB24, and YVU9.

? Does Netscape Conference support full-duplex audio?

Yes, if your audio card has full-duplex audio drivers. If your audio card only has half-duplex audio drivers, Conference will perform auto-switching. With auto-switching, it isn't necessary for the user to manually switch between talking and listening, as Conference will do this automatically. Alternatively, you can install two sound cards and use one for recording and the other for playback. Check with your audio card manufacturer for availability of full-duplex drivers.

? Can I use one Internet phone program to talk to someone using another Internet phone program?

Probably not. Although some Internet phone programs now offer the H.323 compression standard, most programs are not interchangeable. If you want to avoid hassles, don't try to use two different products.

? If I open lots of windows with CU-SeeMe, does that consume more bandwidth?

Most definitely. Every open window consumes bandwidth. If you are only talking to one other person, close all the other open windows to conserve bandwidth.

Note   What is bandwidth? Just as different roads have different speed limits, network lines used to send digital information from one computer to another have their own speed limits. These electronic speed limits are known as bandwidth. Bandwidth is the transmission capacity of a computer or communication channel usually measured in bits per second. Higher bandwidth means information is transmitted at a faster speed.

Can I set up a private CU-SeeMe conference?

Sure. All you have to do is connect to the other person using his or her IP address. You don't need a reflector, just another person ready to chat and the IP number.

Where can I find a list of active reflector sites for CU-SeeMe?

Try these two Web pages:

Michael Sattler's Comprehensive List	http://www.indstate.edu/msattler/ sci-tech/comp/CU-SeeMe/reflectors/ nicknames.html
People'sNet Reflector-Scanner	http://www.face2face.com/CU-SeeMe/

Why does my computer slow down to a crawl while I'm talking to someone using an Internet phone program?

Most likely you are recording your conversation. Double-check to make sure the Internet phone program you are using is not recording every word you say.

I have a Snappy that takes still pictures. Is there any way to make it compatible with CU-SeeMe?

You're in luck. A gentleman by the name of Bill Neisius developed a program called CU-Doodle that will make hardware such as the Snappy compatible with CU-SeeMe. You can find out more about CU-Doodle from the CU-SeeMe customer support page located at **http://support.cuseeme.com/H208.HTM**, or you can download it straightaway from **ftp://ftp.netcom.com/pub/ne/neisius/cudoodle.zip**.

What's the best sound card to use with Internet phones?

The best sound card to use is something that is Sound Blaster-compatible.

❓ What can I do to get better <u>sound quality</u> with my Internet phone program?

You might try turning on Automatic Gain Control (AGC), a feature built into your sound card that boosts the microphone sound level automatically when you talk. AGC can also reduce the level of background noise it picks up when you aren't speaking. Consult the software for your particular sound card, or the help file for that sound card, for information on how to turn on AGC. Each sound card differs in the way AGC is turned on.

❓ Can I use my Internet connection to talk to people on their <u>standard telephones</u>?

Yes. And amazingly this type of connection offers relatively good voice quality. Check out the best of the bunch, NetiPhone at **http://www.netiphone.com**, or try Net2Phone, located at **http://www.net2phone.com**.

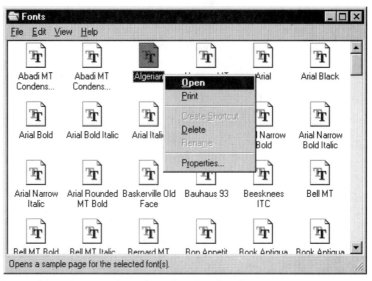

Figure 9-7.   Checking your fonts for damaged font files

❓ My computer <u>stops responding after I launch NetMeeting</u>. Any suggestions?

You may have problems with damaged TrueType fonts. What you need to do is remove the "Fonts for the Family" fonts from the Windows\Fonts directory. You can tell if you have damaged fonts by double-clicking each font in the Fonts folder, as shown in Figure 9-7. If the computer hangs when opening a particular font for display, that font is damaged. You should delete that font and reinstall.

❓ Why does my <u>system beep</u> every time I start CU-SeeMe?

A beep on startup tells you CU-SeeMe cannot find either your video digitizer, the software drivers, or a camera attached. If you have your camera turned off, make sure you turn it on before launching CU-SeeMe to avoid the beeping.

❓ Why does it say my <u>"Video Components cannot be found"</u> when I'm trying to use CU-SeeMe? I know other programs work fine.

Most likely you have your monitor's color depth set too deep. You should set the total number of colors to display through your Control Panel | Display option to no more than 256.

❓ Can I use AOL with Intel's <u>Video Phone?</u>

Intel's Internet Video Phone will not work on any version other than 3.0 of the AOL software. You can check the Help | About AOL menu option to find out what version of AOL you are currently using. If you need to upgrade, use the keyword UPGRADE with AOL versions other than AOL version 3.0 for Windows 95. Other versions do not provide for AOL's servers to assign an IP address to your current session.

Also, for users accessing AOL using a local Internet provider, and accessing their service for content only, the Intel Internet Video Phone with ProShare technology needs the local Internet provider to assign an IP address for the current session.

Searching the Internet

Answer Topics!

Searching the Internet @ a Glance

⇨   Finding information on the Internet can sometimes be an overwhelming chore. With literally millions of sites available, knowing **where to search and how to fine-tune your searches** are the keys to preventing information overload. The best way to find something on the Internet is to know which search engine to use and how to limit your searches.

⇨   But wacky Web pages probably aren't the only things you're in search of. You're probably also interested in **searching for people, files, great clip art, and other things**. There are plenty of places offering search engines for specific types of information you might be interested in finding.

Note   *Don't miss the sidebars. They point you to all sorts of category-specific search sites.*

⇨   If you plan to stake a claim on the wild Web, the key to getting noticed is adding the right information in the exact spots and knowing **how to submit your site to the search engines**.

WHERE TO SEARCH AND HOW TO FINE-TUNE YOUR SEARCHES

? Is there a single place to access all the search engines?

There are several places. One, called Dogpile, is a relatively easy metasearch engine, located at **http://www.dogpile.com**. Another location, Metafind, located at **http://www.metafind.com**, searches through six search engines returning links and organizing the results. It retrieves 10 links from AltaVista twice, 10 from Excite twice, 50 from HotBot, 25 from InfoSeek, 10 from OpenText, and 50 from Webcrawler.

? Can I search for the title of an ActiveX object embedded in a Web page?

Very few search engines currently offer the ability to search for ActiveX objects directly from the main options listed. However, some search engines let you specify a META search string to be incorporated into your search query. For example, AltaVista offers the option to search for ActiveX objects by typing **object:microsoft** in the search field. This would provide you with links to sites that used the word "Microsoft" in the name of the ActiveX object tag.

Tip   *Looking to invest in a mutual fund? Why not try Mutual Funds online, located at* **http://www.mfmag.com**.

? Is there a more <u>advanced way to search</u> than just using multiple keywords?

Most search engines offer advanced search queries, which offer you the ability to narrow down your search by date range, host location, or type of documents (such as newsgroup postings or Web pages). Look for a link offering a page. Some search engines, such as AltaVista, HotBot, and Lycos, can be set to automatically display advanced search pages. If your favorite engine doesn't offer an option to link directly to it, simply bookmark the Advanced Search page to access it any time you need to.

Most advanced search queries allow you to specify date of last update, options for ranking the results, or specific file types or META search qualifiers as shown in Figure 10-1.

? Which is the <u>biggest search engine</u>?

That's hard to say, since all search engines are constantly updating and adding to their indexes. AltaVista, which claims to have indexed 30 million pages, could be considered one of the biggest, but HotBot is is quickly bypassing AltaVista, claiming to have some 36 million pages indexed. Both InfoSeek and Excite also claim larger numbers, about 50 million pages. But as you'll notice in the following table, when searching for the word "dog," you get far more search results from HotBot and AltaVista than either InfoSeek, Lycos, or Excite. So I'd have to say that although the information may not be as precise or contain the best links, AltaVista wins hands down on volume, with HotBot not far behind.

Search Engine	Results When Searching for the Word "dog"
AltaVista	500,000
Excite	239,770
HotBot	405,130

Search Engine	Results When Searching for the Word "dog"
InfoSeek	366,210
Lycos	8,001
Yahoo	2,358

Remember   In the Internet search world, bigger is not necessarily better. Wading through thousands of hits is one thing; pinpointing exact information or finding quality information is another. That's the advantage directories such as InfoSeek and Yahoo, whose indexes are oftentimes viewed by real humans rather than roving robots, have over the big search engines.

Can I bookmark my search results?

Yes. Some search engines and directories, such as Webcrawler, at **http://www.webcrawler.com**; InfoSeek, at **http://www.infoseek.com**; AltaVista, at **http://www.altavista.digital.com**; Magellan, at

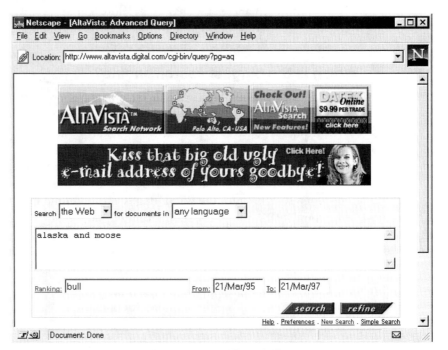

Figure 10-1.   An example of an Advanced Search Page

http://www.mckinley.com; and even HotBot, at **http://www.hotbot.com**, let you bookmark your searches so you can return and examine the results at a later time. First look to see if that option is available through a hypertext link on the search site. If such an option is not available, bookmark it yourself by first running your search, then bookmarking the results. You can add a bookmark by choosing Bookmark | Add Bookmark in Netscape Navigator, as shown here, or dragging the URL to the QuickLinks toolbar in Internet Explorer.

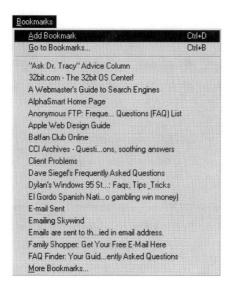

❓ What are <u>boolean expressions</u>?

Boolean expressions are those expressions or search queries where you use the words "and," "or," "not," a combination of two, or all three. These expressions can be combined to allow the construction of very complex queries. AND would narrow a search. For example, typing **movies and Woodie Allen** would return only pages that contain *both* the term "movies" and the name "Woody Allen."

The boolean expression "or" collects both terms specified, so you receive a larger number of results instead of more refined results. The "not" operator lets you search for records that contain the query word or phrase that precedes it but not the term or word that follows it. For example, if you wanted to search for boxers but not boxer shorts you would type **boxers not shorts**. Pages about fighters, not underwear, would be displayed.

Note   *Not all search engines identify boolean expressions by name. Some use a series of symbols, such as "&" for "and" or "!" for "not." Others offer the use of boolean expressions only through their Advanced Search option.*

? I bookmarked my results, but when I try to go back to that page it says <u>Data Not Found—Repost</u>. What did I do wrong?

Most likely nothing. You may still be able to bookmark the page, but you may have to hit the Reload button each time you want to re-create the query.

? How do I make a search engine page my <u>default search page</u> in Microsoft Internet Explorer?

Just follow these steps.

1. Go to the search engine page.
2. Choose View | Options.
3. Click the Navigation tab.
4. Select Search Page from the list box.
5. Click the Use Current button, as shown in Figure 10-2, then click OK to save your changes.

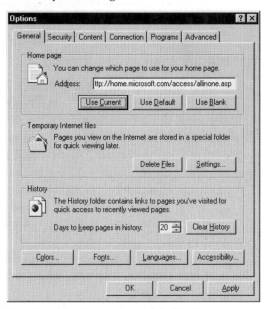

Figure 10-2.   Setting the default search page in Explorer

? What's the difference between a Web directory like Yahoo and a Web search engine like Lycos?

There is less difference now than there used to be, because many search engines are building subject indexes or catalogs based on standard categories like Arts, Entertainment, News, Sports, or Weather. Search engines provide access to information stored on Web pages; you just tell the search engine what you're looking for and it points you in that direction, much like a librarian might in a big library. The more general the search the more pages you'll have to look through.

Directories (such as Yahoo) attempt to organize the Web by dividing it into categories and subcategories. Some examples might include, say, the general category "art" and the subcategory "art museums"; "science" and "astronomy"; "health" and "strokes." Get the idea? If you're looking for information that fits neatly into an obvious category, it might be wise to first search a Web directory.

The advantage of a search engine is that it lets you look for things that just may not be categorized into neat little topics and subtopics. For example, say you are looking for your friend Wendy Robertson's home page. Web directories would not have a category called "Your Friends," so searching for your friend in one of them would probably give you few or no results. But if you used a search engine you probably could find Wendy's home page with ease, because it indexes so many sites.

 Tip · *Lycos lets you search not only for Web pages, sound files, and pictures but also for your UPS packages. You can find Lycos at* **http://www.lycos.com**.

? Why do some search engines return duplicates in the results?

Many times sites will have multiple copies of the document in different directories or the same document on different servers. Search engines such as HotBot attempt to recognize identical pages and group them in the "alternates" category. Also, a single Web server may have multiple host names or be referenced not only by the host name but also by the IP address. CGI scripts, which generate dynamic documents, can also produce multiple copies. Check the date of the page to ensure you are getting the most recent copy.

❓ Sometimes I search and get <u>error messages</u> instead of search results. What's wrong?

Sometimes you'll encounter error messages such as "Database not available" or "Too many accessing server. Please try again." This means the search engine is simply too busy to handle your request. You might try searching again in a few seconds or minutes.

You might also encounter 404 errors when you click a link for a Web page in a search query result. 404 errors simply mean the page has been moved, deleted, or renamed. You can try shortening the URL to see if you can find a starting point. For example, if you can't find **http://www.mysite.com/pages/help.html**, try removing the individual page, "help.html," in the Location field of your browser. If dropping the individual page doesn't work, try just accessing the domain itself; for example, try **http://www.mysite.com**. The site may have a directory listing active pages.

Tip   *A real movie buff? Why not search the Internet Movie Database for your favorite movie. The database can be found at **http://us.imdb.com/**.*

❓ Can I find <u>files with specific extensions</u>, such as all RealAudio files?

Some search engines—HotBot, for example—allow you to specify file types. You can click on Media type and select the file type you want HotBot to search for—even the extension of the file type. For example, if you type **linkext:ra** HotBot would find all the files on the Web that end in .ra, which means it would find Real Audio files embedded in Web pages.

❓ How do search engines <u>gather their information</u>?

Search engines use software programs called robots, spiders, or crawlers to sort through all the information found on the Internet. In addition, sometimes human beings intervene to catalog some of the data into categories. A robot is actually just a software program that automatically looks for, then follows hyperlinks from one document to the next. When a robot discovers a new site, it sends information back to the search engine and creates an indexed entry for it. If this link had previously been indexed, the robot updates the information about the location of this site. How quickly and comprehensively robots carry out these tasks varies from search engine to search engine.

The Top Ten Tips for Searching the Internet

⇨ Don't use just a single word in your search. Instead, use phrases, or at least multiple words, to make your search specific enough to produce manageable results.

⇨ Use boolean search strings, such as Music AND Reggae or Music+Reggae (depending upon how the search engine allows you to mix and match your search strings).

⇨ Specify those things you don't want included in a search, usually by either using the word NOT or putting a minus sign in front of the word you want omitted.

⇨ Use the right search engine, directory, or index for the job. Search engines are best used when you are looking for something out of the ordinary, like a bagel toaster, whereas directories or subject guides are best used to quickly find health, news, or weather sites.

⇨ Click "More Like This" links if you want the search site to bring back more results closer to what you are looking for.

⇨ Let the search engine do the job of plowing through your search results. Use your engine's "Search These Results" feature.

⇨ Read the help files for each search engine or directory to learn more about the available features and options. Sometimes the simple addition of **url:** or **domain:** before your search will help you find exactly what you want. Remember, not all search engines work the same way or use the same META search strings.

⇨ Capitalize the names of people, places, and names of companies.

⇨ Use double quotes around phrases you want to find, as in "American Revolution."

⇨ Try using a site such as Search.com, **http://www.search.com**, to search multiple databases at once or to help you find the right search database or engine for the job.

Tip   *You can track your FedEx package at FedEx's Web site, located at* ***http://www.fedex.com***.

? Can I make a search engine my home page?

You bet. In Netscape Navigator, follow these steps:

1. Choose Options | General Preferences.
2. Click in the "Browser starts with" field.
3. Type the URL for the search engine you want to make your home page, as shown in Figure 10-3.
4. Click OK to save your changes.

? Can I find out how many Web pages are indexed within a particular search engine?

Yes. You can search virtually all search engines using the exact search expression **URL:http**. The search engine should respond with the total number of documents matching this criterion. Since this expression specifies pages with the letters *http* in them, and since every Web page starts with "http," you get the total number stored in a directory.

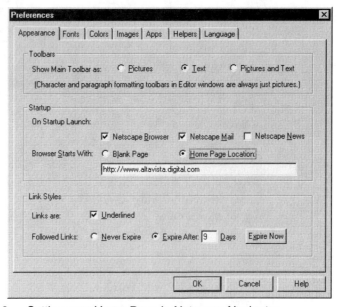

Figure 10-3.   Setting your Home Page in Netscape Navigator

? Do search engines index every single document on the Web in their databases?

No. That would be almost impossible to do, because the Web is constantly changing. However, most major search engines store anywhere from several million to 50 million Web pages in their directories, and those directories are updated on a daily, weekly, or monthly basis.

Tip   *Want to check on your stocks? Try searching by ticker symbol at the PC Financial Network, located at* ***http://www.pcfn.com.*** *You can search not only for daily quotes but also for news about the company. You can also search the Lipper Fund Index and Zacks Company Reports.*

? Can I use a search engine to look for Java applets?

Some, but not all search engines offer the option to search for specific types of files. Look for a drop-down menu option allowing you to search for different file formats, or peruse the help file for instructions on what META search strings can be used. For example, with AltaVista you can type the following in the search field: **applet:cafe**.

? How do I keep postings out of Usenet archives?

Most search engines offer the ability to specify a posting option called the "X-no-archive" flag, which, if followed by the word "yes," will keep the posting from being archived in the search engine. This flag must appear in the header of the newsgroup article; for example, **X-no-archive: yes**.

? How do some search engines know what my last search was or who I am?

Most search engines that offer this feature—like HotBot, at **http://www.hotbot.com**—use one of two different mechanisms to determine who you are and what your last search was. The first method, called a "cookie," is actually a text file stored on your computer that is written to and accessed by the search engine each time you visit the search engine's site. The cookie file contains information such as login name, password, and the last time you visited the site.

Some search engines also support what are called "Fat URLs," which are URLs that point to a page specifically created for you when you click to save your settings. The fat URL can be bookmarked, thereby saving your settings for the next time you access the search engine.

 Note   Wired Magazine's *HotBot search engine contains over 50 million documents in its database and allows you to search for certain media types, such as GIF files or ZIP files, in addition to ordinary Web pages. HotBot is located at **http://www.hotbot.com.***

? I know I can get a <u>list of search results</u>, then search within those results, but is there any way I can do both at the same time?

It depends on the search engine. InfoSeek lets you search and also lets you specify within that search more specific information. For example, if you were looking for horses, but wanted to search the results InfoSeek gave you for stallions, you would type **horses | stallions**. Excite is another search engine that also allows you to search again within the query by simply clicking next to the results, then lets you provide additional search text to use to find results within your initial results.

? Now that I've found the document I want, is there a quick way to <u>locate the keywords</u> I used for the search?

Once you've found the Web page using a search engine, you can use your browser's Find option (usually in the Edit menu) to locate the word or words you are interested in on that individual page, as shown in Figure 10-4. This option will only search on the current page, not on the entire Net.

? Is there some way I can <u>match words exactly in newsgroup postings</u>?

If you type in a proper name or a word in uppercase letters, the search engine will match them. For example, if you wanted the search engine to find all postings containing the first name Bill, you would type **Bill**, not **bill**. Or if you wanted to find all postings with the word "NASA," you would type **keywords:NASA**. This would match all news articles with the word "NASA" in all caps in the keyword list.

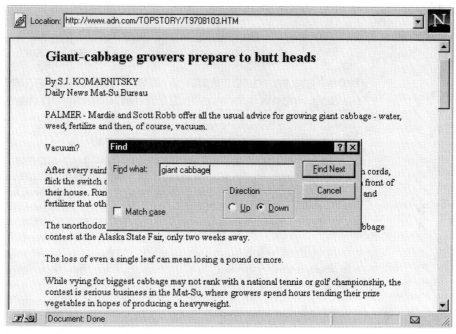

Figure 10-4.   Using the Find option in the Netscape browser

❓ Can I search for <u>newsgroup postings</u>?

Yes, most definitely. Usenet newsgroup archives can be searched using
AltaVista, InfoSeek, Excite, Reference.com, Search.com DejaNews, and
Lycos, to name just a few. Check the drop-down options of your favorite
search engine or directory for the ability to search newsgroups. If you
don't see that option, try DejaNews, at **http://www.dejanews.com**.
DejaNews is the preeminent newsgroup archive on the Web.

❓ How do I find <u>newsgroup postings</u> by a particular e-mail address?

First, select Usenet Newsgroups as the search selection, either from a
drop-down list or radio button option. Next, type **from:ckirk@alaska.
net** in the search string field.

This would match all newsgroup articles with the e-mail address
ckirk@alaska.net in the From: field. Replace **ckirk@alaska.net** with
whatever e-mail address you are searching for.

Remember   *You must first select Newsgroups or Usenet from the section of the Internet you want to look in. Otherwise, the search engine will search for Web pages with the words "from:address@domain" in them.*

? I typed the word "computer" and the search engine said "no documents were found." What's going on here?

Many search engines routinely exclude common words or phrases, called *stopwords*, in their directories. They do this because otherwise the resulting query would return an unmanageable number of results. Some search engines even ignore words beginning with a number, like 1st, so try not to use numbers unless absolutely necessary.

 Tip   *What's the best place to search for businesses? By far, Zip2.com is. Not only do you get results instantly, but you can also get door-to-door directions to the business from your location most anywhere in the United States.*

? Can I use normal English-language expressions in search engines?

Many search engines, such as Excite, InfoSeek, and Lycos, let you type questions, and the search site will supply answers. For example, if you wanted to know what telnet was, you could type in the question, **What is telnet?** and the search engine would respond with links to pages that answer or reference that question. Some sites, however, require you to enclose your question in quotes.

 Tip   *Want to search for news about your town? Try Excite's NewsTracker search engine, located at* **http://nt.excite.com**. *If you wanted to search for news articles about Anchorage, Alaska, you would type* **Anchorage** *in the search field.*

? I've found a link I want to explore, but I don't want to lose the search query list. How can I open a link while keeping the results page open?

You can view more than one Web page at a time by opening up another browser window. Simply right-click the link in your search results and choose "Open in New Window" from the pop-up menu. This opens a new browser window to the link you've chosen and keeps the results window open as well. Use the ALT-TAB keystroke combination or the Window menu to bounce back and forth between open windows.

? How do most search engines <u>rank the results</u> I get?

Normally, search engines rank results in one of the following ways:

Word Frequency in Document   The more times the word or phrase you've searched for appears in the document, the higher the page is ranked. The uniqueness of the word is also a factor and will bring the document up in rank.

Search Words Used in the Title of the Web Page   Pages that contain your search word or phrase in the title of the page will be ranked higher than those that don't.

Search Words in Keywords   Pages that have added a META tag containing the specific keyword you've searched for will be ranked higher than pages that don't have any META tags in them. However, pages with the keyword in the title of the page usually rank higher than META-tagged pages.

Length of the Web Page Itself   Shorter documents containing the keyword or phrase will be ranked higher than longer documents.

? Some engines mention a <u>robot</u>. What is a robot?

Search sites, such as HotBot or AltaVista, are actually composed of two separate pieces: a Web site and a Web-crawling robot. The Web site (the visible part you've been using to find information) responds to your searches by consulting a database, sometimes called an index, of information about all the documents on the World Wide Web. The robot is the automated program that goes out searching the Web, bringing back URLs and information about each URL it finds. So you could consider the robot the electronic librarian for your search site.

? How often are <u>search engines and indexes updated</u>?

Some sites update their indexes once a day, while others may update them weekly or monthly. If the site is updated daily, this will probably be done late at night. Most sites allow you to manually update or submit pages, and those changes could take anywhere from a minute to a whole day. Check the search site for more information about when those updates are implemented.

❓ Is there a place to <u>search mailing list postings</u>?

Reference.com is one good place to search for mailing list postings. However, you might first see if the mailing list has an archive you can search. Individual mailing list archives may be more readily available or go back further than Reference.com does.

Tip   Search.com offers links to virtually every search engine on the Web, plus topic-specific databases. Best of all, you can conduct searches from one simple page. You can find Search.com at **http://www.search.com**.

❓ Is there a place I can go that will let me <u>search multiple search engines at once</u>?

There are many multisearch locations. On some pages however, you may not be able to choose as many options for your search as you would if you went to the search engine's main home page. Here are some of the more widely used all-in-one search pages:

Name	Location	Engines it Searches	Comments
All 4 One	http://all4one.com/	Excite, Lycos, AltaVista, and Yahoo	Somewhat confusing if you don't know how to handle frames, but feature allows you to focus in on one engine's results if you prefer.
Find-It!	http://www.iTools.com/ find-it/find-it.html	AltaVista, OpenText, Yahoo, Shareware, DejaNews, IAF	Offers a single interface to multiple search engines.
Internet Sleuth	http://www.isleuth.com/	Choose from 2,000 search databases	Excellent site, with ability to select multiple search engines. Go here first before going anywhere else.

Name	Location	Engines it Searches	Comments
Savvy Search	http://www.cs.colostate.edu/ ~dreiling/smartform.html	Yahoo, Webcrawler, DejaNews, Galaxy, PointSearch, FTPSearch95, Shareware.com, UsenetAddresses, AltaVistaNews, AcronymAndAbbr, Webster, Roget, WhoWhere?, InReference, YellowPages, Magellan	You can pick and choose which engines to search. Very easy, but produces lots of results if you're not specific.
Search.com	http://www.search.com	Choose from over 3,000 search databases	Great site, but not as straightforward as Internet Sleuth. Certainly has links to just about every type of database you'd ever want to search.

Tip   *Looking for articles on health and fitness? Try searching Time Warner's PathFinder search option at* **http://cgi.pathfinder.com.**

? Is there some way to <u>search a particular domain</u> for pages?

Some search engines allow you to tailor your query so it includes only one particular host by placing the word "host:" or "domain" before the query. For example, if you wanted to search the domain alaska.net for the word "fishing" with AltaVista, you would type **host:alaska.net fishing**. This would display only pages within the alaska.net domain that contained the word "fishing." If you wanted all the pages in this domain that are indexed in the search site's database you would simply type **host:alaska.net.**

? ## Is there a way to <u>search for particular newsgroups?</u>

Yes. Most search engines let you search for a specific newsgroup by specifying a META string qualifier. For example, with AltaVista, if you type **newsgroups:rec.running** you would only be searching in the recreational running newsgroup.

? ## I keep coming up with pages that contain my <u>search query</u> <u>in the links rather than in the text of the document.</u> Can I tell the search engine to look only in the text and not in the title or hypertext links?

Yes. For example, with AltaVista, if you wanted to find the word "McDonald's" in text but not in links which point to the McDonald's Web site you would type **text:McDonald's**.

 Tip   *Need some divine inspiration? The best place to search for Bible scriptures or what the Bible says about all sorts of things including love, hope, marriage, and sin, try the Bible Gateway, available in a variety of languages at* **http://www.bible.gospelnet.com**.

? ## Can I <u>search for text within the links of a Web page</u> itself?

Some search engines offer the ability to search links by specifying a META string before the text you are looking for. For example, if you were using AltaVista and looking for the word "cheeseburger" in the list of links in a Web page you would type **anchor:cheeseburger**. Then AltaVista would search the Web for every page having "cheeseburger" in a hypertext link.

? ## How do I <u>search the titles of Web pages</u> instead of the text within?

Most major engines let you search the titles of Web pages. The titles appear in the title bar of the page and are used when you bookmark a page. If you include **title:loveline** in your query, the search engine will return all pages with the word "loveline" in the title. Check to see if the search engine offers this feature in a drop-down list or in advanced search options.

? Is it better to search for a page using a <u>single word or a phrase</u>?

It's far better to be as specific as you can be, and that means using multiple words, not single words. If you're looking for Web pages on Maltese, the word "dog" will bring up thousands upon thousands of Web pages. The phrase "maltese for sale" will bring up only those pages that have to do with selling those loveable little fur-covered dogs. Here's a quick example from AltaVista's search engine:

"Dog"—500,000 pages
"Dogs fur"—200,000 pages
"Maltese"—10,000 pages
"Maltese for sale"—3 pages

? Can I search for <u>specific domains</u> such as all educational domains?

Yes. Most search engines allow you to specify the type of domain that holds the pages you want to view. For example, if you were interested in seeing pages stored on education-related servers and you were using InfoSeek's search engine you would type **site:edu**. With AltaVista you would type **domain:edu**.

The results would be a list of links to pages stored on sites with the domain .edu in the URL. Other domains you can search for are .com, for commercial sites, .net, for networking sites, country-specific domains such as .fr for France or .uk for the United Kingdom, or .gov for government.

? Is there a way to <u>speed up my searches</u>?

The speed of your searches may be dictated by the traffic on the Internet, so you might try searching at a less busy time. Remember too, that some search engines update their indexes late at night, so you may see some slow down then as well. You can also try entering detailed search phrases so the listing of results will take less time to appear—and less time for you to plow through. Try turning off images in your Web browser (if the search site allows it) so you don't have to wait for banner ads and graphics to display.

Caution   *Some search services, like HotBot, **http://www.hotbot.com**, force you to keep the graphics turned on so you can click on the various button options.*

Can I search the subject line of newsgroup postings?

Most search engines that allow you to search for newsgroup postings also allow you to search the subject lines. For example, if you were using AltaVista to search the Usenet and you wanted to search for messages where the subject was "running" you would type **subject:running**.

You can also combine the subject with other words to search for within the postings themselves. For example, if you typed **subject:for sale hibachi** you would find hibachis for sale in newsgroup postings.

Tip   *Need help potty-training Fido? For information about your pet's care and feeding try searching AcmePet's database at **http://www.acmepet.com**.*

Are there any terms I shouldn't use when searching?

Many marketers of Web sites realize that first-time searchers commonly use terms such as sex, free, shareware, Web, Internet, and Windows. So they include these words in their sites even though their sites may have nothing to do with such keywords. For this reason it's best to avoid using easily targeted marketing words when searching. Be more specific. And don't use words like Web, computer, or Internet. These words are filtered out in most search engines simply because they are ubiquitous on the Internet.

Tip   *Looking for that fantasy football site? Check out SearchSport, http://www.oldsport.com/search/intro.htm. SearchSport lets you search for any sport you're interested in.*

Can I use wildcards in my searches?

Yes, but each search engine uses its own wildcard character, so read the Help file on what that character might be. For example, Lycos uses the $, whereas AltaVista uses the *. So if you were searching with AltaVista and you wanted to find all the pages that had the word "invest" or "investment" or "investiture" in them, you would type **invest*** in the keyword or phrase search field.

? Can I create a <u>Windows 95 shortcut to a search page</u> and place it on my desktop?

Yes, and it's incredibly simple to do. All you have to do is click and hold down on the link to the search engine you want and drag that link to your desktop. Later, you can double-click on the shortcut to bring up the search page with your default browser.

SEARCHING FOR PEOPLE, FILES, GREAT CLIP ART, AND OTHER THINGS

? How do I get a directory to <u>delete my name from its listings</u>?

Usually you would contact the directory's support e-mail address. When you write, make sure you include your e-mail address, telephone number, full name, and street address. For example, if you wanted to remove your name from the People Finder directory site you would send an e-mail to **feedback@infospace.com**, and they will suppress your listing in People Directory.

Tip *Looking for some great recipes? Check out Epicurious, at http://www.epicurious.com. This site boasts over 5,000 recipes.*

? Is there a search engine I can use to <u>find people by their telephone numbers</u>?

Several major search engines used to offer this feature (called a *reverse directory*) but stopped because of concerns about privacy. However, you are in luck. One company, PC411.com, offers not only the ability to search by phone number but also a connection to MapQuest so you can see where the person lives. You can find PC411.com at **http://www.pc411.com**.

Tip *Looking for maps of exotic destinations? Try searching City.Net's map database at **http://www.city.net**.*

? I need to find a picture of a telephone. Can I search for image files by object name? In other words, it would be great if I could specify the word "telephone" to search for pages that contain the image files I'm looking for.

Some sites, like HotBot, allow you to specify exactly what you want to search for by using a drop-down list, as shown in Figure 10-5. If the site you are searching doesn't offer a simple drop-down option, sometimes you can specify image files to search by typing a certain keyword before the filename and type. For example, with AltaVista you would type **image:telephone.jpg**. This will display a list of pages that have image files with the name "telephone.jpg."

? I'm a Web master and I'm looking for JavaScripts. Is there one place I can go to search for what I want?

There are a ton of great sites for Web masters, but one quick place to search for Web page design products such as Javascript is The WebMaster's Reference Library, located at **http://www.webreference. com/**. There you can search for 3-D elements, JavaScripts, or design information and graphics.

 Remember   *You can also use META keywords in most major browsers to search the entire Web for Java applets or ActiveX applications.*

? Is there a good place to find legal information?

Try LawCrawler, **http://www.lawcrawler.com**, an excellent site where you can search for all sorts of legal information and have access to law reviews, the Constitution, and Web-based legal sites.

? Can I search for personal Web pages?

Yes. As a matter of fact, many of the search and e-mail directories offer cataloged personal Web page searches. You can find personal Web page directories on WhoWhere, at **http://www.whowhere.com**; Four11, at **http://www.four11.com**; InfoSeek, at **http://www. infoseek.com**; or Excite, at **http://www.excite.com**. This option is quickly becoming very popular, so check the "What's New" link of your favorite search site to see if it has been implemented.

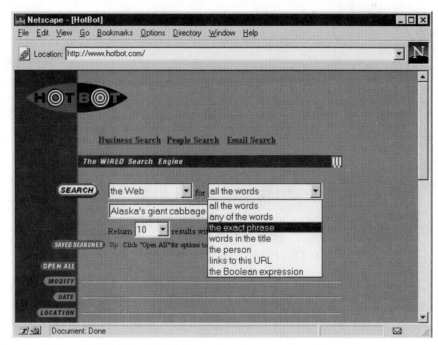

Figure 10-5.   HotBot—a site offering many drop-down options

 Where can I <u>search for someone's e-mail address</u>?

Tons of directories are popping up all over. The most common and largest at this point are listed here.

Name	URL
555-1212	http://www.555-1212.com
BigFoot	http://www.bigfoot.com
Four11	http://www.four11.com
Internet Address Finder	http://www.iaf.net
WhoWhere	http://www.whowhere.com

Note   If you don't want your name included in any of these phone/people databases, contact each individual company and let them know. You'll find the contact information on their main page. Usually they'll delete it within a week.

? How can I find out <u>who is linking to my site</u>? Can I use a search engine to do that?

Yes, you can. Most search engines, such as Lycos and AltaVista, allow you to search for sites that are linked to a particular URL. For example, if you type **link:http://www.alaska.net/~ckirk** in the AltaVista search field, the search results page will list all sites that link back to that page.

HOW TO SUBMIT YOUR SITE TO THE SEARCH ENGINES

? Do search engines take advantage of the <u>ALT tags</u> I've included to describe my graphics?

Yes.

? Should I submit my <u>entire site</u> to a search engine?

You should be somewhat selective about what you submit to a search engine to ensure you pick the right category and site and include the correct URL for your main page, and a brief accurate description. You should not include every single page, as the results that might turn up on a search query would be confusing to the user. Pick only the top levels and add no more than four or five.

Besides, after you submit your site, most search engine robots will take the single main URL, search it, then add the additional links of your site. Don't waste your time. Spend it submitting your site to other search engines and letting all your friends and relatives know about your site.

? How do I use <u>META tags</u> in my Web page?

First, you place all META tags in the header of your document. There are three main META descriptors you can use. They are as follows:

Descriptor	Usage	Example
description	The description keyword can be used to control the content of your document's abstract in the search-results page.	<META NAME="description" CONTENT="This page about Maltese is part of a larger site about dog breeding.">

Descriptor	Usage	Example
keywords	You use the keywords META tag to assign special search keywords to your document.	The following tag can be used within your Web page at the header to add the keywords "dog", "dogs", "breeds", and "breeding" to a page focusing on Maltese. <META NAME="keywords" CONTENT="dog,dogs,breeds, breeding">
robots	This is used to prevent a search engine from indexing your page. Check the search engine for proper syntax or to find out if you need to include a robots.txt file specifying exactly what directories should not be indexed.	The <META NAME="robots">

How can I keep my Web page out of a search engine?

The robots.txt file is placed on your site to tell the search robots which directories are allowed to be included in their indexes and which are not. If you prefer that your site not be indexed by a search engine, you would create a file called robots.txt and place it in the main directory of your site, then reference that file with a META tag pointing to the location of the file in your server's directory.

How many keywords should I include?

The best thing to do is use only two or three keywords that best describe the context of your site and make sure those words appear in your title and in the first part of your Web page. Also, keep in mind that keywords you consider crucial may not be what people use when searching. So it's a good idea to include a fairly comprehensive description below the keywords you use.

I know that it's possible to create a link to a particular search engine directly from a Web page. How is that done? Would I have to pay to use that option on my own page?

The HTML code needed to include a search field from a particular search engine is relatively simple. Most search sites will provide you with the actual HTML code, and you can simply copy and paste it directly into your page. However, before you do this you should read the user agreement. Although you don't have to pay to do this, there may be restrictions on exactly how you can refer to the search site.

Here is the actual HTML code for incorporating a search field that links directly to AltaVista:

```
<FORM method=GET action="http://altavista.
                 digital.com/cgi-bin/query">
<INPUT TYPE=hidden NAME=pg VALUE=q>
<B>Search <SELECT NAME=what>
<OPTION VALUE=web SELECTED>the Web
<OPTION VALUE=news>Usenet
</SELECT>

and Display the Results <SELECT NAME=fmt>

<OPTION VALUE="" SELECTED>in Standard Form
<OPTION VALUE=c>in Compact Form
<OPTION VALUE=d>in Detailed Form
</SELECT></B><BR>
<INPUT NAME=q size=55 maxlength=200 VALUE="">
<INPUT TYPE=submit VALUE=Submit>
</FORM>
```

? I've heard people say that using META tags in my Web page ensures that my site will be included in the various search engines. Is that true?

Meta tags will help you control your site's description, but not all engines support them. They will not guarantee that your site appears first in a search engine's resulting queries. If you want to check to see exactly how your site measures up to others, try Rank This!, **http://www.rankthis.com**, a site that will take your URL and see if it's listed in the top 200 search engine links for that particular keyword or category.

? I have moved to another server. How do I get links to my old pages deleted from a search site?

Oftentimes, the search robots will discover that your old pages are no longer valid and will delete them from the index. However, you should check with the site to see if there is the option to delete specific URLs.

? Should I <u>pay a service to submit my site</u> to all these search engines?

There really is no need to pay a service since many major search engines will find your site anyway. Also, there are plenty of sites you can use to submit to multiple sites for free. If you don't have the time, are not good at figuring out what categories your site falls under, or simply don't want the hassle, then by all means pay for it. If you are paying someone to create your site from scratch, consider adding this to the contract.

? How do I make sure my page is <u>ranked high on the list of search results</u>?

There is really no way to ensure that your Web page will come up higher in search results. However, if you use terms that describe what you are about early in your page, and specific terms in your title, hypertext links, and text, you might have a better chance of getting a higher ranking. You can also use the META tags to add a few invisible keywords.

The Web is getting so large that your chances of having your site ranked high using very common terms, such as "computer software" are pretty slim. Your best bet is to get as specific as possible when cataloging or adding META strings to your pages and include as many keywords as you possibly can.

? I've seen people <u>repeat phrases or keywords</u> in their Web pages, sometimes several hundred times, in small fonts or by using colored fonts that appear invisible on the page. Does this make it more likely a search engine will pick up the page?

Some search engines do pick up pages with multiple occurrences of words, but the rule of thumb is if the text is not placed within ALT or META tags and the text is not visible in a browser it won't be visible in an indexed search engine.

? Do I need to <u>submit my Web pages to a search engine</u>?

Most definitely, submit your key pages to search engines. Be sure to completely read instructions on submitting your pages to a particular search engine so you'll know exactly what the idiosyncrasies of that search engine are and the recommended ways to index your site in its database. Here is a list of sites, both free and fee-based, that allow you to submit your Web pages to multiple search engines:

Site	URL	Fee?
Broadcaster	http://www.broadcaster.co.uk/	No. Offers the ability to submit your site to over 200 search engines
FreeLinks	http://www.freelinks.com/	No. Lets you submit information to their indexes
Register-It	http://www.register-it.com	Yes, but also offers limited free submissions
Submit-It!	http://www.submit-it.com	No. Lets you submit information to hundreds of search engines

? Once I've <u>submitted a site</u>, is there anything else I should do?

⇨ Check your link at least once a week to make sure it appears in the search engine. Sometimes URLs/pages can disappear from indexes, especially if the engine has had a major software overhaul. If you don't see it, resubmit it.

⇨ Make sure you resubmit your site regularly, especially when you make changes. Doing so will ensure that the most up-to-date information your browsing visitor needs is displayed.

⇨ Find other directories or sites that may want to link to your site and let them know you'll link to them.

? Do I have to use <u>text</u> on my Web page in order for it to be included in a search engine? Can't I just use an imagemap?

Although you can use an imagemap, you should use text as well. If you don't, you should at least use the META tag within the header area of your document. Search engines index the text from the various Web pages they visit. If your page doesn't contain the proper descriptive text, the search engine probably won't list it when queried.

Where should I place the <u>text I want included in an</u> <u>indexed search engine</u>?

The best location is high on your Web page, outside any tables. Consider not making your main page a framed page; some search engines have a hard time indexing framed pages. Remember, your visitors can always bookmark subsequent pages, but search engines may not be able to handle special HTML formats that look cool but don't provide the engine with enough text-based information. Also, be careful when using CGI-generated pages. Most search engines cannot index these or when indexed, then clicked to by a user could result in error messages. And above all, leave out any special characters as some search engines simply don't know how to handle special characters.

Which META tags <u>are supported</u> in most search engines?

Almost every major search engine supports the use of META tags embedded within the Web pages themselves. These tags give you some control over how the pages are ranked and how they appear in search results. META tags that are supported include "keywords," "description," "author." Some allow for the use of robot tags so you can even prevent your page from being indexed.

chapter

11 Answers!

Creating Web Pages

Answer Topics!

Creating Web Pages @ a Glance

⇨   Now that you've browsed your share of pages, the idea of creating your own Web page trickles through your mind. And why not? It's relatively easy to do. Once a few **basic questions about Web page creation** are out of the way, you'll be able to stake out a claim on the wild, wild Web and publish with the best of them.

⇨   If you're currently connecting to the Net via an online service, you might be surprised to know that **publishing pages on commercial services** such as America Online or CompuServe is relatively easy.

⇨   Once you've gotten the basics down, there are plenty of **advanced Web design options** you can use to spruce up your page—from advanced HTML coding to implementing Java and CGI scripts—the sky's the limit. You may soon realize, for example, that you've outgrown your original home and may need to start looking for options for hosting your site, design tips, and ways to announce your site to the world. You'll find plenty of resources for each available on the Net.

⇨   If you plan to get really serious publishing pages, you'll probably be interested in **setting up your own web server**. Although it's not too difficult, you will need to know what hardware and software is available, and a few tricks on how to implement your own server.

• • • • • • • • • • •

What Is a Web Page?

A Web page is simply an ASCII text file comprised of special commands called tags which Web browsers can interpret and render as a page on your screen. Web pages don't "contain" images, rather they contain pointers to where graphic files are stored on a server.

BASIC QUESTIONS ABOUT WEB PAGE CREATION

? ## Do all browsers support <u>animated GIFs</u>?

Not all browsers support animated GIFs—some only display the last frame, some only the first. Netscape Navigator 2.0 and Internet Explorer 3.0, and higher versions, support the animated GIF, or GIF89a, file specification and fully display all frames in their animated sequence.

? ## What's the easiest way to incorporate <u>animation</u> on my Web page?

By far the easiest way to animate your Web page is to use an animated GIF. Animated GIFs are just like those little flip-books you used to make when you were a kid. An animated GIF is a single file comprising a series of image layers (or frames) and embedded instructions that control how the image layers are presented (for example, for how long or how many times). The end result is a short animation. One of the best programs available for building animated GIFs is GifBuilder. You can find it at Shareware.com, **http://www.shareware.com**, or you can get it directly from the programmer, Yves Piguet, at **http://iawww.epfl.ch/Staff/Yves.Piguet/clip2gif-home/GifBuilder.html**.

? ## What is <u>anti-aliasing</u> and should I be using it in my images?

Have you ever run across a web page where the graphics look fuzzy with jagged edges? Most likely the designer didn't use anti-aliasing, which is a process that programs like Photoshop use to smooth out the jagged edges in graphics. The anti-aliasing process smooths graphics files by adding in more colors between the other colors. Any graphic you have with lots of curves, angles, or lines should be anti-aliased.

? ## Where can I get <u>artwork</u> for my Web pages?

There are a variety of sources on the Web that offer free, unrestricted artwork for inclusion on your Web page. Here are some of the more popular sites and clip art they offer:

Name	Location	Artwork Offered
The ClipArt Collection	http://www.ist.net/clipart/index.html	A wide assortment of artwork and links to other clip art sites
Net Creators Icon Page	http://www.geocities.com/CapeCanaveral/3348/	All sorts of animated GIFs and icons for Web pages
The ClipArt Directory	http://www.clipart.com	Has a huge list of clipart and artwork-related links
Clip Art Warehouse	http://www.fxmm.co.uk/	Huge assortment of clipart—some commercial, most free
The Free Graphics Store	http://ausmall.com.au/freegraf/index.htm	Lots of very clean, crisp artwork for downloading (updated weekly)
True Realities	http://trureality.com/anime.htm	Some fantastic animated GIFs
CompuServe's Tools & Tips	http://ourworld.compuserve.com/ourworld/tools/education/wmspruce.html	Lots of links to some great buttons, graphics, and horizontal rules

How do I set the <u>background color</u> of a Web page? Should I create a GIF and use it as a background, or is there an easier way?

You can use a GIF but there is an easier way. It's called the Body Background Color tag, or BODY BGCOLOR. With it you specify the color code you want to use within the page. For example, if you wanted to use white as a background color, you would include this in the header of your Web page:

```
<BODY BGCOLOR="#FFFFFF">
```

 Note   *#FFFFFF is the RGB color code for white.*

? I can't seem to get my <u>background colors</u> to work. Any suggestions?

Make sure the background color tag is in the proper location on your Web page. The following example shows where the BODY BGCOLOR tag should be placed:

```
<HTML>
<HEAD>
<TITLE> Title</TITLE>
</HEAD>
<BODY BGCOLOR=color>
</BODY> </HTML>
```

? How do you add a <u>background picture</u> to a Web page?

Use the body background tag and specify the filename of the GIF or JPEG you want as the background. Here's an example:

```
<BODY BACKGROUND="background.gif">
```

This would place background.gif behind the text and graphics of the Web page.

 Caution   Make sure your background doesn't overwhelm the rest of the elements on the page. And make sure the text is still readable after placing the background in your page.

? I've published my page, but now I <u>can't see it</u>. What's the problem?

If you don't see the page, first check to make sure you know the exact URL the page has been assigned and that you're typing it in correctly. Remember that the Web is case sensitive. Also, make sure you have the proper rights for access to your directory. If you don't know how, contact your provider for more information. You can also make sure that the uploaded information is standard, ASCII text and not some native file format.

? ### What control do you have over the <u>color of the text</u> on a Web page?

The colors of the different types of text in a web page can be set by the page's author using the following HTML tags:

Text to be Colored	The Tags to Use
Standard text within the document	<BODY TEXT="#RRGGBB">
Links	<BODY LINK="#RRGGBB" >
Visited links	<BODY VLINK="#RRGGBB">
Selected link (one that's been clicked on)	<BODY ALINK="#RRGGBB">

 Note   *RR, GG, and BB are two-digit hex numbers (00-FF) representing the amount of red, green, and blue in a particular color. For example, "#FFFFFF" represents white and "#000000" represents black.*

? ### How many <u>colors</u> should I use when designing a Web page? My monitor can display millions and millions of colors. Is the same true for Web pages?

Most browsers such as Netscape use only several hundred colors. Netscape uses 216 colors to be exact. When designing Web graphics you should design with your Control Panel | Display | Settings set to no more than 256 colors, as shown in Figure 11-1.

? ### How do I put a link on my page so someone can send me e-mail?

You can place the mailto: tag on your page. If someone clicks the mailto: link and the browser is capable of bringing up their e-mail client, the address you include in the mailto: link will be placed in the To: field of the new e-mail message window. The mailto: tag works like this:

mailto:*e-mail address*

For example, if the link is **mailto:ckirk@alaska.net**, the link places **ckirk@alaska.net** in the To: field of a new e-mail message.

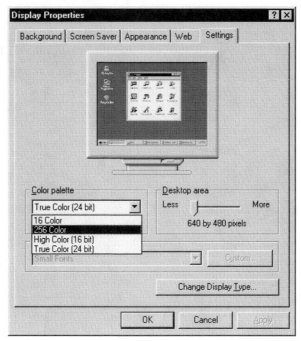

Figure 11-1.   Changing the display

❓ I've just uploaded my Web page but the <u>graphics aren't visible at all</u>. What did I do wrong?

More than likely, one of the following two things happened: you may have uploaded the graphics incorrectly (e.g., to the wrong directory or not at all), or you may have misspelled the graphics filenames or omitted the filename extensions referenced in your Web page.

❓ Are there any <u>graphics embedded</u> in the browser software itself?

Netscape has a wealth of embedded graphics you can use. Just use the following tag in your Web pages: <IMG SRC="internal-xxx-xxx"> and replace the xxx-xxx with the name of the embedded graphic you want to use. You don't have to worry about uploading the graphics since they are embedded in the Navigator application.

Tag	Icon
internal-gopher-index	
internal-gopher-sound	
internal-gopher-binary	
internal-gopher-unknown	
internal-gopher-menu	
internal-gopher-text	
internal-gopher-image	
internal-gopher-movie	
internal-gopher-telnet	
internal-icon-delayed	
internal-icon-notfound	
internal-icon-baddata	
internal-icon-insecure	
internal-icon-embed	

? Why do some Web pages end in .htm and others in .html?

It simply depends on the server and the server options used. Windows/DOS-based servers can use only three letter file extensions while Unix and Windows NT systems offer longer filename extensions.

? How do you see the HTML code used to create a Web page?

Most browsers offer a View | View Document Source option, as shown in Figure 11-2, that lets you see how a Web page is constructed. This will display the HTML code used to create the Web page.

? Why does my Web page look different on different computers?

There are several reasons why pages look different from computer to computer. Some of the reasons include the following:

⇨ Different monitor resolution capabilities

⇨ Different monitor sizes

⇨ Different monitor color palettes

⇨ Different browsers

? Can a mailto: link fill in the subject line as well? I'd like to have people subscribe to my newsletter without having to type the word "subscribe" in the subject line.

Although this is possible, not all browsers support a mailto: link with a default subject line. If you want to be adventurous and you feel the majority of your visitors will be using Netscape version 2.0 or above, the following is the HTML code you would use:

mailto:*address*?subject=*subject*

For example, if your address is **webmaster@mysite.com** and the subject line should be SUBSCRIBE LIST, the HTML code would look like this:

mailto:webmaster@mysite.com?subject=SUBSCRIBE LIST

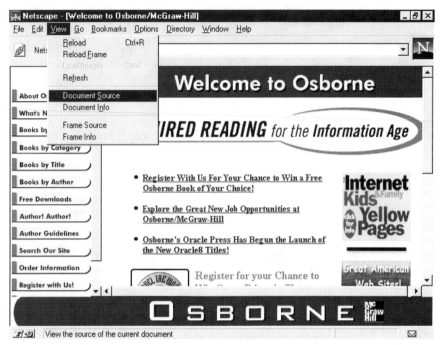

Figure 11-2.   Displaying the source of a document

If you know your visitors are using Lynx or NCSA Mosaic for Windows, use this HTML code:

mailto:webmaster@mysite.com title="*subject*">

   Caution   *Remember these tags are browser-specific and assume the user has configured his e-mail application correctly. If the visitor is not using the appropriate browser, the link will address the e-mail message incorrectly. Your Web page should explain the potential hazards or provide alternative methods for those people using other browsers.*

? How long will it take before my page is available on the Web after I've uploaded it to the server?

It doesn't matter whether you are publishing a page with an independent service provider or on a commercial service like CompuServe or AOL. Regardless of the service provider, it only takes a few minutes for a Web page to become available to the entire Web, as long as there are no publishing restrictions.

Tips for Writing Good HTML Code

⇨ Always comment your HTML code. This will help others who maintain your site know exactly where to add or delete features. For example, if you want to let someone know where an imagemap starts, you would place the following comment line above the code:

```
<!-- client-side map for buttons begins here -->
```

⇨ Use templates whenever possible. Create a standard design layout, then use and reuse that same layout to keep things consistent.

⇨ Leave large spaces between page elements, and liberally space the code to make it easier to read. Remember extra spaces are ignored with HTML.

⇨ Keep your case consistent. Although, with the exception of sections, anchor, and frame names, HTML is not case-sensitive. But to make it easier to read and discern from regular text, type all HTML code in uppercase.

⇨ Place the date of last update, the author's name, and the name of the product used to create the page at the top. This way, others who are maintaining the site will know exactly who did what, when, and with what, and can go back and use the same tool if necessary.

⇨ Always use relative instead of absolute pathnames when referring to graphics or other linked documents stored on the same server. That way if you move the site you won't have to retype all those pathnames if your directory structure is the same.

❓ How do I get my photos on my Web page if I don't have a scanner?

Tell your film developer to put your photographs on either Kodak PhotoCDs or Kodak Picture Disks, or use a process called "Floppy Shots." All three options let you take pictures with a normal camera and film, but when you get your prints back you also get either a PhotoCD or a 3.5" floppy disk for Macs or PCs. You can have up to forty pictures on a floppy disk and about a hundred on a PhotoCD with no additional installation or software required. You can then place those pictures on your Web page.

 Note   *If you use CompuServe and want to find a participating "Floppy Shots" dealer nearest you, either GO FLOPPY or try **http://ourworld. compuserve.com/ourworld/tools/education/wmscan.html**.*

❓ What's the quickest way to reduce the size of a graphic file?

The quickest way to reduce a graphic file's size is to reduce the numbers of colors used in its palette. Reducing the picture down to a small number of colors (let's say less than 20), reduces the file size greatly. Reducing the height and width of the file also affects its storage size.

Or check out GIF Wizard, an online utility that first shows you how much your graphics can be reduced, and then actually reduces them for you. You can find GIF Wizard at **http://www.gifwizard.com**. Click on your country's flag to enter the site. GIF Wizard also offers a search utility for finding graphics on the Net.

❓ Can I view the source of a page without having to go directly to the page and select "View Source?"

You can view the source of any URL by typing the following command in the Location field of your Netscape browser:

    view-source:*URL*

For example, if you wanted to view the source of Netscape's home page you would type:

    view-source:http://www.netscape.com

This will display the source of the file, just like the View | Document Source option does.

❓ Can I view the source of a Web page with something other than just Netscape so I can edit the page immediately?

If you'd like to use your favorite text processor to view and edit the Web page, follow these steps in Netscape:

1. Choose Options | General Preferences

2. Click the Apps button. You'll see the following box:

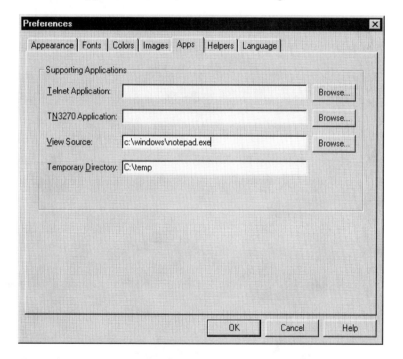

3. In the field where it says "View Source" enter the full pathname where your text processor is stored, or click the "Browse" button to point to the location of the text processor.

4. Click OK to save the changes.

Is there any way to tell if someone is stealing my graphics or text and using it as their own on the Web?

You can certainly do searches using popular search engines like AltaVista to see if any of your unique content is being lifted. Make sure to give your graphics unique names or add some unique text to your Web page. Then use a search engine to locate graphics with the same name or pages with your unique words.

To search for graphics with a particular name, use your Web browser to search AltaVista, located at **http://www.altavista.digital.com**, and type the following:

image:*image name*

For example, if you were looking for a file called siegelhead.jpg, you would type:

image:siegelhead.jpg

and all pages that contain that file embedded in them would be listed. You can also try HotBot's search engine, shown in Figure 11-3, which lets you choose the particular media type you want to search for.

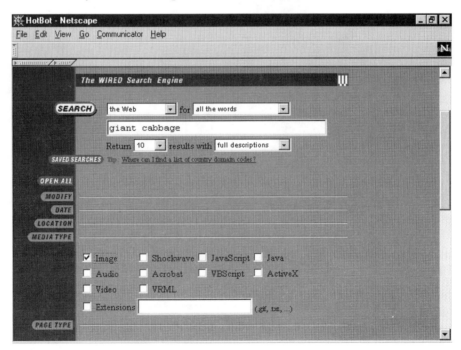

Figure 11-3.   HotBot's Media search feature

What are transparent GIF files?

Transparent GIFs are graphic files that have a transparent background instead of a particular color. That means the color of the Web page will show through any spots on the GIF that does not include color.

How can I include a watermark to mark my graphics?

Internet Explorer versions 2.0 and 3.0 support *watermarks*, the ability to mark your graphics. You can watermark images with the following HTML tag:

```
<BODY BACKGROUND="myimage.gif"
BGPROPERTIES=FIXED>
```

What size screen should I design my Web pages for?

The standard screen size does not exist. Millions of people view Web pages with hundreds of different types of monitors and there are literally thousands of screen sizes for which you could design. Your best bet is to design a page for a monitor no larger than 13 inches and to make the page resolution independent. Some sites place visual guides on the page telling the visitor to adjust their browser window to a particular length. Such visual aids help the visitor know exactly for what size screen the page was designed.

I've seen some pages with lots of white space. How does the designer get that effect?

You can create "white space" by either using nested <BLOCKQUOTE> tags, or by using a single-pixel spacer image that you can create in programs such as Photoshop, Image Composer, or PaintBrush. A single-pixel image, when used properly, will give you more control over the placement of images and text. On the other hand, nested <BLOCKQUOTE> tags will create white space but will not give you exact placement of text and graphics since the tag will adjust relative to the size of the browser window.

PUBLISHING PAGES
ON COMMERCIAL SERVICES

? **Once I've published my Web page on CompuServe, what will the address be?**

When you start the publishing process, you will be asked for an address you want to use for your home page. The address you choose for your home page also pre-registers you for a mail alias. For example, if you choose jane, your Web address (URL) will be **http://ourworld.compuserve.com/homepages/jane**, and your e-mail address would be **jane@compuserve.com**.

? **What am I allowed to put on my home page if I'm using CompuServe? Can I put my business on CompuServe?**

As with any online service, your home page must match the operating rules set forth by the service provider and CompuServe has relatively strict rules about what they allow. Inappropriate material such as profanity, pornography, illegal, or copyrighted material on any home page is strictly forbidden and could lead to the termination of your account. Check GO RULES for more information. And yes, you can place your business Web pages on CompuServe, as long as you follow their rules.

? **What is AOLPress? Do I have to use it to create pages on AOL?**

AOLPress is America Online's specialized software that helps you create and publish pages on the Web. You don't have to use it but it does make the publishing process easier.

? **How can I have my Web page detect the browser being used to view my site?**

You can either use a script or the server you are using may offer META capabilities. However, you can also include a client-side link without any programming. For example, take a look at the following code:

```
<HTML>
        <META HTTP-EQUIV="Refresh" CONTENT="3
        URL=http://www.mysite.com/netscape.html">
        <HEAD>
        <TITLE>Please wait while we detect your browser.</TITLE>
        </HEAD>
        <BODY>
        <H2>Please wait while we detect your browser.</H2>
        Using Netscape? The Netscape enhanced version of this
        page will automatically load. If you are not using
        Netscape, <A HREF="http://www.mysite.com/others.
        html" >Click Here</A>
```

When visitors come across this site, those not using Netscape will click and be taken to the correct page. Netscape users will be taken to the Netscape page automatically.

? If I cancel my account with CIS or AOL, what happens to my home page?

If either your CIS or AOL account is terminated for any reason, your home page will be deleted. Save your home page and graphic files to your local hard drive before terminating the account. You can quickly upload the saved information to another service provider and be up and running in no time.

? Can I use CGI scripts in AOL?

AOL members cannot run their own CGI scripts. However, there are a few standard CGI scripts you can incorporate into your Web pages, including a counter, a guestbook, and imagemaps. Check **http://members.aol.com/wwwadmin/index.htm**, or use the keyword WEB DINER for more information on the CGI scripts that are currently available for use on your Web page.

? How do I spread the contents of a column across cells in a table?

If you want to spread header information across two columns, use the COLSPAN attribute in your table cell tag. With COLSPAN, you can specify how many columns of the table the cell should span; the default is one cell. Here is an example:

<TD COLSPAN=2>This will span across two columns</TD>

? How do I use cookies?

A "cookie" is information saved to the client's machine in a file called cookies.txt. The cookies.txt file can include the last time the client visited the site, the password or login name, or other useful information. To implement cookies in your site, use the following format in a Web page:

Set-Cookie: NAME=*VALUE*; expires=*DATE*; path=*PATH*; domain=*DOMAIN*;secure

Note   *See Netscape's home page at* **http://www.netscape.com** *for more information on implementing cookies on your site.*

? Is there an additional cost to place Web pages on AOL or CIS?

Both services offer the ability to create and place Web pages on their server as part of your membership. However, standard connect charges may apply, depending on the payment plan option you've chosen.

? How do I display the current date and time in a Web page?

The server you are using must offer this option. If it does, use a server-side include. The syntax of such an include is dependent upon the server. Check with your server administrator.

? I've changed my Web page, but when I go to view it I don't see the changes. What could be the problem? I've waited several hours after uploading before checking.

If you are sure you've saved the page in text format with the .html or .htm extension, try holding down the SHIFT key while you click the Reload button in your browser. Your Web browser may still be caching the old page and not getting the new page from the server. If that doesn't work, try clearing the memory cache in your browser's preferences menu.

? **How do I add <u>e-mail notifications</u> when my Web page changes? Does that require an elaborate script?**

> A free service called NetMind URL-Minder does just that. You can find NetMind at **http://www.netmind.com/**. All you do is register your site and include some HTML code in your Web page. Complete instructions can be found at NetMind's site.

? **I'd like to show how I made my Web page using <u>examples of actual HTML code</u>. How do I do that without having the code interpreted?**

> If you want to include examples of HTML code, you have to use special characters to replace the < and > so the text between the brackets is not interpreted as HTML codes. Type &lt to replace the < and &lm to replace the >.

? **How do I get rid of the <u>extra spaces at the top</u> of my framed page?**

> You could use the MARGINHEIGHT attribute to control the upper and lower margins of a frame. MARGINWIDTH can be used to take care of space around the left and right margins within a frame. If you want to incorporate either of these two attributes, your FRAME tag should look like the following:

> ```
> <FRAME NAME="URL" SRC="FILE.html" MARGINWIDTH=0
>     MARGINHEIGHT=0>
> ```

? **I've published my page on CIS, but I've forgotten the URL. Is there a way to <u>find my page without the URL</u>?**

> If you forget the URL of your home page you can search the OurWorld Home Page database located at **http://ourworld. compuserve.com/** or you can submit your page again and your URL will be displayed.

? **I've created a mailto: form, but the results always come back as one long line of text with + signs in between each word, along with other extra symbols. How can I easily format the responses?**

You can use several shareware utilities to strip away those extra characters. Search Shareware.com's Web site, located at **http://www.shareware.com**, using the keyword mailto. You'll find at least 10 files such as WebParser and FormReader. Some even use Java to parse out the form information removing any extraneous characters.

? **How do you get frames to go away when linking to a different, non-framed page?**

All you have to do is put the following tag near the top of your Web page:

<BASE TARGET="_parent">

This will cause the frames to go away when linking to pages outside the framed area.

? **Does CompuServe offer any graphics I can place on my home page?**

Use GraphFF, the Graphics File Finder (shown in Figure 11-4), if you want to add graphics to your page. You can also search the Web for GIF or JPG files to add to your page. Just make sure you have consent of the copyright holder before you place any graphics or photographs from another source on your page. You can also go to the Tools and Tips page, located at **http://ourworld.compuserve.com/ourworld/tools/education/wmspruce.html**, for more links to graphics that can be used on your home page.

? **What is Home Page Wizard? Do I have to use it to create pages on CompuServe?**

Home Page Wizard is CompuServe's authoring tool aimed at making the task of creating a home page and placing it on CompuServe's servers easy. It offers a wide range of features including drag-and-drop editing, an extensive number of templates, and plenty of tips and help. There is even a test feature that lets you test your

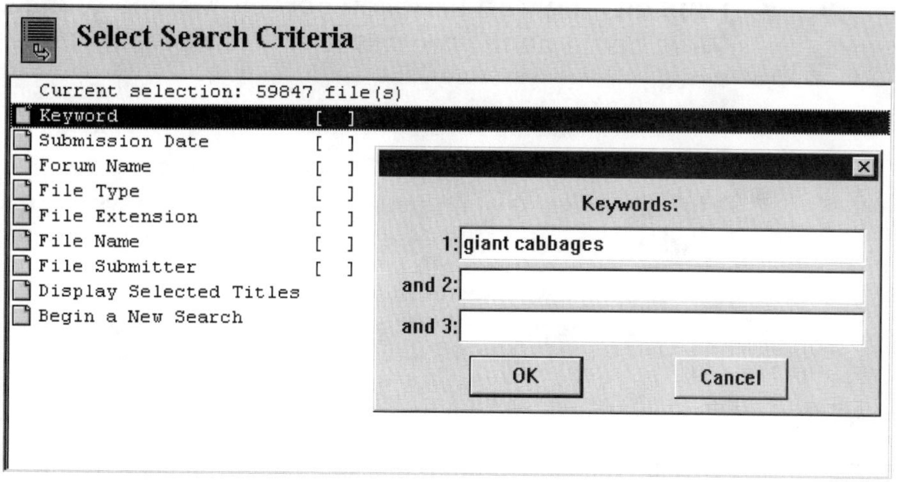

Select Search Criteria
Current selection: 59847 file(s)
Keyword [ ]
Submission Date [ ]
Forum Name [ ]
File Type [ ]
File Extension [ ]
File Name [ ]
File Submitter [ ]
Display Selected Titles
Begin a New Search
Keywords:
1: giant cabbages
and 2:
and 3:
OK
Cancel

Figure 11-4. CompuServe's Graphics File Finder

page before uploading it. Although you don't have to use Home Page Wizard (shown in Figure 11-5) to create pages for placement on CompuServe, it is recommended, because the Wizard is designed specifically for CompuServe and it uploads all the graphics and text pages together.

OUR WORLD
HELP Publishing Web Pages
Download Windows 3.1x Publisher
Download Windows 95/NT Publisher
Download Macintosh Publisher
click here!
Where ideas are not just shaped. They are STRUCTURED.
CSi
COMPUSERVE FORUMS® Where You Belong

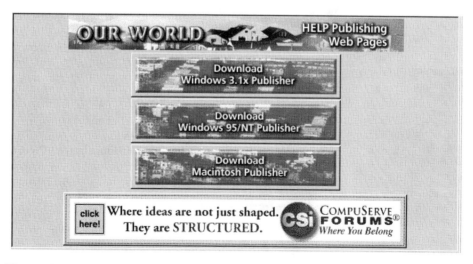

Figure 11-5. CompuServe's Home Page Wizard main menu

? I see an icon with a broken corner, instead of the image. What could be the problem?

Maybe you used an image file format your browser does not understand. Make sure you only use GIF or JPG files.

? Instead of seeing an image, I see an icon with a question mark where the image should be. What's wrong?

Most likely the server cannot find the image you are referring to in your Web page and instead simply shows either a broken icon or an icon with a question mark in it. First make sure the directory you specify for the image is correct and that you are using the <IMG SRC> tag. Otherwise your image will end up looking broken, as shown here:

Also, make sure you've spelled the tag and filename correctly.

? What is an imagemap?

An imagemap is a graphic image, either GIF or JPG, that has links to other pages or sites referenced in it. When a user clicks a region of the image, if the image has been identified as an imagemap, the server looks up the coordinates supplied in the Web page that were clicked-on and finds the URL referenced for those particular coordinates.

An excellent example of an imagemap would be a map of the United States. You click on a state, and the coordinates defined for that state take you to the Web page for the state.

In order to assign links to different areas of an image, you'll need to use an imagemap tool. Some HTML editors include this option. An excellent imagemap creation tool for Windows is MapEdit. You can find it by searching Shareware.com's index at **http://www. shareware.com.**

? Can I use imagemaps with AOL?

If you use AOL's page creation tool called AOLPress, you can use imagemaps. Use the keyword AOLPRESS for more information, and you'll see a screen much like that shown in Figure 11-6.

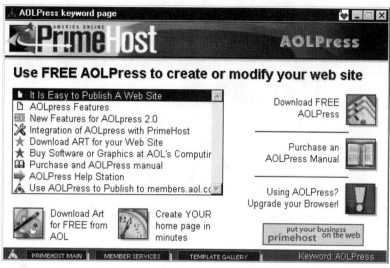

Figure 11-6.   AOLPress

❓ What are <u>Interlaced GIF files?</u>

Interlaced GIFs, unlike normal GIF files, don't load from top to bottom but rather load in layers, improving in quality as they are loaded.

❓ Is there a <u>list of all the currently supported HTML tags</u> available on the Web?

You can find an entire list of currently supported tags at **http://www.w3.org/pub/WWW/MarkUp/Wilbur/**. If you prefer a downloadable reference, try the Web Design Group's Windows help file at **http://www.htmlhelp.com/reference/**.

❓ Can I let <u>other people upload</u> to my AOL site?

AOL allows you to have an incoming directory—a kind of drop-box—which allows others to upload files to your directory. Only you will be able to read or view those files; no one else will have access to those files. The only limitation to this option is the 2MB restriction AOL imposes per screen name.

Remember   You can have up to five different screen names per single AOL account. If you need to create more space, just create another screen name.

How do I reset the page counter on AOL?

If you want to track visitors monthly, weekly, or daily, you can reset your Web counter by following these steps:

1. Use the keyword MY PLACE
2. Click the My Place icon
3. Click the .odometer file to select it.
4. Hit the DELETE key.

When I try to upload a file to my personal Web space on AOL, I get a PC Error 255. What am I doing wrong?

"PC Error 255" or "Remote PC Error 255" simply means the file you are trying to upload is still open in either your HTML editor or text processor on your computer. Make sure you close all files before uploading to ensure you don't get this message.

If I create a page on AOL, can people who aren't AOL members see it?

Anyone with Web access will be able to view your page. Although some features like certain chat rooms or areas such as Oprah are only available to AOL members, the AOL member servers and the files stored on them can be viewed by anyone with Web-browsing access.

Can I replace the Submit button in a form with an image?

Yes you can, if you use the following tag,

<INPUT NAME=*ButtonName* TYPE=image
SRC="http://*location/image.gif*">

where *ButtonName* is the name you want to give the button, and *http://location/image.gif* is the location and name of the image you want to use.

Is there a way to <u>upload multiple files</u> to the AOL server?

If you use a TCP/IP-based FTP program such as WS_FTP you can. AOL's FTP option only allows uploading one file at a time. To find out about the programs AOL recommends for FTP, use the keyword MY PLACE and follow the links.

What will be the <u>URL</u> of my page if I use AOL?

Your page would contain the screen name you used when you first logged on. For example, if your screen name were KIRKCL, your Web page URL would be **http://members.aol.com/KIRKCL**.

Note   *What about the "/screename" spelling? OK, the /screename portion of the URL is not case sensitive even if your screen name is in upper or lowercase. However, all file names listed after your screen name are case sensitive, so make sure you use only all upper or all lowercase when naming your Web pages.*

Note   *Most Web servers are set up to display a file named index.html if the browser just types in the name of the directory, as in **http://www. alaska.net/~ckirk**. If there is a file stored in the ~ckirk directory, then that file will be displayed when the browsing visitor requests this URL. If there isn't a file named index.html, the Web server will respond to the request by displaying a file listing of that directory. Therefore, if you are unsure what name to use, try index.html or index.htm if you want that Web page to appear instead of a directory listing when the URL is requested.*

I'm on America Online (or CompuServe). Can I put up <u>my own Web page</u>?

Both America Online and CompuServe offer the ability to publish Web pages at no additional cost outside your normal connect and membership charges. AOL offers a maximum of 2MB of disk space for your Web pages per screen name (10MB in all if you use all five screen names). CIS offers 5MB per account. Use the AOL keywords MY PLACE or CompuServe's GO INTERNET for more information on setting up your own page. The AOL My Place screen is shown in Figure 11-7.

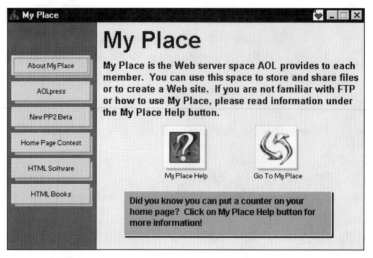

Figure 11-7.   My Place, the Web page creation site available to AOL members

❓ Where do I go to set up a Web page within CompuServe?

From the main menu select the icon for the Internet or GO INTERNET, then click the button for the Home Page Wizard. You'll find all the instructions for publishing a page on the Internet through CompuServe.

❓ Can I put up a Web site for my business on AOL?

Yes you can, but read AOL's terms of agreement before placing any material on AOL's servers. Use the keyword TOS for more information about what's acceptable.

❓ Where is the project stored after I'm done using Home Page Wizard? I can't seem to find it anywhere.

Your project should be stored in the directory containing your project's name. For example, if you named your project homepage, all the project files should be stored in the ~hpwiz\project\homepage directory.

ADVANCED DESIGN ISSUES

? **How can I add an access counter to my Web page?**

Counters are usually CGI scripts that link to or generate GIF graphics representing the number of times a page has been accessed. To add a counter, first check to see if your Web server already has one that you can reference in your Web page. AOL, for example, offers a free CGI script just to help you track visits to your site; for instructions, simply check out **http://members.aol.com/wwwadmin/counter/counter.htm.**

If you don't have a counter available, check one of the following company locations for instructions on how to use *their* counter on your page:

Counter Resource	Location	Features
Jcount	http://www.jcount.com/	Offers free Java-based counters and scrolling marquees
WebTracker	http://www.fxweb. holowww.com/tracker/	Offers free and fee-based tracking
Live Counter	http://www.chami.com/ prog/lc/pnp/	Offers plug-and-play counters
Yahoo's List of Counters	http://www.yahoo. com/Computers/World_ Wide_Web/Programming/ Access_Counts/ or http://www.yahoo.com/ Business_and_Economy/ Companies/Computers/ Software/Internet/World_Wide _Web/Log_Analysis_Tools/	A fairly comprehensive listing of for-fee and free Web counters along with log analysis tools

? **Why does it seem as if some of the attributes in some of the tags in my Web pages are ignored?**

If you are using an attribute value that contains non-numeric characters, it must always be enclosed in quotes. For example, if you specify size in percentages, the following format must be used: WIDTH="50%".

What are some of the <u>best sites for Web designers and Web masters</u>?

There are many sites dedicated to designing Web sites. The following are some of the more useful sites with links to thousands of other sites:

Site	Location	What it Offers
Web Design Group	http://www.htmlhelp.com	Lots of links to references for design, FAQs, and HTML codes.
The Web Developer's Virtual Library	http://www.stars.com	A wealth of information about adding multimedia, Java, ActiveX, and more to your site.
Developer.com	http://www.developer.com	Lots of Java and VRML information and links.
ActiveX.com	http://www.activex.com	If you're looking for ActiveX information this is the place to go.
Builder.com	http://www.builder.com	Excellent site with lots of references, how-to tips, reviews of HTML editors, and links to resources.
Internet/HTML Design Guide	http://griffin.multimedia. edu/~library/guide.htm	Not flashy but has lots of down-home HTML information along with lots of links to other sites.
Web Page Tips and Resources	http://www.ccim.com/ webzine/webtips.html	Lots of links for the beginning Web master.

Sometimes I see little <u>blue dots trailing a graphic</u>. What's causing this?

A trailing blue dot may appear after an image due to the way the image tags have been used. A dot appears after an image when there is white space after the image tag. Here is an example:

```
<A HREF="mypage.htm"><IMG SOURCE="me.gif"> </A>
```

This code will display a blue dot after the image because of the space preceding the </A> tag.

How can I keep my page from being <u>cached</u>?

Use the META tag to specify the expiration of the content of your page to prevent the information from being cached in a browser. Make sure the expiration date is at some point in the past.

<META HTTP-EQUIV="Expires" CONTENT="Tue, 04 Dec 1993 21:29:02 GMT">

How do I <u>center a table</u>?

The best way to center a table is to use the <TABLE ALIGN=CENTER> tag. However, this may not work in some browsers. So you might consider putting the <CENTER> tag around the entire table.

What is <u>CGI</u>?

The Common Gateway Interface, or CGI, is a standard for external gateway programs to interface with information servers, such as HTTP servers. A plain HTML document retrieved by the Web server is static, meaning it exists in a constant state or that it doesn't change. A CGI program, on the other hand, is executed in real-time, and it can output dynamic information.

How can I keep my Web page, and the photographs and images on it, from being <u>copied from my site</u>?

You can't really prevent people from viewing the source of your Web page nor from copying graphics from your site. But you can "watermark" your graphic files and make sure you clearly note all material is copyrighted and should not be reproduced without the express written consent of the copyright holder. The best way to internally watermark your graphic files is to place your logo or some symbol within the graphic to make it easily identifiable.

I've tested my framed site with several browsers. Sometimes the <u>display is blank</u>. How do I fix this?

You should include links or content for those browsers that don't support frames. This is accomplished within the <NOFRAMES> section in the main frame Web page. If you don't use the

<NOFRAMES> tag, browsers such as Netscape version 2.0 or Internet Explorer 2.0 will display as a blank page. Browsers that do not understand frames simply ignore all tags relating to frames and display only those elements within the body. Just make sure you don't put your <FRAMES> tags within the body. The following example shows how you would construct such a page:

```
<HTML>
<HEAD>
</HEAD>
<FRAMESET COLS="80,100%" FRAMEBORDER="yes"
  FRAMESPACING=0>
<FRAME SRC= NAME= >
<NOFRAMES>
<BODY>
Content for non-frame-compatible browsers
</BODY>
</NOFRAMES>
</FRAMESET>
</HTML>
```

? What main <u>elements</u> should my Web page have?

Like any good story, your Web page should have a beginning, middle, and end. The following shows the essentials that every Web page should have:

⇨ <HTML> This tells the browser what markup language is going to be used; in this case it's HTML.

⇨ <HEAD> This sets up the area where the header information such as comments, META tags, and titles will be placed.

⇨ <TITLE> This will title the page, making it easier for people to bookmark the site, or search for keywords within the title that match their interests.

⇨ </TITLE> This closes out the title tag, telling the browser where the title ends and where other elements can begin.

⇨ </HEAD> This closes out the header section.

⇨ <BODY> This tells the browser where the body information starts.

⇨ </BODY>   This tells the browser where the body information ends

⇨ </HTML>   This tells the browser where the page ends.

❓ What are some common <u>errors</u> I should look out for when checking my Web page?

Problems with Web pages can range from simple misspellings to problems with frames or forms. Here is a list of the most common problems:

⇨ Misspellings of tags

⇨ Open tags (i.e. the closing tag is missing)

⇨ Tag elements that have been placed in the wrong section; e.g., <FRAMES> tags in the body text

⇨ Misspelled filenames and filenames that are referenced incorrectly

---

Top Design Tips

⇨ Make sure your site has a clearly stated goal. When people visit it, they should know what you're offering them.

⇨ Always sketch out the page and site designs before creating the site. Never try to design directly in an HTML editor.

⇨ Be consistent with your design and design elements. Use the same navigational bars or references throughout the site.

⇨ Content is King. Make sure you have interesting and valuable content that pertains to the audience browsing your site.

⇨ Don't just link to be linking. Make sure your links have some relevance to what's contained on the page or site.

⇨ Use attractive color schemes, with complementary colors for text, links, and backgrounds. Aim for readability, not for the greatest variety of colors.

I've seen links that display an <u>explanation of the link</u> in the status bar when you move your mouse pointer over them. How can I get my links to do that?

Those links are using JavaScript. Remember, however, that not all browsers are capable of displaying JavaScript. Here's an example of such a script:

```
<A HREF="main.html" TARGET="main"
onMouseOver="window.status='Back to the first page'; return
true"><IMG SRC="home.gif" ALT="home" BORDER=0
HSPACE=0 VSPACE=0 ></A><BR>
```

Note   *Looking for some good Web-design books? Two of the best are David Siegel's* Designing Killer Web Sites *and Roger Black's* Websites That Work. *You won't find tips on how to create nifty HTML code; instead you'll find excellent design ideas on how to create sites that people can easily navigate and enjoy. If you're a programmer at heart, rather than a designer, and are looking for some good design ideas, pick up one of these books.*

 How can I create a <u>form to upload a file</u>?

A new ENCTYPE attribute for the FORM tag has been implemented in Netscape Navigator 3.0 and allows you to write forms that let the user input a file instead of just text data. The following is an example of such a form:

```
<FORM ENCTYPE="multipart/form-data"
  ACTION="_URL_" METHOD=POST>
Send this file: <INPUT NAME="thefiletosend" TYPE="file">
<INPUT TYPE="submit" VALUE="Send File">
</FORM>
```

Remember   *Not all browsers will work with this form. You should provide an alternate method if other types of browsers will be used.*

I've made the text smaller than the default font size with the <FONT> tag, but there appears to be a <u>gap between the last lines</u> of the text. What can I do to fix this?

This phenomenon is a quirk in HTML. The easiest way to fix this is to add the <BR> tag immediately after the closing </FONT> tag.

? **I've added a file to my Web page for downloading but when the link is clicked, instead of downloading the file, a page full of <u>gibberish</u> is displayed. What did I do wrong?**

You didn't do anything wrong. A couple of things could be the problem. Your Web server may not have its MIME types configured properly, or the browser may not have the correct plug-in installed. The best thing to do is to compress the file with a program such as WinZip and place the zipfile on your site. With the exception of GIF, JPG, or sound files, when a file is not zipped it will usually display as text.

? **<u>How much should I charge</u> for my Web-page design services?**

It depends. Are you a graphic artist? Do you know how to program in CGI? How extensive are the pages you are building? HTML is relatively easy to learn with programs such as PageMill, HotDog Pro, and FrontPage. But knowing how to code in HTML is not as important as good design or the ability to interface databases with Web sites. The going rate ranges anywhere from $25 per page to several hundred dollars per hour. Base your fees on how valuable you think your abilities are, then compare them to other design services within your geographic area.

? **Is there a place I can go to see <u>how my page will look</u> in a particular browser?**

You could try the Web Page Backward Compatibility Viewer at **http://www.delorie.com/web/wpbcv.html**. It will display your page as it would appear using the browser you specify.

? **Is there a place to see <u>how my site ranks</u> in various search engines based upon the META tags I've used?**

You can try a service called Rank This!, located at **http://www. rankthis.com**. You supply the search phrase someone would use, then your page's URL, and Rank This! will tell you where your page might be found in various search results.

Where can I find out about the <u>Link Exchange and Banner Advertising programs</u> I see on the Web?

One of the best places to go to get the real low-down on what's hot, what's not, and what's a scam is a site called Web Site Banner Advertising located at **http://www.ca-probate.com/comm_net.htm**. This site has a massive amount of links explaining virtually every banner advertising campaign going, along with research information into the effectiveness of banner advertising.

Instead of changing the contents of the frame, my <u>link opens a new window</u>. Why does this happen?

Most browsers such as Internet Explorer are case-sensitive and interpret target frame names by their case. For example, if you define a frame called "LINK1" and have an anchor that links to "link1," the target name will not be recognized and Explorer will open a new window instead.

How can I get a <u>linked file</u> to show up in a particular frame?

First, specify the name of the frame you want to target by including the following tag:

```
<FRAME SRC=file.html NAME=main>
```

Next, include this name in the TARGET attribute of your link:

```
<A HREF=link.html TARGET=main>
```

How do I get all of the <u>links from my table of contents frame to fill the whole screen?</u>

In the source file for all your pages you should place the following line:

```
<BASE TARGET=_top>
```

This sets the default for the page to fill the entire screen with the contents of the page.

? **I've placed my pages in my home directory, but when I access the URL for my directory, I get a listing. How can I make the URL go directly to a Web page instead of to a directory listing?**

It depends on your server, but in order to have a URL go directly to a Web page instead of a directory listing, you must place a file named either index.htm, index.html, home.htm, or home.html in the directory. For example, if your URL pointed to **http://www. alaska.net/~ckirk**, if you placed a file called index.html in the /~ckirk directory, the contents of index.html would display. If there is no index.html file, a directory listing would display instead.

? **How do I redirect a link without modifying my server?**

You can use the META tag, specifying the refresh rate and content for the META tag to display after the refresh time has elapsed. If a browser linked to this example, the page would display for three seconds before taking the browsing visitor to the link newpage.html.

```
<HTML>
<HEAD>
<TITLE>The Old Link</TITLE>
</HEAD>
<BODY>
<META HTTP-EQUIV="REFRESH" CONTENT="3;
  URL=newpage.html">
This page has moved. Please wait and I will take you to the
new page.
</BODY>
</HTML>
```

? **Why won't my section links work?**

If the links to your page sections are not working, make sure you have the section name reference spelled the same within your page. Then make sure you are using the same case throughout. The NAME tag is case-sensitive, meaning you must use the same case when referencing the section throughout your document.

For example, this will work:

```
<A NAME="Reference1">
<A HREF="#Reference1">
<A HREF="page2# Reference1">
```
But this will not work:
```
<A NAME=" Reference1">
<A HREF="#reference1">
<A HREF="page2#reference1">
```

❓ How can I embed a <u>sound</u> into the background of a page and have it play automatically?

Use the EMBED tag. But before you do, consider placing the tag close to the bottom of the body section since it may take some time for the sound file to load. The EMBED tag looks something like this:

```
<EMBED SRC="sound.wav" height=4 width=4 autostart=true
    hidden=true>
```

You can also use the <META> refresh tag and place the URL of the audio file in the CONTENT field of the <META> tag.

If you are designing sites specifically for Internet Explorer you can use <BGSOUND SRC=URL> which automatically plays the sound specified in the SRC attribute. Add the LOOP attribute followed by a value to loop the sound file, or use LOOP=INFINITE if you want the sound to play continuously.

Note   *If you have problems having MIDI files play, check your server to make sure the proper MIME types have been set to play MIDI files. Check with your ISP if you aren't running your own server.*

❓ Is it possible to have different <u>submit buttons</u> that do two different things on a single form?

Yes. First you need to give each button a name and value in order to determine which button was clicked. Browsers display the value attribute you use and will send the value to the server as well. A form could have the following tags:

```
<INPUT TYPE=SUBMIT NAME=member VALUE="I want to
    become a member">
```

```
<INPUT TYPE=SUBMIT NAME=moreinfo VALUE="Please send
me more info before I join">
```

? Is there a way to <u>superscript or subscript</u> text in a Web page?

Not all browsers recognize the <SUB> (SUBSCRIPT) and <SUP> (SUPERSCRIPT) tags, but for those that do, such as Netscape Navigator, these tags will display a smaller font compared to the default font of the page.

? How can I make sure my pages have the proper <u>syntax</u>?

A good place to go to have your Web page checked is Doctor HTML, located at **http://www2.imagiware.com/RxHTML/**. This site will check links, spelling, and form structure. You can also visit the Web Validator at **http://www.webtechs.com/html-val-svc/** or use the Kinder, Gentler Validator at **http://www.ee.surrey.ac.uk/FAQ/ checkhtml.html**. If these don't work for you, try the Web Design Group's Validator at **http://www.htmlhelp.com/links/validators.htm**, or Bobby at **http://www.cast.org/bobby/**. Bobby, shown in Figure 11-8, will check compatibility with specific browsers and offers indications of links that work for the physically disabled.

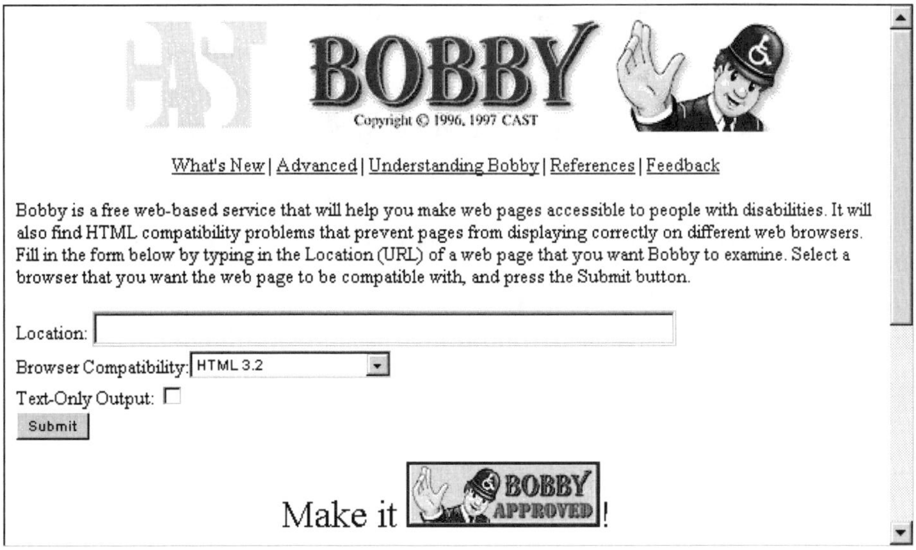

Figure 11-8.   Bobby's main screen for validating your Web pages.

More Design Tips

⇨ Create a search option if your site is complex.

⇨ Use white space liberally. You don't have to fill up the screen from end to end. Using white space makes things easier to read.

⇨ Limit use of large graphics. Not everyone has a high-speed connection. Try to keep large graphics to under 50KB.

⇨ Re-read the text in your site for clarity and spelling errors.

⇨ Watch out for "dead links." Make sure you have links on all pages to take the user back to the main page or to other pages. Use navigational aids or buttons at the top or bottom of the page to give people the ability to go back to the beginning.

⇨ Make sure you include an e-mail link to the person responsible for creating and updating the Web site.

⇨ Change or add new content periodically and let those who have visited your site know of the updates.

⇨ Create your own "hot list" and update it weekly.

? I've added a title tag to my page, but I don't see the title appear at the top of the window. What did I do wrong?

Most likely you haven't placed the <TITLE> tag in the HEAD section of your page, or you've forgotten to close off the tag with </TITLE>.

? How do you troubleshoot a CGI script that doesn't seem to work properly, even if you don't know much about it?

The first thing to do is go through the script looking for any obvious problems such as references to non-existent directories or files. After you've done that and run the debugger, try to execute it from your account at the command line. If you can execute it with no problems, your script may not work due to improperly set file permissions within your directory. The script may be calling for files in other directories that have not been given proper read/write access. If that's not the problem, ask your administrator to view the error logs and to help you isolate the problem.

❓ How do I get the text on my page to have that typewriter look?

To get that typewriter look, use the <TT> tag. <TT> stands for teletype text. Place the text you want affected between the opening <TT> tag and the closing </TT> tag.

❓ I'd like to include video on my site. What are the most widely used video formats?

There is a variety of popularly supported video formats including QuickTime, MPEG, and AVI. If you want to include video files for downloading, place a link to the file along with the complete filename, such as **http://www.mysite.com/movie.avi**. If the browser is capable of understanding the file format, it will automatically play the video once the file has been downloaded to the browser's cache.

The streaming video formats becoming widely used are Vivo, available at **http://www.vivo.com**, Streamworks at **http://www. streamworks.com**, and RealVideo, available at **http://www.realaudio.com**.

SETTING UP YOUR OWN WEB SERVER

❓ How do I get banners to rotate on my server?

There are several shareware, external CGI scripts you can get for your Web server. There is one called Banner Push that lets you rotate banners randomly. Every time the page is reloaded, a new ad will display. You can find this CGI script at **http://www.windows95.com/** in the Web Server Miscellaneous tools section.

❓ Should I let users run CGI scripts off my server? I heard this can cause security problems.

Although CGI scripts can open up all sorts of security holes in your server, there are a few things you can do to ensure you don't leave your server wide open to security breaches:

⇨ Never run your server in the root directory of your operating system

⇨ Restrict access to the directories the CGI scripts will run from and access

⇨ Check every CGI script before putting it out for public consumption

? Is there a site that compares all the various Web servers?

Probably the best place to go is a site called Web Compare. This site lists virtually every server available for every platform and details the costs, platform, features and how the major servers stack up against each other. You can find Web Compare at **http://webcompare. internet.com**. Another great place to check out is Serverwatch, located at **http://www.serverwatch.com**.

? How much does it cost to host a site?

Depending on what you want, and which service you choose, site hosting can range anywhere from $25 per month to thousands of dollars. The larger the site and the more options you need, the more expensive the hosting service will be. Average costs of a medium-sized, hosted service will usually run you about $150 per month.

? How do I get my own domain name, like mysite.com?

First, you need to find a service provider or Web-hosting service that will provide you with a Web server to store your files. Your ISP or web hosting service can register your domain name for you, or you can do it yourself, provided they give you pertinent information such as the IP address of the server storing your site and contact information for their technical support.

Next, you need to register your domain name with InterNIC, the company registering the bulk of the domain names. You fill out a form and pay $100 to register for two years the name you choose. Many of the most common or interesting names have already been taken, so you may need some imagination to come up with a unique name. You can find InterNIC and the registration forms at **http://www. internic.net/**.

Note *InterNIC may not be registering domains in the future. The interim Policy Oversight Committee (iPOC) announced in July, 1997 that it was accepting applications for other organizations to register domains, so by the time you get around to registering your domain name, there may be more than one company to choose from. Check the Internet Society's Web page at* ***http://www.isoc.org/*** *for news on other companies offering such services.*

Where can I find a **FAQ page** specifically for Web servers?

One of the better places to go is the WWW FAQ page, located at **http://www.sinica.edu.tw/www/faq/boutell/index.htm**. This site offers a wealth of links for both Web servers, Web browsers, and Web authoring. You might also try checking the following sites for good Web administrator support:

Web Site	Location
Web Developer	http://www.webdeveloper.com
Web Review	http://www.webreview.com
Developer.com	http://www.developer.com
Web Master Magazine	http://www.cio.com/WebMaster/
Web Monkey	http://www.webmonkey.com

How can I **fine-tune my server**?

Although a lot depends on the operating system software, there are a few things you can do to fine-tune just about any server.

⇨ Make sure you have enough RAM memory to support the server and any multiple applications you have running concurrently. Most servers recommend at least 32MB of RAM memory for a standard Windows 95 or Windows NT server. You may consider upgrading that to at least 64MB.

⇨ Examine the hard disk you are using. If you are using standard EIDE/IDE drives you may consider upgrading to a SCSI drive. SCSI drives offer faster throughput than standard EISA drives. Also, consider placing the log files on another drive, if possible, and make sure the log files are cleaned out consistently.

⇨ If you are writing CGI applications, consider using the server's Application Programming Interface (API). Using the server's built-in programming interface will speed up processing of external applications.

⇨   Restart your server on a regular basis. A good restart will clear out memory that may be slowing down the processing of your server.

⇨   Make sure your Internet connection is capable of handling the volume of data being transferred. Sometimes the slow down isn't related to the server, but rather the service provider's data connection.

Are there any free Web-hosting services?

If your service provider can't host your Web pages, you can try other sites offering free home pages. Here's a partial list, along with the "catch" each has:

Site	Location	Catch
GeoCities	http://www.geocities.com	Offers 2MB of free space for all personal sites.
HomeFree	http://www.homefree.net/	You just have to put a small advertisement for HomeFree at the bottom of your Web page.
Free Home Page	http://free.websight.com/free/	Commercial pages need to be cleared with the system administrators first, and you are limited to only one page.
Phrantic.com	http://www.phrantic.com	They've been hosting the Internet homeless since 1994. You're limited to 3MB of space and no commercial advertising.
AngelFire	http://www.angelfire.com	No pornography and a valid e-mail address must remain on your page, but you can advertise your business.

Site	Location	Catch
Planet Tripod	http://www.tripod.com/planet/	You only have 200KB of space for your pages and advertising is automatically attached to your page. You can purchase more space and options with their premium membership.
Cybercity	http://www.cybercity.hko.net/	Offers the best deal of any free Web page hosting service including 5MB of space, CGI programming, and more. One downside is that the servers are located in Hong Kong. You also have to credit Cybercity and put up with some e-mail advertising.

? What <u>hardware and software</u> do I need if I plan to do it myself?

You will need a computer that can run Web server software and that is connected to the Internet. You can use anything from a 486/66MHz computer, to a Macintosh IIci, to a Pentium Pro, or a PowerMac. When selecting a server, remember the following: speed is not as important as memory. The more RAM memory you have the faster your server will serve up Web pages. Processor speed is mainly needed when your site offers database searches or uses external CGI or Java-type programs. You can find a variety of Web server software at TuCows.com, located at **http://www.tucows.com**.

? Can I run <u>multiple servers</u>, including my Web server, on a single machine?

Web servers listen for requests on ports that other servers do not listen to, so you shouldn't have a problem. Depending upon how much RAM you have, you should be able to run several servers, whether they be Web servers, FTP (file transfer protocol) servers, or e-mail servers.

? What are the popular Web servers available for PC and Mac computers?

There are hundreds of Web server software programs, some shareware, some freeware, and others commercially available. For a list of shareware and demoware Web servers, check TuCows at **http://www.tucows.com**. For Windows 95, check **http://www.windows95.com**. Other popular Web server software programs are listed here:

Server Software Program	Platform	Requirements
Microsoft Internet Information Server	PC	486/66MHz or above, running Windows NT
WebStar	Macintosh	68040 or above running System 7.1 or above
Netscape FastTrack	PC	486/66MHz or above, running Windows 95 or Windows NT
Luckman's Web Commander	PC	486/66MHz or above, running Windows 95 or Windows NT
O'Reilly's WebSite	PC	486/66MHz or above, running Windows 95 or Windows NT

? How do I find out if someone already has registered a domain name I'm thinking of using?

You can search InterNIC's Whois database to see if a domain name has already been registered and by whom. Their Whois search database, shown in Figure 11-9, is located at **http://rs.internic.net/cgi-bin/whois**.

? How can I add a search option to my site?

Check with your server administrator to find out if the server offers a search facility. If it doesn't, check out a company called Netcreations that allows you to link directly to their search engine to allow visitors to search your site. You can find Netcreations at **http://www.Netcreations.com/pinpoint/**. If you are running your own server, the

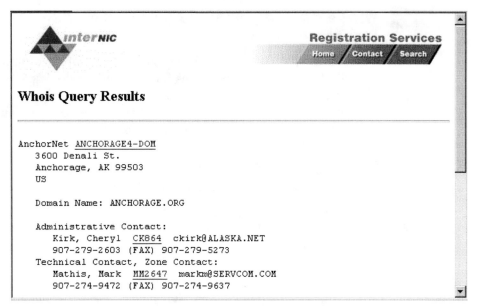

Figure 11-9. Searching InterNIC's Whois database

search engine you use will be based on the operating system platform you are running. The following table lists the various search engines available for certain platforms:

Search Engine Software	Platform	Where to Get More Information
Topic	Unix and Windows NT	http://www.verity.com
Excite	Unix and Windows NT	http://www.excite.com
RWPSearch	Windows NT and Windows 95	http://www.rpro.com
FoxWeb	Windows NT and Windows 95	http://www.foxweb.com (Allows searching a FoxPro database)
AltaVista Search	Unix and Windows NT	http://www.altavista.digital.com
DB/Text	Windows 95 and Windows NT	http://www.inmagic.com
Microsoft Index Server	Windows NT working with IIS Servers	http://www.microsoft.com

? ### What are the advantages to <u>setting up my own</u> <u>Web server</u>?

When you set up your own server, you have complete control over the content, external programs, and tracking options implemented on your server. You can add whatever CGI scripts, Java applets, or plug-in options you want. In addition, you have complete control over whether to offer streaming audio or video.

? ### Are the standard <u>U.S. designations</u>, like .com and .net, the only top-level domains I can get?

No they are not! The Kingdom of Tonga allows you to register your domain under their top-level domain designator. For example, if the domain name Disney.com is already taken, you could register the name Disney.to with the Kingdom of Tonga. Notice that the top-level domain is not .com; it is .to, the top-level domain designator for Tonga. You can register your domain name with the Kingdom of Tonga through their registration service found at **http://www.tonic.to**.

? ### Which is better—<u>virtual hosting</u> or setting up my own site?

If the service you are using offers all the features you want, then virtual hosting is much easier. You don't have to worry about making sure the server is up and running 24 hours a day. You don't have to worry about keeping track of error logs and running reports because most virtual hosting sites offer access reports. You should only consider running your own server if you have the technical knowledge and staff to keep the system up and running all day, every day.

If you do have the staff and the technical capabilities, and your virtual host is limited in the amount of space or additional features it has available, or if you find the virtual host is sluggish due to high traffic, you should consider setting up your own Web server.

If you are still unsure whether you should host your own Web site, check the Web Site Planner at **http://www.nua.ie/wp/**. This little survey will help you understand exactly what to concentrate on when setting up a server.

? What is <u>Web hosting</u>?

Web hosting is like renting space on someone else's server, leaving all the day-to-day, server-related maintenance issues to someone else. When you rent space on a hosting service, you don't have to buy your own server, configure the software, or keep the statistics. Most hosting services will offer the following:

⇨ Domain Name Registration

⇨ A certain amount of disk space to store your site

⇨ Access to CGI scripts for such things as counters

⇨ Monthly statistics on the number of accesses to your site

⇨ Backup of your site

⇨ E-mail addresses for your site

? I'd like to offer <u>Word, Excel, and Adobe PDF</u> files on my server. How do I do that?

Each Web server offers what is called a MIME-type configuration file. This file tells the server how to handle different types of files identified by the three-letter extension of the file. Most servers allow you to modify and add to the MIME configuration file through the server administration program used to administer the server.

chapter

12 **A**nswers!

Nifty Things on the Net

Answer Topics!

Nifty Things on the Net @ a Glance

⇨ There's more to the Internet than just the Web. Because the Internet was
    created using a wide variety of Unix-type servers, there still exists today a
    multitude of **Internet resources and tools** you can use to find out all sorts
    of interesting network information, such as whether a domain is active or
    the route things take to get from one server to the next. You may have
    heard of some of these tools, such as finger or Telnet; whereas others, such
    as Gopher, are slowly fading into the distance as Web servers take over
    more of the role of previous types of server software.

⇨ One of the most frequently asked questions about the Internet is "**What are
    the best sites for**…". There are millions of Web pages, but a few stand out
    in certain categories, such as travel, computing, free stuff, and
    entertainment.

⇨ A wide assortment of strange and ordinary gadgets are connected to the
    Internet. And with a simple Web browser you can view these
    miscellaneous net features. Everything from CB radios to hot tubs are
    connected for your viewing pleasure.

USEFUL INTERNET RESOURCES AND TOOLS

 ### Where would I get an **Archie Client**?

Archie is a software tool that lets you search the Internet for publicly
accessible files stored on FTP servers. Archie lets you search for

359

keywords in file or directory names and will point you to the locations of those files. You can get Archie clients for Macs and Windows-based computers. However, Archie is quickly being replaced by Web-based search sites such as Shareware.com, located at **http://www.shareware.com**, Download.com, located at **http://www. download.com**, or Filez, located at **http://www.filez.com**. You can search for Archie clients at any of these locations.

? How do I find out if a Web server, e-mail server, or other server is actually up and running?

You can use the ping command. The ping command lets you check to see whether another system is currently up and running. The general form of the ping command is

ping *domain*

Ping will respond, telling you whether the domain is alive and well.

? What does finger do?

Finger is a network utility that lets you check on specific information about a particular user or groups of users (see Figure 12-1). When you "finger" a user on a network, oftentimes you can find out the following information:

⇨ The person's user ID

⇨ The person's full name

⇨ If the user is currently working on the network

⇨ When the user used the network last

⇨ When the user last read his or her e-mail

⇨ A phone number, address, or office location

⇨ Information that the person has specifically prepared for the public to read in what is called a .plan file.

Note   *No word in the English language rhymes with month.*

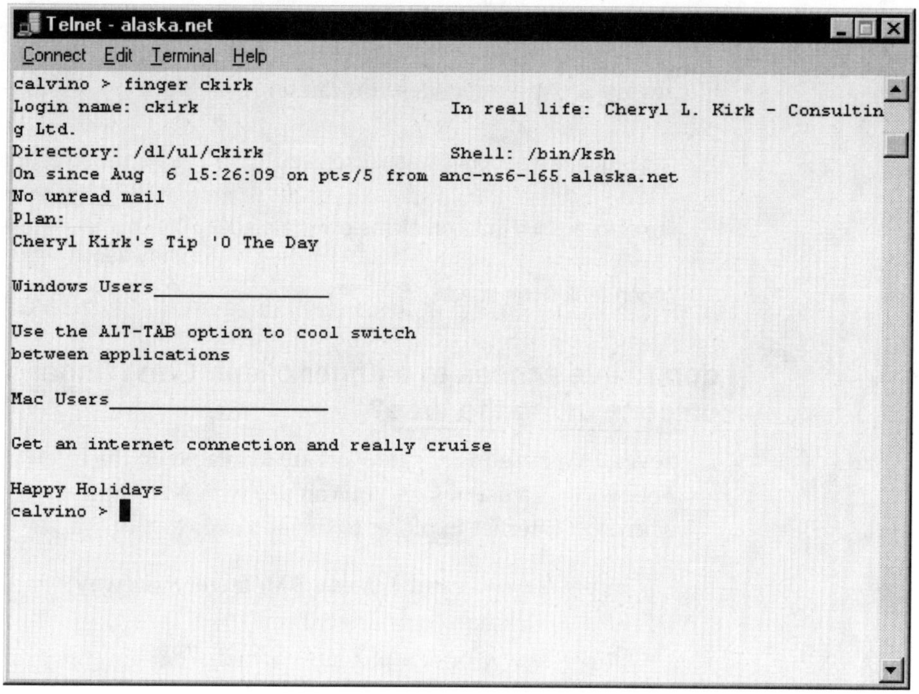

```
Telnet - alaska.net                                              _ □ X
Connect  Edit  Terminal  Help
calvino > finger ckirk                                                ▲
Login name: ckirk                    In real life: Cheryl L. Kirk - Consultin
g Ltd.
Directory: /dl/ul/ckirk              Shell: /bin/ksh
On since Aug  6 15:26:09 on pts/5 from anc-ns6-165.alaska.net
No unread mail
Plan:
Cheryl Kirk's Tip 'O The Day

Windows Users_____

Use the ALT-TAB option to cool switch
between applications

Mac Users_____

Get an internet connection and really cruise

Happy Holidays
calvino > █                                                           ▼
```

Figure 12-1.   Fingering your friendly author

❓ Can I finger for other information?

You bet you can. Normally you just type **finger** *username@domain*. But there are a variety of other ways to use it. Here are some common uses:

Command	What It Does
finger	Shows everyone who is on your network now
finger ckirk@alaska.net	Shows information about the user ckirk in the domain alaska.net
finger cheryl	Shows all the user IDs that have the word "Cheryl" in the name

Also, finger .plan files have been set up to relay everything from baseball scores to the latest earthquake information. Here are some always active finger sites you can try:

finger quake@geophys.washington.edu	Information on the most recent earthquakes
finger forecast@typhoon.atmos.colostate.edu	For hurricane forecasts in the Atlantic region
finger drink@csh.rit.edu	Checking the Coke machine

? I don't have access to a finger client. Can I finger someone using the Web?

Several Web-to-finger gateways are available on the Internet. Following is a list of sites you can use with Netscape Navigator or Microsoft Internet Explorer to finger a site:

http://www.cs.indiana.edu:800/finger/gateway
http://rickman.com/finger.html
http://www-bprc.mps.ohio-state.edu/cgi-bin/finger.pl

? What would I use Gopher for? Someone said their information is on a Gopher server. Do I need a special client to view what's on a Gopher server?

Gopher, developed at the University of Minnesota, (Go Golden Gophers!) is a way to distribute documents on the Internet. Before the introduction of the Web, Gopher was the choice for presenting information hosted on servers in a straightforward nested menu structure. This nested menu resembles PC directories, with directories and subdirectories branching off. The files listed on a Gopher server may be stored locally or could be pointing to files stored remotely on other Gopher servers.

Gopher servers could store text or binary files, directory information, and image or sound files. They also offer gateways to other types of servers, such as Web servers, Archie servers, or Whois servers. Gopher servers are more akin to FTP servers in that they do not allow for displaying graphical information as Web servers do. Gopher servers are slowly being phased out in favor of Web servers. You can use your Web browser to view the contents of what's in a

Gopher server. Since the information is stored as text and clickable links, you won't see much difference in the way you navigate or read information off a Gopher server.

How do I make my own .plan file?

First create a text file with the information you want to be included in your .plan file. You may try using a text editor on your Unix system. Save the file with the name ".plan". That's all you have to do.

Warning   *Only one person in 2 billion will live to be 116 or older.*

How do I make my .plan file visible to everyone on the network?

You'll need to use a Unix command, chmod, to let others read your .plan file. Chmod lets you set the attributes to a file so others can read, write, or execute files in a directory. When your account is set up, the normal default is to prevent others from reading files in your own directory. In order to make it possible for others to see the .plan file in your directory by using the finger command, you need to make your directory readable and executable by others and your .plan file readable by others.

To make your directory readable and executable by others, type the following command:

    chmod 755

To make your .plan file readable by others, type the command:

    chmod 644 .plan

What software do I use to ping a site?

You can use a Telnet client, but Windows 95 also has a utility specifically for pinging a site. If you are connected to the Internet, try bringing up the DOS prompt, then typing at the C> prompt:

    ping *domain*

The system should reply, telling you whether the domain is alive and well.

? What is a .plan file

A .plan file is basically a text file that's displayed anytime someone
fingers you. You can include anything in your .plan file including
URLs, e-mail addresses, regular addresses, or quotes of the day.
Some plan files offer information about earthquakes or weather
information. Due to security issues, not every server allows everyone
else to view a user's .plan file.

? What is Telnet used for?

Telnet is a software tool that lets you log on to remote computers,
essentially turning your computer into a dumb terminal. Unlike
modem terminal software, Telnet software is used to connect to other
computers, not through a modem, but through the Internet. In other
words, Telnet software does not have dialing capabilities, and it
supports relatively few terminal types. Telnet is often used to log on
to university, government, and library computers and mainframes.

Many government and university systems still use mainframe
computers that are not yet connected to the Web but are connected to
the Internet via Telnet. If the system you want to access is such a
system, you would need to use a Telnet client.

? Do I have a Telnet client on my computer?

Yes. Windows 95 has a built-in Telnet client. To launch it, follow
these steps:

1. Click the Start button.

2. Select Run.

3. Type **Telnet** and click OK or press ENTER.

4. Choose Connect | Remote System, and then enter the name for
   the remote system you want to connect to. That system will be
   stored in the Telnet preferences under the Connect menu the next
   time you launch Telnet.

? What is Traceroute for?

Traceroute is a software network tool for displaying the path that
data packets take when they travel from your machine to another
Internet host. If you want to check your network connection using the
Windows 95 program called tracert, open a DOS window and type
tracert.*domain*, or try this Web page version of Traceroute:

http://tracer.maxim.net/

The following is an example of what Traceroute would display:

```
traceroute to flex.net (205.218.188.1), 30 hops max, 40 byte packets
 1  anc-cr3-e1-1.alaska.net (206.149.65.254)  2 ms  1 ms  1 ms
 2  agis-alaska.seattle1.agis.net (206.43.44.5)  68 ms  48 ms  68 ms
 3  a1-0.737.santaclara1.agis.net (206.43.44.242)  136 ms  80 ms  148 ms
 4  198.32.136.72 (198.32.136.72)  123 ms  103 ms  90 ms
 5  core3-hssi2-0.SanFrancisco.mci.net (204.70.1.13)  107 ms  221 ms  137 ms
 6  core1.Dallas.mci.net (204.70.4.217)  262 ms  360 ms  290 ms
 7  core1-hssi-3.Houston.mci.net (204.70.1.122)  180 ms  285 ms  287 ms
 8  border4-fddi-0.Houston.mci.net (204.70.3.99)  273 ms  220 ms  246 ms
 9  flexnet-inc.Houston.mci.net (204.70.39.50)  247 ms  230 ms  234 ms
10  tron.flex.net (205.218.188.1)  366 ms  379 ms
```

Note   *Back in the mid- to late 1980s, an IBM-compatible computer wasn't considered 100 percent compatible unless it could run Microsoft's Flight Simulator.*

How do I use the Windows 95 Traceroute client?

To use it, all you have to do is bring up the DOS prompt and type the following:

tracert *domain*

For example, if you wanted to measure the number of hops between your domain and another domain, say, flex.net, you would type

tracert flex.net

What is Veronica?

Veronica is a service that maintains an index of titles of Gopher files and lets you search the titles of those files by keywords. Veronica is used with Gopher-based information to help you find files without having to do a menu-by-menu, site-by-site search. You can access Veronica from most top-level Gopher menus.

What can I use Whois for?

You can use Whois for looking up the names, addresses, phone numbers, and e-mail addresses of people or companies who have registered domain names on the Internet. An example of a couple of domain names are mcgraw-hill.com and alaska.net.

> *Tip*   *Whois is a network tool that lets you query information pertaining to a particular domain name, such as mcgraw-hill.com.*

? Where can I find a <u>Whois database</u>?

A simple Web-based Whois interface is located at **gopher://rs. internic.net/7waissrc%3A/rs/whois.src**. You can also try Internic's Whois database page at **http://rs.internic.net/cgi-bin/whois**.

WHAT ARE THE BEST SITES FOR...

? What sites should I use for booking an <u>airline reservation</u> or general travel-related information?

I'd start with Microsoft's Expedia, a completely automated travel site where you can book reservations, find out about hotels, rent a car, and catch up on the latest travel information. Check out Expedia at **http://www.expedia.com**, shown in Figure 12-2. Expedia offers secure transactions for booking with a credit card.

TraveloCity is another excellent site for planning your travel, and it offers an option to search for bulk and courier discounted fares. You'll find TraveloCity at **http://www.travelocity.com**.

City Net, at **http://city.net/forms/reservations**, offers secure transactions, meaning you can book a flight with your credit card. The interface is incredibly simple; it's one of the easiest travel sites to navigate. Don't forget to check out Epicurious's travel search option found at **http://www.epicurious.com**. Here you can search for that perfect romantic bed and breakfast or find the ski resort that caters to your level of expertise.

With a name like Travel.com, you'd expect links to virtually every travel-related site on the Internet. And you get it at **http://www. travel.com**. Whether you're looking for airline reservations or hotels to stay in, this is an excellent source for anything relating to travel.

Figure 12-2.   Booking an airline reservation via Expedia is a first-class experience.

Another excellent source is PCTravel, one of the first travel sites on the Internet. You can find PCTravel at **http://www.pctravel.com/**. And if you're just looking for a comprehensive list of travel-related links, try the Comprehensive Travel and Relocation Service at **http://www. millionaire.com/travel/ related.html**.

❓ What are the best book sites?

Are you reading or buying? The major booksellers, such as Barnes & Noble, are online, but so are "virtual bookstores," such as Amazon (see Figure 12-3) and Computer Literacy. Some of the best book sites are

Figure 12-3.   Amazon.com is one of the best virtual bookstores.

listed in the following table. Some let you read excerpts, others let you purchase online, and some point you to links relating to books and book publishing.

Site	Location	What It Offers
Amazon.com	http://www.amazon.com	Purportedly the largest bookstore on the planet, this site offers tons of reviews of books, links to many authors, and the ability to buy over 2.5 million books. It's one of the best places to go if you want to buy a book.

Site	Location	What It Offers
AnyBook	http://www.anybook.com	Are you looking for an out-of-print book or books from specialty publishers? AnyBook might be able to help, although it's not as extensive as Amazon.
Barnes & Noble	http://www.barnesandnoble.com	Also touting themselves as the largest bookstore on the planet, they offer lots of links, online ordering, and catalog searching for your favorite book or author.
Book Stacks	http://www.books.com	Like Amazon, Book Stacks offers the ability to order any book from their inventory online. They offer discounts up to 40 percent on some books, along with links to authors and online chats with authors.
BookWire	http://www.bookwire.com	Interested in books? This is the place to go. They have every type of link imaginable, from links pointing you to mailing lists discussing books, to links to every major book publisher— truly an extensive site for the book lover.
Computer Literacy	http://www.cbooks.com	This virtual bookseller focuses on computer-related titles. They include links to computer-related trade shows, along with reviews and a searchable database.

Site	Location	What It Offers
The Internet Public Library	http://www.ipl.org	This is the first public library on the Internet with lots of interesting links to newspapers, magazines, and online books. They also cater to children, offering many links to young people's reading material. They offer a special searchable database pointing you to various texts online.
Project Gutenberg	http://www.promo.net/pg	It's fine literature digitally republished. Looking for Mark Twain's work? What about the complete text of Alice and Wonderland? There's no reason to buy the classics anymore, they're online here at Project Gutenberg.
SmartBooks	http://www.smartbooks.com	Want to read more about the Internet? This bookselling site is devoted exclusively to books about the Internet.
The Virtual Bible	http://www.mit.edu:8001/ people/aaronc/bibles.html	Want to search the biggest selling book of all time? This site has links to all sorts of search engines and online versions of the Bible.
The Write Page	http://www.writepage.com/	This site offers lots of links to authors, titles, and writers' resources.

❓ What are the best computer-related sites?

There are a ton of computer-related sites, but a few stand out for the depth of information and navigational ease. Whether you're looking for pointers to shareware, places to buy computers, or news and reviews of hardware and software, these sites are good starting points:

Site	What It Offers	Location
CINet Central	A wide variety of computer-related news, how-tos, and hardware and software reviews	http://www.cnet.com
ZiffNet	In-depth reviews on hardware and software, plus a huge shareware index directory	http://www.zif
Windows95.com	Excellent source for all kinds of Windows 95 software	http://www.windows95.com
TuCows	Huge depository of reviews on shareware and freeware with links for downloading	http://www.tucows.com
OnSale	The place to go if you're into buying computer stuff at cheap prices; run like an electronic auction house, this site also includes options for buying all sorts of electronic gear	http://www.onsale.com
The Internet Product Finder	Links to virtually every Internet-related commercial software and hardware product available	http://tips.iworld.com

❓ What's the best Web site for checking my e-mail while I'm on the road?

Without a doubt, the easiest way to check your POP e-mail is Hotmail, shown in Figure 12-4. You'll need to follow the sign-up procedure. Once you have signed up, you'll click the Options button and then the POPmail button. Now you can read your e-mail, forward it, reply to it, or send new messages. You don't need to configure anything; your e-mail stays on your server, so when you get back home, you still have a copy of each message received.

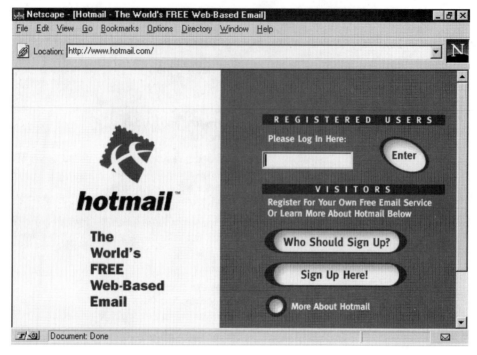

Figure 12-4.   E-mail on the road is a breeze with Hotmail.

? What are the best e-zines and online magazines on the Net?

The Web is full of e-zines, and labeling one "the best" is rather subjective since most cater to specific tastes. So if you are looking for your favorite or best e-zine, why not try searching the e-zine database, at **http://www.dominis.com/Zines/**. Every type of e-zine imaginable is indexed in this search engine. From health to the military, from fashion to cooking, whatever you fancy, you'll be able to find an e-zine to match your particular tastes. NerdWorld also has a long list of e-zines for your viewing pleasure, categorized by type and geographic location. You can find the list at **http://www.nerdworld. com/trees/ctr30.html**.

In terms of commercial ventures both in the print and online world, here is a list of the more popular sites:

Site	Location	What It Offers
Feed	http://www.feedmag.com	This site offers articles on cultural and political issues relating to technology that are well designed, well written, and fun to read.
Salon1999	http://www.salon1999.com	This excellent literary site offers an interactive magazine of books, arts, and ideas. Some big-name columnists grace Salon's pages.
American Journalism Review List of Magazines Online	http://www.newslink.org/ mag.html	If you're looking for your favorite magazine, you might find it here in this comprehensive list.
The Electronic Newsstand	http://www.enews.com/	Billed as the ultimate magazine site, you can subscribe, search, or read many of your favorite magazines from this Web page. They also offer a roundup of what's appearing in your favorite magazines.
List of Electronic Magazines	http://www.abc.hu/unix/ magazines.html	If you're looking for an online magazine, this is a great place to find one, arranged alphabetically.
Word	http://www.word.com	This is one of the original e-zines, with a classy look and all sorts of features on culture, the Net, new media, and current issues.

 ## Is there a place that has links to all <u>FAQs</u> about the Net?

One of the best places for links to FAQs is the FAQ Finder, located at **http://ps.superb.net/FAQ/**. There you can even search for the subject of the FAQ you are looking for.

Tip *One of the best places on the Net to learn how to do everyday things, such as sharpen a knife, shine leather shoes, spin a basketball, or childproof your home, can be found at Learn2.com, located at* **http://www.learn2.com/**.

❓ Where do I find the best <u>free stuff</u> on the Net?

Sure, information is free, but there's also a ton of stuff you can register, call, or write for, all sent to you absolutely free. The following table lists some of the best sites that point you to everything from free e-mail accounts and Web hosting services, to free toothpaste and magazines.

Site	Location	What It Offers
Free Things on the 'Net	http://idt.net/~jusric19/ free.html	This site has lots of links to lots of free stuff on the Web.
Free-Stuff.com	http://www.Free-Stuff.com/	This is the ultimate site for finding free stuff. Very well designed, it comes complete with a search engine for finding exactly what you want without having to pay for it.
Free Stuff on the Web	http://www.galaxymall.com/ Galaxy/free/	Nothing fancy, this site just offers links to where all the free stuff is, arranged by category.
Games and Giveaways	http://www.playhere.com/ giveaway.htm	This site offers links to more than just what's available on the Web.
The Complete List of Free Stuff on the Internet	http://rsg.simplenet.com/ free.htm	This one's not the slickest interface but certainly has a load of links—over 300—to stuff you can get free over the Internet.
The Web 100	http://www.Web100.com	If you want to know what's hot, check out this site. It lists the 100 top Web sites voted on by Web users and updated hourly.

? ## What are some of the best print <u>magazines</u> focusing on the Net?

Ziff-Davis' *Internet Magazine*, is located at **http://www.zdimag.com**. The Net, located at **http://www.thenet-usa.com**, and *Internet World*, located at **http://www.iworld.com** are available in just about any bookstore. Others, such as *The Web Magazine*, located at **http://www. webmagazine.com** and a British publication called *.net*, are excellent sources of Net-related information and lists of links. You should be able to find these magazines in the larger chain booksellers. If you want to shop on the Internet you might try Internet Shopper, or if you've always wanted to know the stories behind the people who are behind the Web sites, try reading Internet Underground.

? ## What are the best <u>movie and entertainment</u> sites?

If you're interested in movies, or you're a TV buff, the Internet is the place for you. Here are some of the more interesting sites for movie and entertainment buffs:

Site	Location	What It Offers
Mr. ShowBiz	http://www.mrshowbiz.com	Anything relating to show business can be found here—news, gossip, links to star bios, box office charts, and more. (See Figure 12-5.)
The Discovery Channel	http://www.discovery.com	This is one of the best companion sites to the cable TV channel.
E! Online	http://www.eonline.com	The dishy entertainment channel channels its energy into a Web site with lots of good insider gossip about the stars. It also has tons of links to TV shows, movies, and reviews.
Comedy Central	http://www.comcentral.com	Looking for a few good laughs? This is the place to go.

Figure 12-5.   All the showbiz info you could want

Site	Location	What It Offers
TV Guide	http://www.tvguide.com	You'll find lots of TV gossip, reviews, and information on your favorite soaps, stars, and TV shows.
Box Office Online	http://www.boxoff.com	Archives of movie reviews, the latest news on new releases, and links to other online resources about movies are located here.
The Internet Movie Database	http://www.imdb.com	This is the definitive source for information on virtually every movie ever made.

Site	Location	What It Offers
MovieWeb	http://movieWeb.com/ movie/movie.html	This site offers links to all major movie houses along with QuickTime movie clips.
MovieLink	http://www.popcorn.com	Looking for a movie in your area? Search the MovieLink database.
Film.com	http://www.film.com	Reviews, movies on tapes, and more. Excellent site if you are looking for movie reviews of films already out on tape.

? What are the best <u>music</u> sites?

Music is definitely taking over the Internet. If you just want to find your favorite band's official Web site, or check out a clip of the latest Foo Fighters CD, there are plenty of sites offering lots of music and music label-related information.

Site	Location	What It Offers
The Ultimate Band Site	http://ubl.com	If you're looking for a band and links to that band, you can't miss this site. (See Figure 12-6.)
CDNow	http://www.cdnow.com	This is the world's largest online electronic music store that lets you hear, browse, and buy CDs.
Classical Net	http://www.classical.net	This excellent site has thousands of links to sites relating to classical music.
Live On-line	http://www.live-online.com	This is a great site for finding online and live music events on the Internet. It also includes a digital jukebox where you can cue up your own songs.

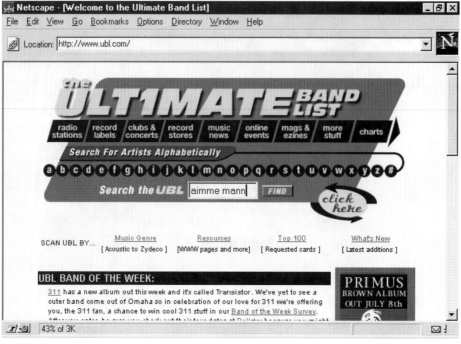

Figure 12-6.   Use the Ultimate Band List to find all your favorites.

Site	Location	What It Offers
AudioNet	http://www.audionet.com	This site offers links to radio stations that are connected to the Internet and can be heard by using the RealAudio player.
Timecast	http://www.timecast.com	Go to this site for pointers to live concerts, live radio stations, and lots of online music.
Festival Finder	http://www.festivalfinder.com	Are you looking for a music festival to go to, or traveling to another state and want to know if your favorite band is playing? This is the site to visit.

Site	Location	What It Offers
Soundz - The Music Nexus	http://www.soundz.com	This eclectic site has all sorts of information on music, including history, sound files, links to bands, and more.
The Daily .Wav	http://www.dailywav.com	This is the place to go for some great midi and .wav files.
Yahoo's List of Recording Companies	http://www.yahoo.com/ Business_and_ Economy/Companies/ Music/Labels/all.html	If you're looking for a Web site for your favorite label, this is the place to go. It offers links to almost all the majors plus many smaller and independent companies.
The DJ	http://www.thedj.com	Here you'll find free music, all the time. You choose the type, the DJ plays it for you using the RealAudio player.
Classical Insites	http://www.classicalinsites.com/	For everything you'd ever want to know about classical music, this is the site.

 ## What are the best <u>news</u> sites?

Although it depends on whether you want regional or local information, some of the best news sites are mainly the big boys. Also included in this list are links to various newspapers and news gathering sources. Again, there are a ton of news sites on the Internet. Also check out the various search directories, such as Excite, **http://www.excite.com**, or InfoSeek, at **http://www.infoseek.com**. Search directories are also getting into the news tracking business, and they offer pointers to lots of daily news from around the world.

Site	Location	What It Offers
ABC News	http://www.abcnews.com	This site has U.S. and international news with lots of links to other sources. (See Figure 12-7.)

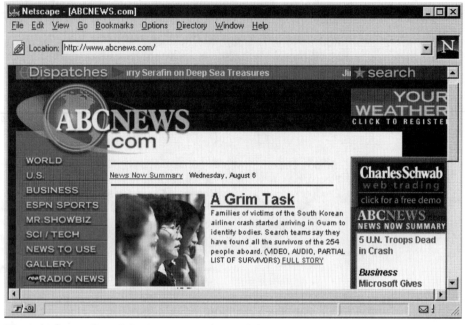

Figure 12-7.   Get all the latest news from ABC.

Site	Location	What It Offers
CNN	http://www.cnn.com	Here you'll find global news with links to technology-related features.
MSNBC	http://www.MSNBC.com	This site offers global news with links not only to technology but also to many entertainment and lifestyle-related features.
NewsLink	http://www.newslink.org	Use this site to find online newspapers in your geographic location. It also has links to magazines and e-zines.

Site	Location	What It Offers
The New York Times	http://www.nytimes.com	Some say this is the best newspaper in the country, both on paper and on the Web.
Reuters International News	http://www.reuters.com	Here you'll find excellent international news and photographs, along with closing stock market prices and scrolling up-to-the minute news.
The Financial Times	http://www.ft.com	That pink paper from over the pond is now on the Web.
NandONet	http://www.nando.net	Go to this site for lots of links to news from around the globe. It takes advantage of lots of Java, so be prepared.
Yahoo's List of News-Related Links	http://www.yahoo.com/News/	You'll find an extensive list of news-related links. Also check out Yahoo's news tracking software to keep track of up-to-the minute news.
PointCast	http://www.pointcast.com	Although not officially a news site, PointCast's software feeds you news, weather, entertainment items, and stock quotes continuously, displaying feeds through the specialized PointCast software and through the PointCast screen saver.

What are the best <u>sports</u> sites?

There are thousands of sports-related sites on the Web, many with up-to-the minute updates, sports scores, and links to fantasy leagues

you can join online (see Figure 12-8). But for information about a
particular league or a particular team, your best bet is to go directly to
the source. Here are some of those sources:

Site	Location
ESPN	http://www.espn.com
Sports Illustrated	http://www.sportsillustrated.com
The Official Site for the NFL	http://www.nfl.com
The Official Site for the NBA	http://www.nba.com
The Official Site for Major League Baseball	http://www.majorleaguebaseball.com
The Official Site for the NHL	http://www.nhl.com
Runner's World	http://www.runnersworld.com
NandONet's Sports Server	http://www.nando.net/SportsServer/
GolfWeb	http://www.golfWeb.com

 Note   *The first toilet ever seen on television was on* Leave It to Beaver.

Figure 12-8.   One of the big boys in sports information

MISCELLANEOUS STUFF ON AND ABOUT THE INTERNET

Tip   *If you're looking for a list of interesting devices connected to the Internet, a good place to start is the home page,* Thingys Connected to the Internet, *located at* **http://marconi.w8upd.uakron.edu/users/search/interact.html**. *You should also check Yahoo's list of* Interesting Devices Connected to the Net *at* **http://www.yahoo.com/Computers_and_Internet/Internet/Entertainment/Interesting_Devices_Connected_to_the_Net/.**

? Is there really a <u>Coke machine</u> connected to the Net?

There is more than just one Coke machine connected to the Internet. At last count the total number hovered around just under 20. Although you can't get a wet, cold Coke delivered to your desktop, you can check the status of how much Coke is in a machine, when the last purchase was made, and what the refill levels are. Two of the best places to find out more about Internet-connected Coke machines is The UCC Drink Machine, located at **http://www.ucc.gu.uwa.edu.au/drink/** and Lloyd's Coke Machine, located at **http://www.ugcs.caltech.edu/~walterfb/coke/coke.html**, where you can actually interact with a real Coke machine.

? Can I <u>connect my TV</u> to the Net?

Well, in a way, you can use your TV as a kind of monitor or display for displaying Web pages and e-mail messages with a device called WebTV. WebTV is a little black box with computer "smarts" in it. About the size of a VCR, it has a 33.6Kbps modem built into it and sells for under $300. The unit uses a standard television set as its display and standard phone lines to connect to a local service provider. The actual WebTV units are made by Philips-Magnavox and Sony, and they offer a wireless remote for surfing from one Web page to the next, or a wireless keyboard that you can use to write e-mail messages. You can find out more about these amazing little boxes at **http://www.Webtv.net**.

Note   *In every episode of Seinfeld there is a Superman somewhere.*

? Can I get my e-mail messages on my pager?

It depends on the company providing you with your paging service, but companies such as SkyTel offer the ability to receive e-mail messages on your pager or send messages to a pager from the Internet. All you need is an alphanumeric pager in order to see the messages. Many services can also send you the latest news, sports scores, stock quotes, and weather information.

Note   *Isaac Asimov is the only author to have a book in every Dewey-decimal category.*

? Can I get my e-mail, voicemail, and fax mail all in one mailbox?

A company called Jfax offers an all-in-one mailbox that can store voicemail, e-mail, and fax mail, then route the information to you wherever you might be. You can find Jfax at **http://www.jfax.com**. One thing to note, however, not all areas are covered by a local phone call.

? Can I send a fax over the Net?

Yes, you can, but you may not find it that easy. Several gateways set up across the globe connect the Internet to phone systems, allowing you to fax something to someone directly from the Internet. The best thing to do is read The Phone Company's Remote Printing Service instructions, located at **http://www.tpc.int/tpc_home.html**, for more information on how and where you can fax something to someone.

? Can I get information on my computer without being logged on to the Net?

The AirMedia NewsCatcher is a little black pyramid-shaped box with a pager built in that connects to any Windows-based PC. It captures information coming over the paging networks and delivers it directly to your PC through the serial port. The box itself is manufactured by Global Village, makers of Global Village modems. You don't have to be logged on to the Internet in order to get the latest sports scores, news, weather, or entertainment information, but if you are, you can quickly click various links to take you directly to Web pages with more information.

The AirMedia NewsCatcher sells for under $150 and includes a free one-year subscription to basic services. If you would like to know when mail has arrived in your e-mail box, you can purchase that feature for an additional charge. For more information about AirMedia, check out their home page at **http://www.airmedia.com**.

 Note   *Lincoln Logs were invented by Frank Lloyd Wright's son.*

? Is there really a <u>hot tub</u> connected to the Net?

Paul has had his hot tub connected to the Internet for quite some time. Now he's added his refrigerator for your benefit. But that's not all. If you feel like waving to the cats, you can, by sending a signal to a robotic arm in Paul's humble abode. You'll find all these wacky options at **http://hamjudo.com/cgi-bin/hottub** on the Web.

If that's not enough for you, you can also check the temperature in the Chez Oxford House wine cellar and find out what the wine of the day is. Their hot tub is linked up as well. You'll find Chez Oxford at **http://mckusick.com:451/**.

? How do I get my <u>name up in lights</u> at Netscape's Engineering Department?

Have you ever wanted to see your name scroll by in lights on a sign like the one in New York's Times Square? If so, point your browser to **http://home.netscape.com/people/mtoy/sign/index.html**, shown in Figure 12-9.

In the middle of the engineering department at Netscape, there is a computer attached to the Internet and also attached to a scrolling sign. Just type in a message, and it will appear on the sign for all those Netscape hackers to see.

? Where's this <u>Netscape FishCam</u> I've heard so much about?

Netscape, the company, has a special "FishCam" pointed directly at the company's fish tank. Besides seeing a continuously updated picture of Netscape's fish tank, the page also has plenty of other links to FishCams across the globe that are connected to the Internet. But best of all, you don't have to worry about overfeeding them or forgetting to feed them while you're on vacation. To get to the FishCam, bring up a Navigator Web page, then press CTRL-ALT, F.

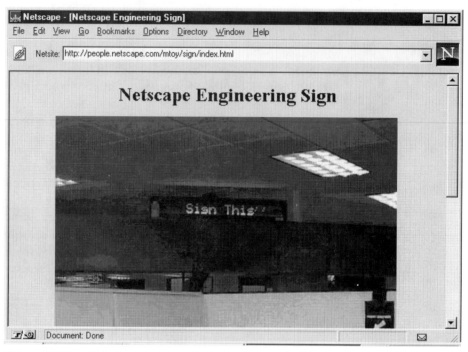

Figure 12-9.   Put your name, or whatever else, up in lights.

 Note   *Montpelier, Vermont is the only U.S. state capital without a McDonald's.*

❓ Can I page someone using the Net?

You sure can. All you need to know is the service they are using, their pager number, and a link to a couple of paging links. Try these:

Company Offering Service	URL
Wildfire's Multiple Paging Options	http://www.wildfire.com/w3p/wwwpager
SkyTel's paging service	http://www.skytel.com/Paging/
USA Mobile's paging service	http://www.usamobile.com/epage.html

 Tip   *Did you know that Leonardo da Vinci invented the scissors?*

What pocket organizers or palm-top computers connect to the Net?

The world of palm-top computing is getting pretty darn crowded. Now virtually every palm-top computer offers some form of modem connection to the Internet or to commercial online services such as CompuServe or America Online. Many now come with Windows CE installed. CE, a slimmed down version of Windows 95 specifically made for palm-top computers, offers the ability to run modified versions of Word, Excel, and Internet Explorer, making the palm-tops that use the Windows CE software miniature versions of your Windows desktop computer.

Two of the best units to consider are the Philips Velo, which comes with a built-in 19.2Kbps modem and Internet Explorer already installed, and the latest incarnation of the Newton, with dramatically improved handwriting recognition software and connections to the Internet. Besides those, here are a couple of other palm-top computers to consider and their manufacturer's Web pages:

Palm-Top	Company	Location
Newton	Apple Computer	http://newton.apple.com
Pilot	U.S. Robotics	http://www.usrobotics.com
Compaq PC Companion	Compaq	http://www.compaq.com/us/common/prodinfo/handhelds/index.html
Zarus Hand-Held PC Companions	Sharp	http://www.sharp-usa.com
Casiopeia	Casio	http://www.casiohpc.com
Philips Velo	Philips	http://www

Can I connect my shortwave radio to the Net?

You can, and someone already has. Check out **http://www.chilton. com/scripts/radio/R8-receiver** to see and hear how it's done. And then when you're ready, check out **http://rob.acol.com/radio/cb/** for all sorts of links relating to CB radios on the Internet.

Note   *February 1865 is the only month in recorded history not to have a full moon.*

? Can I get real-time <u>traffic reports</u> on the Net?

Yes, you certainly can, although not all major cities offer Internet links from their traffic cameras or sensors to their Web pages. One that does is the Twin Cities, located at **http://www.traffic.connects.com/**, which provides a graphical map representing the various freeways. Sensors on the freeway are sent to a central computer, which in turn massages the data and represents average speed throughout the various freeways.

You can check out traffic cameras at the following locations:

Region	URL
San Francisco area	http://www.kpix.com/traffic/cameras/
Boston Bay traffic cam	http://www.smartraveler.com/boston/ liveimage.html
Washington D.C. area	http://www.erols.com/tvn/
Arizona Department of Transportation	http://www.azfms.com/Travel/camera.html
Wilmington Delaware traffic cam	http://www.inet.net/trafficam/
Philadelphia	http://www.trafficam.com
Seattle - Washington State Department of Transit	http://www.wsdot.wa.gov/regions/northwest/ nwflow/ or http://trafficview.seattle.sidewalk1.com/

? What other <u>wacky things</u> can I do over the Net?

You can do all sorts of things. Here's a quick list of some of the more bizarre ways to waste time on the Web:

What You Can Do	URL
Print a message to an Imagewriter Printer	http://www.yikes.com/printer/
Watch and operate an interactive railroad	http://rr-vs.informatik.uni-ulm.de/rr/
Create your own personalized message with refrigerator magnets	http://www.northcoast.com/cgi-bin/fridge
Talk to Rob Hansen	http://www.inference.com/~hansen/talk.html
Flush anything you want down the toilet	http://www.geocities.com/SouthBeach/9438/toilet.html

What You Can Do	URL
Virtually blow some chow and see the results in seconds	http://www.xvt.com/users/kevink/sick/sick.html
View what's happening in the Oval Office (yeah, right…)	http://www.morecrap.com/ovl.htm
TV Today—watch TV from around the world, complete with your own TV changer	http://www.tvtoday.de:9600/onlinetv/TVframeset.hbs
Remotely observe the sky with the University of Iowa's telescope	http://inferno.physics.uiowa.edu/REMOTE_OBS/remote_index.shtml

A **A**nswers!

Internet Error
Messages

Answer Topics!

Internet Error Messages @ a Glance

You're bound to run into an error message or two while surfing the Internet. Maybe you're having **connection problems**, or maybe you're getting lots of **Web browser error messages** when you try to connect to certain servers. Determining the cause can sometimes be very frustrating. Maybe your newsgroup server is down and that's why you're getting all those **Usenet newsgroup and NNTP Server errors**. Could you be typing in the wrong FTP login when you get all those cryptic **FTP errors**? Or maybe you simply have a wrong e-mail address when those **e-mail errors** pop up. No matter what you're doing, if you spend any time on the Net sending e-mail, viewing Web pages, or transferring files, error messages are inevitable. This appendix lists the most common errors you'll run into, explains what they mean, and tells what, if anything, you can do to prevent them from happening again.

Remember   *Not everything can be fixed by tweaking your Web browser or your Internet connection. Oftentimes the only way you can fix problems on the Internet is by letting the Web master, the newsmaster, or the postmaster know there is a problem.*

CONNECTION PROBLEMS

It can be difficult to pinpoint connection problems and where certain connection errors may be coming from. They could result from problems with your system software, your modem, your telephone line, or problems with your Internet service provider or the Internet itself. Here are a few errors you might encounter and ways to combat those error messages:

Error	What It Means	Possible Location of Problem	Resolution
A request to the host has taken longer than expected	You are trying to connect or process a request on a system that is very busy.	The host or domain. You'll often get this message on America Online.	The system is too busy to process your request now, so you can either wait, and try again later, or log off, and then get back on at a less busy time. You might also check the version of the connection software and upgrade if necessary. This could also point to a problem in your communications driver.
Received no carrier from modem	The software didn't hear a dial tone when it told the modem to dial the phone.	Your telephone line or modem connection.	Make sure the telephone line is plugged into the back of the modem in the correct jack. Make sure your phone extensions are on the hook and that no one else is using the phone. Make sure you have disabled call waiting. Check your modem profile and ensure you have the latest UART chip installed.
Too many consecutive transmissions	Your software is not receiving the proper information.	Your communications driver, your modem setup, or your memory.	This problem could be caused by insufficient memory, improper modem setup, or an outdated modem driver. Make sure you have enough memory, are using the correct modem initialization string, and have your system resources configured properly.
Packet reflection detected	Your modem is not set up properly to work with the communications software.	Your communications software modem setup.	This error message is commonly found when you do not have the right modem selected in your America Online software. Change the settings, exit AOL, then relaunch.

Error	What It Means	Possible Location of Problem	Resolution
Cannot Initialize Modem	The connection software cannot get the modem to respond properly.	Your connection or networking software or your modem.	Make sure the modem is turned on or that you have tried turning it off and on again, or try rebooting your computer. Also check the modem initialization string to make sure you are using the right one.
Cannot locate the modem	The connection software cannot find the modem.	Your modem or your connection software.	Make sure you have the modem connected to the computer and that you are specifying the correct modem port. Also make sure the modem is turned on.

WEB BROWSER ERRORS

Many Web browser errors have more to do with the site you are trying to connect to than problems with your browser itself. If your system has been working fine, but you are having problems connecting to various sites, the problems could lie within the Internet itself. You might try clearing your memory or disk cache every so often as well. Clearing the cache can also help you avoid common Web browser page-displaying problems.

The following table lists problems you might encounter and what you can do to fix them:

Error	What It Means	Resolution
400 Bad Request	The server cannot figure out the URL you requested.	Check the spelling, and make sure you are using the proper case as well. Try backtracking to see if the domain, at least, is correct.
401 Unauthorized	Most likely, the password you specified is invalid.	Check the password and try again. Make sure you don't have the CAPS LOCK key activated.

Error	What It Means	Resolution
404 Not Found	404 is a result code sent from the Web server software to your Web browser. It means the browser found the host computer, or the server, but can't find the specific document you requested.	First check to see if you typed the URL correctly. URLs are case sensitive, so make sure you typed it exactly as shown. If the URL is correct, the page may have been deleted, moved, or renamed. Back up one level to see if you can find a site index for the host you are accessing.
403 Forbidden Access or Access Denied	The site or page you requested requires special permission, such as a login name or password.	Check to find out what the login procedure is, or double-check the spelling of your name and password. If you still cannot access the page, contact the Web master to find out if the site is restricted by IP address or domain. Your service provider's site may be restricted from accessing the intended site.
502 Service Temporarily Overloaded (could also be Network Connection Refused by the Server or Too many connections)	The site is too busy to handle additional requests.	Try loading the site again, or try accessing it later.
503 Service Unavailable	The server is too busy to handle your request.	Wait a few minutes, then try again. If it's a busy site during a busy time, such as elections or breaking news, it would probably be best to find an alternative site.
Bad File Request	The form or HTML code included in the form you are viewing has an error listed in it.	Contact the Web master to let him or her know there is a problem with the form. Also check to make sure you are using a browser capable of handling forms.
Cannot Add Form Submission Result to Bookmark List	The result of a form you've filled out cannot be saved as a bookmark.	You often get this response when trying to save a search result or result of an archive search. Try saving the previous page where you first searched instead.

Error	What It Means	Resolution
Connection Refused by Host (similar to the 403 error)	The Web site you requested the document from requires special access permission.	Seek the proper access permission or double-check the spelling of your login name or password. Also make sure your domain is not restricted from accessing the site.
DNS Lookup Failed *or* Failed DNS Lookup	The URL cannot be translated into a valid IP address.	Could be that the DNS server, the server used to translate site names to their actual IP addresses, is busy. Or you could have your DNS server configured wrong in your Network Settings. You could also have the wrong URL syntax. Check the URL again for any problems, wait a few minutes, and try the site again. If you are still having problems, double-check with your service provider to find out if there are any problems with the DNS server.
HTTP Server at Compress "xxx".com:8080 Replies:HTTP/1.0 500 *or* Error from Proxy	This points to a problem with the proxy server.	The proxy server is either down, busy, or cannot process the command it received. Wait a few minutes, and if you still receive the same message, contact the administrator of that proxy server.
Gateway Timeout 503 Error	The network connection timed out when trying to access the gateway.	The Internet may be busy, or there may be problems with the gateway used between your ISP and the rest of the Internet.
Host Unknown	The domain name you specified is not in the DNS database or registered.	Double-check the spelling. You may not have typed the domain correctly, or you might have added .edu when it was a .com site.

Error	What It Means	Resolution
File Contains No Data	Your browser found the site, but nothing is contained in the file.	You could try adding port 80 to the URL right after the domain name but before the first directory slash. For example, http://www.mysite.com:80. Or if it's a search, try rerunning the search with a different parameter. If you still encounter this error, contact the Web master of the site.
Helper Application Not Found	You are trying to download or access a file that needs a helper application.	Check the site to make sure you know what application is needed. If you don't have that application, download it. If you do have the application, check the helper application preferences in your browser preferences to make sure you have the right filename and pathname pointing to the helper application.
Cannot Connect to Server	Most likely, you are trying to connect to a secured server using the HTTPS:// protocol.	This could be due to a Web server error or the inability of a Web server to work properly with Internet Explorer 3.x or the beta version of 4.0. Try using a different browser to connect.

USENET NEWSGROUP AND NNTP SERVER ERRORS

Newsgroup and Network News Transfer Protocol (NNTP) errors, those errors spewed out by the newsgroup server itself, can at times seem baffling. But if you have an idea of where the error message originates, you can easily fix your own problems.

Detailed here are common newsgroup and newsgroup server errors you might encounter and ways to fix them:

Error	What It Means	Resolution
Newsgroup Not Found	The browser cannot find the Usenet newsgroup you tried to access.	Make sure you've correctly typed the news server address in your browser's preferences or options menu, then try again.

Error	What It Means	Resolution
The Link No Longer Exists *or* Site Unavailable	Too many users are trying to access the site, or the site is down for maintenance or no longer exists. There could also be problems with line noise. Or perhaps you've typed the wrong newsgroup address.	Wait a few minutes, try reconnecting, and double-check the name of the newsgroup.
TCP Error Encountered While Sending Request to Server	Garbage or erroneous data is on the line between you and the server.	Try again later. If the problem persists, check your network configuration or consult your network administrator.
Invalid Newsgroup	You typed the wrong name for the newsgroup server or used the wrong syntax.	Double-check the spelling, and make sure the newsgroup exists on the newsgroup server you are connecting to.
No Such Message	This indicates an out-of-date message. The message you requested is still in the index but has been removed from the server.	There's not much you can do, except try searching newsgroup archives such as DejaNews.
Could Not Connect to Server	The news server is busy or is down, or you do not have access to the news server.	Wait or double-check the news server preference settings in your browser. You might also have problems with an improperly configured system.
The Message Appears Unintelligible	A binary file, such as a picture, movie, or program, has been posted encoded into ASCII characters.	Most newsreaders include automatic decoding, and this particular message may be using a coding scheme your browser is unfamiliar with. Read the header of the message for details about decoding the file.
Too Many Users	The site is busy.	You may want to try again later.

Error	What It Means	Resolution
Unable to Locate Host	When you tried to contact the news server it was either unavailable or the Internet connection was dropped.	Double-check the spelling, and make sure you still have a valid connection to the Internet. If the problem persists, contact your ISP or network administrator.

FTP ERRORS

Just like the Web, when you FTP, you are connecting to a server. Sometimes the server is busy, sometimes you type the wrong name for the server, or sometimes the server simply isn't available. Detailed here are some of the more common FTP errors you might encounter and ways to work around them:

Error	What It Means	Resolution
Invalid Host *or* Unable to Resolve Hostname	This is FTP's equivalent to the Web browser's 404 error. The FTP program cannot find the site you requested.	Make sure you typed the correct FTP server name in the server name field.
The FTP program connects to the server, then suddenly stops responding	The software could be waiting for a response or could be improperly configured.	Try adding a dash (-) before your login password. This will turn off the site's informational messages, which may be causing a conflict with the FTP program. Double-check the configuration of your FTP program, and make sure you are specifying the correct server connection in your FTP program.
Too many consecutive transmit errors	Most likely, noise has confused the FTP program, and it cannot continue.	You could be experiencing noise on your telephone line, or you may have the incorrect modem initialization string. Check both your hardware and software settings, disconnect, then reconnect and try again.

E-MAIL ERRORS

Most mail errors are caused by misspelling the recipient's name or the domain name or forgetting the @ between the username and the domain. The following table lists some of the more common errors you might encounter and their solutions.

 Remember   *Commas and spaces are not allowed in e-mail addresses, and some services such as CompuServe require you to replace the comma with a period. Check Chapter 3 for more information on how to address a message to a user on a particular commercial service provider.*

Error	What It Means	Resolution
Unknown User	The e-mail server you sent the message to cannot find the user in its database.	You either typed the name wrong, or the user is no longer getting mail at this location. Contact the postmaster at the site by sending an e-mail to postmaster@*domain*, where *domain* is the domain where you normally sent the user e-mail.
Cannot Open Mailbox Mailbox Full	Your mailbox has the maximum amount of messages it can hold and cannot be opened.	Contact your network administrator and have him or her allocate more space for your mailbox, either temporarily or permanently. If you don't normally get large volumes of mail and have started to, work with your administrator or ISP to isolate the source of the additional mail. You may have been mail-bombed.
Warning: Message Still Undelivered After Xx Hours	Your mail message has been delayed.	This could be caused by the mail server on the other end being down or by a break in the connection somewhere along the way. Don't worry about sending another; the mailer program will continue to try to send the message for a set period of time. This is really just an FYI message.
Mail for a mail list stops appearing		This may be caused by a temporary problem at the site or on the Internet. You may have been involuntarily "unsubscribed" by the mail list server.

Error	What It Means	Resolution
Service Unavailable	The mail server you sent the message to is not accepting e-mail at this time.	Check with the person you are trying to send the message to, to see if there are any problems with the site.
Unbalanced	The e-mail address you specified had unnecessary symbols in the address.	Check the address and try again.
There has been an error transferring your mail. I said (or the client said) PASS and the POP server said -ERR Password supplied for (username) is incorrect.	Your password to connect to the mail server is incorrect.	Make sure you've typed the password correctly and do not have the CAPS LOCK key activated.
Mail Server (Host) busy. Please try again.	The mail server is currently overloaded with requests.	Wait a few minutes, then try again. If the problem persists, your ISP may be having e-mail server problems.

Index